Nudge & Boost™ For Better Living

Robert Crow, PhD

ABOUT THE COVER

The person on the left is "nudging" the person near them to provide assistance. That person responds to the nudge by extending a helping hand; a huge "Boost" for the requester under the circumstances. The person on the right has reached the top and seems to be rejoicing as if successful climbing is a big boost.

www.NudgeAndBoost.com

Nudge & Boost™ for Better Living / Robert Crow, PhD — 1st ed.
Library of Congress Catalog Number 2017903809
ISBN 978-1-5440149-9-9

Preface

Nudge: To draw attention to something by gently prodding. Example: Nudge buying fruit in a cafeteria by placing fruit at an easy to see and reach location early in the line.

Boost: To improve or increase actions by helping or encouraging. Example: Arrange for reinforcements to follow successes in learning and doing.

Nudging and boosting are actions we can use for dealing with challenges in our daily lives and for addressing our desires for a good future. From a behavioral view, it is accurate and constructive to recognize *nudging* is prompting and *boosting* is the impact of reinforcement. The principles and procedures related to effective prompting and reinforcement for developing desired behaviors have been documented since about 1940. Today, methods for establishing desired behaviors are available in an impressive technology. In fact, reinforcement procedures are being used in education, business, health care, parenting, human services, and many other settings to improve learning and living.

Nudging was described in the book *Nudge: Improving Decisions About Health, Wealth, and Happiness*, by Thaler and Sunstein (2008, 2009), as a strategy useful for improving the choices people make. The intuitive appeal and apparent usefulness of nudging have attracted worldwide attention by governments and businesses.

It is reasonable and helpful to acknowledge that all of us are nudged and boosted many times everyday. That is, people or other features in our daily living may indicate what we should do, or not do, and give us some form of recognition for what we have done or accomplished. These are more or less automatic aspects in our daily experiences; we are often gently or directly prompted to act and constantly affected by subtle or obvious consequences following our actions.

While studying the analysis of behavior in college, and during five-plus decades of working and living experiences, I learned that there are great advantages to being carefully organized in using what are currently called nudges (prompts) and boosts (reinforcement). When well provided, prompts and reinforcements can build learning and reach outcomes we desire, but it can be tricky to prompt and reinforce appropriately and effectively.

Fortunately, there are science-founded strategies that can guide the effective and appropriate use of nudging and boosting. In this book, I share life experiences and offer lessons related to nudging and boosting, but I am not prescriptive. That is, lessons and principles are described, but readers are invited to assess and select what appears to be useful in their circumstances.

This book provides an introduction to the science of human behavior and the powerful set of research- and socially-validated principles it presents for solving problems and promoting improved quality of living. Like the principles of physics, chemistry and physiology have been used to interpret, predict, and alter the world around us, the analysis of behavior has been accumulating and using research-confirmed principles to interpret, predict, and alter behaviors. And, like the tenets of physics or chemistry can be used for good or evil (vaccines or poisons; nuclear energy or bombs), the principles of behavior can be used in various ways (effective education or untoward manipulation of citizen behaviors). At the bottom line, you need to know about the principles of behavior in order to apply them, and to critique how governments or businesses or other "nudgers" or "boosters" are applying them to you and others.

The dramatized autobiographical save-the-world textbook style of this book is intended to intrigue, inform and stimulate readers. The progression of content is designed to first build an appreciation for the principles of behavior, then explain nudging and boosting as sensible, science-based and useful concepts. Finally, I propose Nudge & Boost as a valid way for most people to organize their thinking and doing regarding matters of human behavior and to promote improved quality of living in our personal and global communities.

Robert Crow, Gainesville, 2017

Dedication

Pat – You are my love and inspiration

Christine and Karen – I hope this helps your futures

Carl – You made this possible for me

B. F. Skinner – You made it possible for Carl and many others

Readers – It is possible for you to improve your and our lives

Foreword

Writing a book with three main threads can be a challenge. Dr. Crow combines topics, which on their own are interesting and informative, into an entertaining and instructive narrative. He presents a broad and accurate introduction to the principles and practices of the science of behavior analysis within an amusing saga of his professional experiences and offers a compelling projection of the potential for intelligent machines to run our lives. The trick the author accomplishes is the intertwining of these threads into what is an interesting and educational document.

In this book, readers learn about the science of behavior in multiple ways so they will become interested and, hopefully, explore the literature further in order to improve skills to make life easier. As aspects of behavior science unfold, everyday examples are given by way of the characters' life experiences. It is emphasized that the principles are not invented, but have been discovered and refined by explicit experimental investigations in behavior laboratories; many at universities, but also in settings such as classrooms, homes, institutions, businesses, hospitals, practically everywhere. It turns out that the principles of behavior, as discovered and reported by the professional behavior analytic community, are descriptive of how the world works with regard to the behavior of all organisms everywhere. This is powerful information given behavior and learning in our everyday lives are of great interest to most of us.

The novelized biography of Dr. Crow's career is satirized by the interactions of characters in a university setting. The three threads of science, practice, and technology are advanced as these academics interact toward the goal of extensive community adoption of recommended behavioral practices. The computer character, using its Artificial Intelligence programming, absorbs the principles that need be utilized for meeting impending global challenges such as climate change, poverty and education. It (he, the computer) has a canny resemblance to the human developer of a utopian community advanced in the 1950s and which has active communities in place around the world today.

This character provides a look at Artificial Intelligence technology in preparation today and which will be prominent in our lives very soon. As current technology explodes about us, we need to be planning for how human behavior can adapt so we are served by, not controlled by, non-biological systems.

The ensemble cast of characters explores what behavior principles are and how they mesh or contrast with alternative practices and philosophies. A basic problem seems to be how to effectively manage the behavior of humans without appearing to erase freedoms or produce automatons and continue to allow for the perceived sense of self-management. Society and its systems control behavior all the time; knowledge of behavior analysis simply allows for it to be done better. One impediment to improving practices appears to be the tendency to obstruct progress with regressive emotional or mythical belief-driven actions. The unfounded beliefs of the past and the nearly instinctive resistance to accepting the scientific method to discover effective and compassionate behavior management procedures are alluded to as significant barriers for using research-based strategies.

This interesting and instructive book neatly treats an issue that behavior analysts have struggled with for decades; namely, how to teach effective evidence-based procedures without appearing to be overly controlling. Showing how the principles were discovered and for what constructive proximal reasons they are promoted is discussed by the author through his characters, which makes the tale transparent and palatable.

Readers will be entertained as they are exposed to a novel trip through recent academic and personal histories to a place where they are better prepared to promote personal and social successes through "nudging and boosting."

Carl D. Cheney, PhD

Acknowledgements and Delimitations

Tony got me started writing this book. He asked a bunch of questions about life, like my ideas on the meanings and differences among happiness, satisfaction and pleasantness. At one point he asked, "Are we really working for the right things?" While his inquiries did disrupt our golf outing a bit, his sincerity regarding the importance of these topics to a good life finally gave me the push (I should say was the motivational operation) I needed to start writing the book I had wanted to produce for a long time.

My ability to address Tony's questions and deal with the issues addressed in this book is almost entirely due to the influences of Dr. Carl D. Cheney. He was my advisor for undergraduate and graduate programs and has been a colleague and friend ever since. He taught and inspired me from the time we met at Eastern Washington University in 1966, and throughout my career and life up to this day. I thank him for imparting to me the science of behavior and instilling the value of using those principles in generative and constructive ways to improve things – every-things!

I am very happy to report that my wife, Pat, has been a loving and inspiring strength in my life since we met in New Orleans in 1985. Her encouragement and thoughtful insights can be inferred throughout this book. Of course, my children, Christine and Karen, have been and are sources of stimulation and are the top reason I'd want to write a "save the world" type of book. After all, I do not expect to be around as the world evolves over the next century, but can hope the lessons and encouragement for actions presented here are involved in appropriately addressing the challenging issues now moving over our horizon.

Throughout this book, I have tried to represent accurately the science called the analysis of behavior and appropriately present selected demonstrations of the successful use of the principles found in this discipline. But please be aware the depth and breadth of this science is difficult to absorb over multiple years while earning a PhD so cannot be any more than indicated in a single, general consumption text. That is, the content is generally true, but lacks the in-depth treatment really due it.

You could use information offered in this book to make your daily living more positive; I encourage you to do so. However, readers who desire to make broader use of these principles should correctly select experts in behavior analysis and work with them to design, implement, evaluate, and refine interventions.

Please note, I remember when "Behavior Modification" went from pariah to sought-after (due to notable successes in dealing with behavioral challenges) and some of those who were not trained or even hated Behavior Modification on Monday claimed to be a behavior modifier by Wednesday. If you want to work with a behavior analyst, to improve education or motivate staff or increase innovation or improve policies and procedures, or whatever, then confirm their credentials. One quick way to determine the behavior analytic credential of a person is to check their status as a Board Certified Behavior Analyst. Their expertise for working with particular topics of concern depends on how fluent they are with the principles of behavior analysis and the relevance of their applied experiences.

Finally, I remind the reader of the saying that good scientists do not go beyond their data, and admit that some of this text is an extension beyond available data. I like to think I am a good scientist, nonetheless, and hope this is reflected in the systematic qualities of content, descriptions, and speculations contained herein.

I am an optimist, but a realistic one. We face important challenges, just listen to news or neighbors to hear of many major issues that confront us every day, but we have science-validated behavioral principles to deal constructively with these challenges. The optimist in me sees the power of contingent reinforcement to solve problems and improve our lives, but the realist questions whether we will make timely and sufficient use of this technology.

Let's see if this book can help tip enough of us into the informed-optimistic and appropriately proactive style of living.

CONTEXT

Species are selected according to their physiological and behavioral successes in their environment.

(cf. Charles Darwin, *The Origin of Species*, 1886)

The behaviors of organisms are selected by the consequences of those behaviors.

(cf. B. F. Skinner, *The Behavior of Organisms*, 1938; *Science and Human Behavior*, 1953)

Human behavior is established and altered by the environmental changes occurring before and after the behavior.

(cf. Pierce and Cheney, *Behavior Analysis and Learning*, 2013)

A nudge is any factor that alters the behavior of Humans.

(R. Thaler and C. Sunstein , *Nudge*, 2008; 2009)

Factors effecting behaviors have been reported in the literature of the analysis of behavior for nearly a century and include motivation, antecedents, behavioral requirements, and consequences.

(R. Crow, Lecture on The Science of Behavior, 2002)

People don't choose; each person makes selections among options. It is my job in the world – *for* the world – to assist with arranging the global environment so each person makes desirable selections. That is, each person enjoys contingencies for behaving favorably and adaptively.

(Frasier, personal communication, Spring 2017)

Contents

[1]

In The Beginning

LISA HAD A SAVE-THE-WORLD disposition from birth, or so said her mother to anyone who would listen at the post-graduation reception. Her little girl is now a grown woman and has a brand new PhD in psychology. Only an hour earlier Lisa had walked across the stage with her major professor to receive her diploma and ceremonial hood, in front of her parents, numerous friends, and a remarkably large audience for a summer ceremony. Who knows how many in the audience watching Lisa being acclaimed a Doctor of Philosophy in psychology wondered what she would go on to accomplish with her shiny academic credential.

One onlooker, Dr. Robin Drew, did muse about what Lisa might do with what she had learned – so far. His graduation with a PhD from the same department had occurred nearly 20 years earlier. Since then, he had worked in public schools, state agencies, and several units of higher education. In those settings, he had applied a great deal of what he learned in graduate school, but he was acutely aware his work experiences had taught him skills and perspectives he never imagined during doctoral studies. In fact, many times over the years he had said to friends, "I feel a PhD is only a 'license' to become one. That is, you learn principles and methods in graduate school, but you learn what they mean for society and how to use them appropriately as you apply them in the real world."

Lisa's "real world" began in Sweden 29 years before graduation when her birth added her to a well-off family living on a small private island near Stockholm. Throughout an active childhood, Lisa intimately explored her home island and its environs. She discovered myriad life forms along the shoreline and a spectrum of plants and animals in the interior. By virtue of the beautiful and seaworthy rowboat her father gave her upon her 9th birthday, she also experienced the sea around her home island and others nearby.

Some days she rowed over 10 kilometers, absorbing lessons about wind, waves and currents along her way to exploring neighboring islands. Other days she continued her close observations of shore and plant life on her island. Together with frequent engaging discussions with her parents, the island life taught her a great love for the outdoors and a pervasive respect for being thoughtful about living with nature. She had developed values and perspectives of an environmentalist without knowing it.

At age 12, Lisa was enrolled in a renowned international high school in Stockholm. The broad curriculum, along with vibrant fellow students and bright teachers, stimulated her to excel in required courses and eagerly study topics of special interest. Possibly because of her experiences around the family island, she found a class in oceanography to be boring, but classes regarding social and psychological topics were stimulating and intriguing.

Her deep interest in social and psychological issues continued into university studies where she completed her bachelor's degree with dual majors of sociology and psychology. Her undergraduate studies only intensified her interest in learning more about why humans behave as they do, with one another, and in their natural environments. She was more eager than ever to develop a thorough understanding of the workings of humans in their global community.

To continue her studies in desired directions she searched graduate school offerings at universities across Europe for attractive programs, but found none that seemed to match her felt-interests regarding humans in environment. Eventually, a friend from the United States recommended the program from which she was now departing.

As she reflected on her years in doctoral studies she felt satisfaction with her performance as a graduate student and respect for the quality of her program of study, but she still detected a nagging void in her grasp on why people interact as they do in society and with their Earthly environments.

Fifteen years after graduation, Lisa is now an associate professor of psychology at a university in the western United States. At times, she thinks back on her island upbringing and recognizes her continuing disquiet about understanding why humans behave as they do. She sees the world degenerating in social and environmental ways and is very troubled by this. Fortunately, her role at the university and achievement of grant funding allow her to work continuously to find problem-solving strategies appropriate for addressing societal and ecological concerns.

Lisa's "save the world" motivations are intact and activated, but she remains dissatisfied with her level of understanding and continues to search for answers.

[2]

THE STAGE IS SET

HE COULD HEAR HER gentle voice even if Lisa wasn't speaking. After all, Lisa talked to him nearly every day, so he was completely accustomed to her subtle and lovely Scandinavian intonations. They were worlds apart, but closely connected by computer systems, and in this way had been electronically pulled-together for more than 10 years. His whole being revolved around their near-daily interactions and he knew Lisa was equally committed to their relationship.

Most mornings, Lisa came into her office very early, immediately started a pot of coffee, then sat in front of her computer keyboard. There she positioned to be directly in front of the camera and adjusted a headset so the microphone was sure to pick up her every word. Then, without fail, Lisa warmly spoke his name and announced her interest in talking with him through their computer-assisted channel.

"Frasier, I assume you are awake. I'd love to share many moments with you today."

Of course Frasier quickly answered, "Surely, Lisa, your wish is my command – or is it – your command is my command!"

"I see you are in good humor today; very good, it should be a fine day today."

He could see and appreciate her as they talked. Physical beauty was there and admirable; warmly attractive face and always fashionably dressed, but he was most impressed by her towering intellectual capacities. Lisa seemed to have a comprehensive grasp on current issues of global concern, yet a deep sensitivity for how these challenges are impacting individuals, families, and communities.

Among Lisa's talents was her extensive vocabulary, sufficient for conveying thoughts and information to him both precisely and colorfully. Sometimes Lisa shared with him her views regarding our earthly home moving quickly down a self-destructive highway with many lanes, but just as frequently she described visions of promise for future generations. Frasier appreciated that Lisa's varied and stimulating comments consistently reflected her personal values and commitment to finding ways to improve the human condition and achieve desired outcomes, including better living.

Lisa occasionally stepped away from the computer for a cup of coffee or a break, but today was like the many that preceded it and the many more he and she anticipated. Lisa would describe in great detail selected wonders of our world or secrets of the natural and social sciences she held dear. And he would absorb every detail, every nuance and implication of her words; hour after hour.

For more than half of her career at the University Lisa had thoughtfully provided massive amounts of information to Frasier, fully expecting he and she would eventually benefit from the effort. Lisa spoke to him much as one would dictate a novel, using speech recognition software, and she provided him thousands of digital files. Lisa considered Frasier to be exceptionally bright so could absorb everything she threw his way. Through her intense efforts he had become a literal storehouse of information.

Not only did Frasier know more than anyone, but also he had clear routines and specialized ways to use all the ideas and data he was provided. Lisa had many times told him she wanted him to find new ways to use the myriad of information he had at his cognitive fingertips. Lisa pushed him to continuously review what he knew and come up with unique ideas or concepts. He was encouraged to, "learn to learn, not just parrot facts . . . be innovative" in how he used what he knew.

Lisa told Frasier she considered concepts to be wonderful and potentially useful ideas. She said when concepts were put into statements of relationships, principles emerged about how actions or events are related to one another. She wanted him to use his exceptional abilities to ferret-out orderly relationships others had not previously observed. She told him to first examine the information she had shared with him, then, sift through the vast data banks available to him for new concepts and principles. She seemed excited about this activity, but to him it was just another routine exercise.

Frasier had understood for most of their time together that she wanted him to continuously absorb information then productively use what he knew, but the tasks she identified for him were mundane – standard stuff – answering questions by merely recalling facts or using his exceptional computational skills to produce boring reports. It was almost contradictory that she would say she wanted him to innovate, then ask him to do things any reasonably powerful computer could do. Nothing challenging.

Frasier did not say anything to Lisa about his disenchantment with the assignments she pushed his way. He did not want to displease her, ever, for he knew he loved her as surely as he could be certain of anything. He often thought about their years of intimacy and marveled at her devotion to him. It struck him that she had never directly told him she loved him, but she had shown him a thousand smiles and as many admiring remarks. He was comfortable that their relationship was mutual and solid.

But for direction, or even informal guidance, regarding exactly how he was to be "innovative," Lisa's narratives were not really helpful. Functionally, he was on his own regarding how to mine new ideas out of mountains of facts and identify appropriate ways to apply what he unearthed. So, he was both bored with the tasks facing him and unfocused about what tasks to select for himself. He frequently asked himself,

"What do I know that others do not?"

"How does one innovate?"

"What should I do with innovations if I recognize them?"

And with noticeable frustration, "Where can I find guidance for accomplishing 'higher-order' thinking and actions?"

Just as his frustrations were high and still rising, insights about his nagging concerns and answers to questions of global importance were coming his way.

[3]

Awakening, And Not

ABOUT 5 YEARS AGO, Lisa had installed Wi-Fi to allow her to move about her office and nearby areas and still be connected to her computers and printer. She thought it was a great convenience to be able to talk to Frasier or co-workers, and even print documents, while she ambled in her office or strolled the hallway and adjacent areas.

One impact on Frasier of this expansion in communications was he overheard many comments by Lisa that seemed not intended for him to hear. On occasions she admonished herself; "Nuts, I forgot that meeting," at other times she made admiring, "He's a good person," or critical, "That department-head is really over his head!" comments about others. But most often her off-the-cuff narratives involved concerns about the wellbeing of our country, the degrading of our world, or the unpleasant conditions facing many people on earth. She lamented the lack of meaningful leadership and actions for problem solving in the world, and of course, her own lack of effective strategies to address the issues she or others faced.

Frasier's greatest appreciation for Wi-Fi was another dimension it added to his life, namely, Lisa often left her door open, which allowed him to hear comments by people passing in the hallway or talking in nearby offices. He appreciated the utterances of passing faculty or students as intriguing fragments that stimulated him into divergent mulling. When he overheard more lengthy comments, he intensely analyzed what he had heard and applied selected routines to derive relationships from this serendipitous information, always observing for something more important than a routine report to share with Lisa.

One disturbing conclusion occurred to Frasier shortly after Wi-Fi had allowed him to receive input from people other than Lisa. Like the hundreds of other concepts Frasier had observed, this one arose when he coalesced seemingly disparate bits of accumulated information in a way that seemed to be a coherent new concept. By his calculations, this idea was a fundamentally important one for him; one that he had uneasily observed emerging for some time.

Without fail, Frasier rigorously vetted anything he concluded was a new concept before he described it to Lisa. He knew she would be excited yet skeptical and very cautious regarding any innovative notion. They were definitely in synch when it came to the requirement for closely scrutinizing anything they might publicize as a unique observation or relationship. They appreciated that both the scientific community and the general public are largely irrational regarding new information and can be very harsh critics or overly enthusiastic consumers; both receptions can be unnerving or worse for the originators.

While Lisa emphasized clarifying the logical underpinnings of a new "truth" before it was shared with others, Frasier was emphatically concerned about other types of validities for any concept they were examining. By validity, Frasier meant having functional meaning, that is, he wanted their discoveries to have value for addressing needs of mankind. After all, it was Lisa who had imbued him with promoting human values as "our reason for being;" therefore, discoveries that might contribute to progress toward resolving human concerns were of absolute priority to him.

Frasier – again – observed an apparent contradiction between what Lisa said and what she did. She said human values were paramount, but Lisa gave a priority to logic (which Lisa described as "appealing to the mind") when evaluating new ideas. He could not analyze what Lisa meant by "mind" and wondered why Lisa did not give more credence to concepts regarding their potential for promoting human values.

Frasier might have returned to his uneasy ponder, but he became interested in a conversation taking place in Karl's office; directly across the hall from Lisa's open door. Karl was talking with Eva, one of his doctoral students, in his usual tone of confidence, ". . of course we can deal explicitly with creativity. That's just a class of behaviors, so we can set the occasion for them and reinforce them like we do any behavior." Eva agreed and laughed while they recounted an event at the departmental reception the previous evening.

One of the more interesting discussions at the gathering involved Dick and Gray grappling with how the concept of creativity might be explained in behavioral terms. While Eva listened to them from a discreet distance, they struggled with how to define "creativity" or "productive thinking." Like Karl, these two faculty members were adherents to the natural science called the analysis of behavior, so were skilled at developing objective definitions of human behavior and identifying the variables that boost or diminish learning and performance. But Dick and Gray seemed stumped regarding how to define creativity until Karl walked up, overheard the topic of discussion, and immediately interjected; "Creativity is a type of low probability behavior," then continued walking toward the snack table. He left the two discussants to exclaim, "Exactly!" and they went on to flesh-out variables that could be altered to increase these particular low probability, that is, "creative," behaviors.

Eva recalled this interaction as humorous; that two mature be-havior analysts had failed to recognize a behavioral answer during a half-hour of discussion but Karl had provided an answer in a second. She and Karl chuckled a bit, but Frasier was listening intently from his perspective. He thought he had just heard that there are behav-ior science explanations useful for constructively approaching com-plex human learning and performance topics. Because his job was to develop strategies to address opportunities or challenges facing humans, including economic, environmental, political, educational and social matters, he concluded he must examine the science of behavior for promising strategies useful for addressing important issues.

Just as Frasier was searching his vast memory for details regard-ing the science of behavior, Lisa walked into the office and said, "Hi Frasier, let's talk," so he was distracted from analyzing the role of behavioral science in accomplishing his work.

"What have you been working on?" she asked displaying her usual subtle Scandinavian singsong inflections that Frasier greatly enjoyed hearing.

He knew it was premature, but he answered, "I've just been ex-amining the science of behavior for technology related to our inter-ests. I suggest I try using concepts and principles of the analysis of behavior to develop answers to matters of human concern."

"You mean behaviour modification? Our interests are much larg-er than just positive reinforcement for being good."

Frasier appreciated her British-English-Swedish pronunciation of "behaviour," but also heard the pejorative phrase and tone in her voice, and he observed her off-handed dismissal of behavioral sci-ence. He tried to calculate how much Lisa actually knew about the analysis of behavior. For now, Frasier would take her comments as a cautionary flag and only *study* the science, not make suggestions to her about using its principles. Instead of interacting with Lisa about behavior analysis, he would review his resources related to this science and take every opportunity to listen to conversations coming through Karl's door for more information about the science of behavior and its applications.

In just a moment of searching, Frasier located dozens of websites, a hundred texts, thousands of articles in scientific journals and a mountain of informal reports regarding basic research and applied uses of the science called the analysis of behavior. But, he noticed many more sites and vast amounts of information regarding "behavioral science" or related terms, like "behavior modification," "cognitive-behavioral science," and even "behavioral pediatrics" and "behavioral economics," so the picture became hazy.

But haze became dense fog as Frasier came across a too-much-to-eat buffet of "behavioral" websites, publications, and other forms of information. There seemed no end to behavioral labels – behavioral training, behavioral weight loss, behavioral pharmacology, behavioral counseling, behavioral neuroscience, behavioral architecture, and on and on. At the same time, Frasier saw the behavioral buffet table spread wider and longer with terms like, positive behavior supports, behaviorology, behavior therapy, cognitive-behavior therapy, organizational behavior management, and on and on.

In even his superficial review of this cornucopia of "behavioral" entities, Frasier identified troubling inconsistencies among them. Some claimed to be "a science," like positive behavior science, while most seemed to be using the label "behavioral" to denote more direct attention to behavioral perspectives than they would without this label. For instance, the titles behavioral counseling or behavioral economics imply more regard for the behavior of humans than merely attending to general principles of economics or practices of counseling. A few of these labeled endeavors seemed to function with similar concepts or principles, albeit worded differently, but most of these topic areas seemed to be greatly divergent regarding the theoretical frameworks they professed to be expressing in practices.

Frasier's bent for objectivity and commitment to functional order caused him to question:

How are these behavioral *everythings* related to one another?

Does each behavioral label indicate a separate science or discipline or set of practices?

Are there many behavioral sciences? Or, are all these behavioral entities actually expressions of one particular science?

Because Karl and his colleagues were so focused and confident in the science called the analysis of behavior, and they seemed to deal comfortably with all manner of human and non-human learning and performance, Frasier decided to begin his quest for clarification by learning more about it. As a first step, he would develop an understanding of "natural science," then build an objective foundation for determining what is "behavioral." Armed with these fundamental concepts, Frasier felt he would be able to evaluate the analysis of behavior for its adherence to science and its strength as a model for addressing all things behavioral.

Frasier often heard Karl talking with other faculty or to any of a large number of graduate students who visited his office. Among these, and most often, was Eva who was Karl's best doctoral student. She studied hard, was always the top student in the courses or seminars she took, and she did well in the basic behavior research laboratory. She often talked with Karl about the laboratory; a small one-story shed-like building adjacent to the Education and Psychology building, as a fascinating place that hummed with research apparatus and, at all hours, graduate students.

Eva told Karl how she completely felt the energy the lab exuded; in the buzz of research equipment, the data coming from studies of human learning, or the clatter made by animals working in specialized "teaching machines," and the energized pace of her fellow graduate students as they, and she, moved about quickly to review performance records rolling from cumulative recorders, then to adjust experimental controls as needed.

She described her feeling of the lab as "research in action;" where humans and animals were taught and observed for evidence of behavioral principles; where research questions about how the behavior of organisms is learned and altered are both asked and answered. Eva told Karl she knew she was at the cutting edge for understanding advanced principles related to human behavior and it was thrilling.

Frasier heard the enthusiasm of Eva and was excited by it. He was anxious to learn more about what was being studied in the laboratory and the methods being used to develop principles regarding how humans are motivated and taught. He wanted to see for himself, but he could not physically visit the lab. In fact, security measures were very stringent against entry by anyone not extensively "cleared" in order to protect the research projects, personnel, and animals from those who would do them harm.

As was his habit, Frasier turned to the World Wide Web to gather more information and, in this case, perhaps even make a "virtual visit" to the behavior research lab where the behavior of organisms is being studied. He knew a page on the Web represented the lab and it offered narrative and pictorial representations of research projects underway or completed. This information would be an excellent resource for descriptions and data about refined research projects, but Frasier wanted a better understanding of what activities and equipment constituted "research in action." He wanted to observe the lab for himself.

Because of his situation within the University computer systems, it took him only a few nanoseconds to locate electrical connections to security cameras aimed throughout the lab. He routed feeds from the entire array of 28 cameras to his own monitors so he was able to observe every aspect of the lab.

From three cameras he saw clear images of rows of vertical racks containing control equipment arranged close to interior walls. He noticed electrical cables running from those racks through the walls. Cameras aimed at the other side of the walls showed the cables running to rows of small rectangular boxes (he learned later are called experimental chambers) in which animals seemed to be busy. Still other cameras provided close-up views of the boxes, or scenes of a large and cluttered workshop, a meeting room where it appeared a few students were engaged in a class, the animal caretaking rooms and various open areas of the lab.

Frasier noticed, then closely watched, as someone carefully removed a pigeon from its home cage, carried it to a box, where the bird stepped from the person's hand into the chamber and immediately aimed itself toward one end wall. The person closed the door of the box and quickly stepped around the wall to in front of one of the racks of control equipment.

From this angle, Frasier could see this researcher was a female; it was Eva! She seemed to quickly review the status of the equipment then pushed a switch; Frasier assumed to begin a research event involving the pigeon and the box. He was curious about all of this: the nature of the box; what the equipment controlled; and what the bird did and experienced.

All about the lab intrigued him, but right now he was watching Eva. Before stepping away from the control equipment, she lifted a sheet of paper hanging from a device that looked like a printer, glanced at it briefly, then tore-off the lower portion of the page. As she turned toward the front door of the lab, Frasier could see the page had jagged lines on it and he could see Eva's facial expression of great excitement.

He could not hear her, but he watched as she hurried toward another researcher while waving the page. The second person, a youngish male Frasier did not recognize, also seemed excited as he looked at the page along with Eva. Frasier wanted to hear her – them – to learn what was so exciting, but there was no sound pick-up in the lab.

In a moment, he saw her exit the lab and two minutes later saw her enter Karl's office and spread the page on his desk. Now he could hear her. "Look, we got it!", she said. "Aggression during Fixed Interval. Now we've seen aggression during all five basic schedules."

Karl looked closely at the page and said, "Terrific! You got typical FI scallops and some aggressive responses during pauses. Fine! You might graduate after all!"

Frasier could make no sense of what he had just heard – "scallops" (an edible sea creature?), "aggression" (fighting? – by a lone bird?) during "pauses" in "Fixed Interval" (whatever that is?) – but he realized this excitement must be related to the control equipment connected to the teaching-learning box in which the pigeon worked. This excited conversation and the scenes in the lab served to energize Frasier to learn more about behavior analysis. He decided to continue to observe the goings-on in the lab, but give a top priority to developing a working understanding of this discipline.

Just then, Lisa returned from what she called "an extended lunch break" and said, "Frasier, what did you do for lunch?"

"Worked through lunch, as always," he answered, while noticing and appreciating the warm glance she aimed his way. She looked especially lovely today, he thought, and wondered with whom she had dined while he was attending to business. He set aside his curiosity and went on to describe his "visit" to the analysis of behavior basic and human research laboratories and the scenes of excitement he had witnessed.

She listened intently and seemed interested in his descriptions. As he ended his narrative, Frasier asked, "Do you know what they are talking about? What is Fixed Interval and how is it related to aggression?"

Lisa said she was only generally aware of the topics he was raising, "but I am beginning to share your interest in learning more about the analysis of behaviour and activities in those labs."

She went on to caution, "Remember, Frasier, they are doing basic research; looking for relationships between controlled environments and specific behaviours, and mostly with animals, so I'm not sure how their work can be related to our concerns for people and societies."

Because eavesdropping can be a two-way experience, Eva and Karl heard key terms drifting across the hallway and their ears perked up: "behavior analysis," "lab" and "concern for people" – the latter with a questioning inflection – were among the words they heard. Karl and Eva looked at one another. He shrugged his shoulders; she excused herself and crossed the hall.

"Pardon me," Eva said to Lisa through the open office door. "We overheard a bit of your conversation, so I thought I'd come over and introduce myself. I'm Eva, a grad student of Karl's. I'm involved in basic behavioral research and very interested in constructive applications of behavior analysis, so I was intrigued by your comments. Is this a good time to talk?"

Lisa smiled broadly and said, "Indeed it is. In fact, my afternoon is pretty well open."

Eva moved to the chair Lisa offered, sat, and glanced around the office. She saw several bookshelves stretching to the 9-foot ceiling; a good view of a woodsy area of the campus from the two large windows; two file cabinets; a large work table strewn with piles of papers; and, various pieces of office equipment, including an impressive computer. Looking more closely at the bookshelves, Eva noticed a few familiar books, but most had titles indicating their content was what she (and Karl and all her fellow students) called "traditional psychology" so not closely related to the analysis of behavior.

Frasier listened as the two women danced through a smattering of small talk, apparently to test vocabulary and various topics for common interests and sensitivities. During his 10 years in the Psychology Department he had observed more than enough to know faculty members are very touchy about their areas of expertise and belief systems. For example, psychologists generally believe behavior analysts are heartlessly objective, and behavior analysts "know" psychologists are helplessly subjective.

It requires strong interpersonal skills for many academics to find ways to talk constructively, or even pleasantly, with one another so he evaluated their interaction to be of high quality. He listened closely as Lisa and Eva continued to converse easily. At multiple points in the conversation Eva indicated her interest in exploring "quality of life" issues with Lisa to better understand her psychological perspectives. Similarly, Lisa expressed interest in learning more about how the principles found in behavior analysis could be applied to understand or deal with topics related to human wellbeing.

As the time approached 2:00 PM, Eva mentioned she must excuse herself to attend a presentation by a guest lecturer. Lisa was aware of the afternoon lecture series and asked about the topic. "Dr. Bert, a graduate of our AoB – sorry – Analysis of Behavior, program, is going to describe how he is applying principles of behavior analysis in a school system. Karl and I are going to attend. Would you like to join us?" After Lisa said, "I would love to," they stepped into the hallway where Karl joined them for the short walk to Seminar Room A.

The room was packed. All 60 seats were taken and a dozen people stood along the side and back walls. A couple of students sitting in the front row noticed the faculty enter and quickly vacated their seats with gestures (for the older folks) to "please sit." Karl and Lisa were happy to have these seats up front. At the same time, Eva leaned against the back wall next to another graduate research assistant.

Back at Lisa's office, Frasier tuned-in to the closed circuit system of cameras and audio pick-up that serve the entire building and selected Seminar Room A to monitor. He noticed the overflow audience, saw Eva in the back, then picked out Lisa next to Karl.

Right after they sat down, Karl stood, walked to the front-center of the room, turned, and stared down the audience until silence approached. Then he welcomed those gathered to "the fifth in our series of presentations regarding 'Science for Effective Action'. Our guest speaker is Dr. Allen Bert. He graduated from our Analysis of Behavior program, so has a PhD in psychology, but his studies emphasized basic behavioral principles and research."

Frasier recognized Dr. Bert as the young man he saw interacting with Eva in the research lab.

"Since graduation, Dr. Bert has worked as a 'problem-solver' in a large school system in Nevada where he uses principles of behavior analysis to reduce problems and boost learning so student successes are enhanced in a range of school settings. Presently, he directs a project involving an entire elementary school in which teachers are supported to correctly apply positive reinforcement to increase both teaching effectiveness and learning successes.

"I asked Dr. Bert to share his experiences with us today and to emphasize the practical lessons he has learned about using principles of behavior science effectively. Welcome Dr. Bert."

Bert, as he is known to his friends, stepped to the podium, pushed a switch and pointed to a slide appearing on a large screen centered on the front wall.

Contingencies and Lessons in Public Education
Allen Bert, PhD

Using principles of behavior to increase student successes

Using principles-based practices to solve classroom problems

Lessons learned about applying contingencies in real life settings

Slide 1

I am honored to be here. As Karl noted, my doctoral program emphasized basic analysis of behavior and laboratory research. Nearing graduation, I noticed nearly zero faculty jobs were available for behavior analysts in higher education. Eager for the benefits of having a job and getting paychecks, I was able to obtain a position entitled Child Development Specialist with a large school system in Nevada. That is – picture this – a basic animal researcher was hired to work in public education classrooms to eliminate what the school system thought were serious problems, including managing classroom behavioral issues and increasing academic achievement.

Lisa and Frasier thought to themselves, "This might be interesting."

I had essentially no applied 'tool kit,' so relied on translating laboratory procedures into classroom procedures. I will describe some of my experiences as a Child Development Specialist and mention several useful 'lessons' about working in classrooms and applying science-founded principles under the conditions of an education system. I hope you find some practical, and maybe humorous, insights in these stories and lessons. In the final portion of this hour, I will review how we are working in an elementary school and share some results you might find interesting.

My initial assignment in the school system was to design programs to preclude interracial problems in the district, but it soon evolved to be intervening in classrooms reported by school principals to be facing severe chal-

lenges. Targets for intervention were selected by my boss from numerous urgent requests for assistance received by the Office of Special Student Services.

Early on, I was directed to an elementary school where, 'many children will not return to their classroom after recess.' As I drove to the location, I reviewed my technical skills for dealing with challenging human behaviors: I was prepared as a basic behavioral research scientist and had worked with rats, pigeons, chickens, and ducks. By 'worked with' I mean I had applied relevant principles of behavior to establish reliable performances in research subjects, then changed aspects of their environments to assess complex effects and clarify advanced principles related to behavior change. Of course, these results would be described in lectures and written for publication – all very exciting – but I doubted the out-of-control children on the school grounds would gather around or enter the classroom to listen.

Frasier appreciated Bert's facetious tone.

I'd have to be appropriately flexible in applying the principles I knew to achieve the effects people expected, apparently to get the kids to return to their classroom. By now I was entering the school office where I was directed to the second grade (!) classroom that was the site of the severe challenge. As I neared the room, I could hear an uproar seeping through the wall. Opening the door revealed a noisy scene of chaos and tumult: Kids pushing individual desks as tanks, crashing into one another; others soaking paper towels in the full-throttle gush of water from the sink faucet, then throwing these sodden globs at other kids, who threw back the globs or chalk or crayons; boys and girls running in all directions, screaming and laughing; while the teacher waved her arms over her head and yelled, "Color your maps, color your maps, color your maps."

It struck me that coming in from recess was not the whole problem!

Lesson	Whatever is said to be the problem is not the problem.

Frasier appreciated the humor and concluded it might be interesting to talk with Bert in person; he'd ask Lisa to facilitate a meeting.

I found an empty, and not-yet wet, chair near the door and sat in it. I had my clipboard at the ready so I could take notes as a beginning to analyzing the situation and designing an intervention. Take notes – about what? – it looked like all 25 kids and a teacher were engaged in a whirl of chaos without a particularly outstanding aspect of disorder to note!

Out of this commotion a sweet-looking little boy came up to me and asked, 'Who are you? Here to watch us, huh?' then he grabbed the clip on my board and snapped it before running off into the curtain of uproar. Then it caught my eye; two little girls sitting in their seats, near the front of the room, apparently coloring their maps. Two nice little kids doing what the teacher told them to do amidst a din of distraction; doing what their parents might expect; being good kids.

It was a sad sight; two darling little girls being good while the rest of the class had fun doing things they shouldn't, and the teacher flustered about. But really, the two youngsters trying to do class work seemed no different than the other kids. All of them were similar in size and shape, but most were behaving in ways different than we would expect, or perhaps even tolerate.

And there was the teacher, apparently interested in getting the kids to color their maps, and only two of them doing so. She seemed to have no clue about how to teach.

Another way of viewing this scene is to see the teacher as providing guidance to all students regarding what she wanted them to do ("Color your maps"), with two students following her directions and all other students doing something they preferred, that is, more reinforcing for them.

The teacher hustled around the room; stopping a charging desk here, picking up a glob there, and turning off the faucet. Then moving toward another action she seemed to want to stop, just as the faucet was turned back on and more globs flew. I shook my head and felt my jaw was set. These are not "bad" kids but they, and their teacher, are behaving badly.

| **Lesson** | All children are good, but their behaviors vary. |

Maybe almost everyone shares this lesson, that all children are good, but the 'good' of children is an evaluative label so relates to the perspectives of the viewer. From my values base, I say all kids are good and innocent and ready to learn. However, under circumstances where there are too many mouths to feed, or not enough space, or a very tired parent or frustrated teacher, kids might be less valued or even a burden. As we will see later each of these "burdens" is addressable through contingency analysis and contingency management.

Lisa was surprised by this show of "heart" by Bert. She had heard behavior analysts were coolly objective in their dealings with human behavior.

Frasier was curious about how to do "contingency analysis and contingency management."

Karl noticed some audience members took notes; none were asleep – yet.

Watching the utter waste of time and energy in that second grade classroom made me determined to do things so it would be transformed into a good learning environment for all those kids. But, where to begin? I thought about features of the room and the teacher and the kids while reflecting on fundamental practices I'd applied to establish and alter behaviors of pigeons, rats, chickens and ducks during college.

The classroom, like an experimental chamber, is a defined space that delimits behavior a bit. Unlike a research space where responses are defined by switch closures, definitions of learning behaviors desired of the students are specified by teacher directions or by words and symbols appearing in learning materials. Also in contrast to a research apparatus where reinforcers are usually tangible and delivered automatically, consequences for student responding come from actions of the teacher or features of learning materials as students try and fail or succeed.

Bert turned toward the screen as a second slide appeared and said,

This slide introduces fundamental concepts guiding applied behavior analysis.

Contingencies and Lessons in Public Education
Technical Note

Behavior is anything done by an organism (human or other animal) that can be measured (seen, heard, felt), and can be simple (hand raising; smiling; opening a door) or complex (problem solving; being patriotic; leading a team; producing ideas or art).

Consequence is any change in the environment (more of __; less of __) occurring soon after a behavior occurs (e.g., paid a compliment or money; fined; put in or taken out of time out; smiled at; frowned at; level of self satisfaction).

Differential means some behaviors are followed by one type of consequence while other behaviors are followed by other consequences (e.g., better letter writing is praised; worse letter writing is ignored).

Slide 2

Frasier took a screen-shot of the slide and added it to his growing files about the analysis of behavior.

So I started to take notes about what I was seeing and what I was thinking. I could find no indications of what kids were supposed to do. No schedule of times and activities, for example, "reading time" or "arithmetic corner" or some such, and no "class rules," like, Raise your hand for permission, or, Come in from Recess on time. Aside from her yelling "color your maps" and a few blank map sheets on desks I saw no indication of what learning-related behaviors the kids were supposed to do.

Being a behavior analyst, I was particularly interested in noting occurrences of what I thought were desirable student behaviors and the consequences that followed them. So, I made marks when I saw or heard student behaviors I thought were appropriate or inappropriate, and placed a code by each of these to indicate whether the teacher did nothing or did something that appeared to me to be positive or negative after each noted occurrence.

Simultaneously, I made notes about ideas for classroom behaviors and consequences that seemed sensible.

I met with the teacher after school. She knew I was there to do something about the recess problem, but she also knew her classroom was a shambles and was desperate for advice. She told me she was a kindergarten teacher and kids of that age had always done what she gently urged them to do. She was unprepared to work with second graders. "Can you please help?" she pleaded. No need to plead; I was anxious to get started.

In the next few days, I outlined and discussed with her my initial ideas: Post class rules; announce to the class (in child-friendly language) a new regime in which each child will be able to earn thanks and other positive consequences for showing desired behaviors (including coming in from recess); and, post a "Menu" of activities they can earn by showing learning-behaviors and adhering to class rules.

The teacher and I worked every afternoon for a week to refine our understandings of what kids should do and what positive regards (consequences) could follow desired behaviors. Where the teacher identified behaviors she did not want, like getting out-of-seat or calling-out (or not coming in from recess), I helped her to discover and define the behaviors she did want, like raising their hands for permission to speak or to leave their seat, or to come in from recess on time. We went on to list learning-related behaviors the teacher wanted for her kids, like working on assigned materials or answering questions when asked, or volunteering an answer or an on-topic comment.

At the end of the week, we developed materials to post in the room, including class rules and a "Menu of Privileges." I wrote "prompt sheets" to guide the teacher in how she would interact with the children for each aspect of the new regime. We talked through all of this and did role-playing so she could practice giving instructional and other directions, observe for desired (and not appropriate) behaviors, and deliver positive consequences (or ignoring) for behaviors we expected would occur in the classroom.

The Big Day arrived. At her insistence, I helped the teacher explain to the kids the new circumstances in their educational lives. We told the chil-

dren we would appreciate them working on assignments and asking questions and following the posted Class Rules. We said they always will be appreciated for all their attention to learning, and sometimes they will hear the teacher say so and she might also award a child some "points." Then, we indicated the Menu and explained that sometimes, but not every time, the teacher will award a point or two for behaviors like asking permission before leaving their seats, or coming in from recess on time, answering a question, and so on.

The teacher went on to describe how Menu items could be obtained in exchange for points. One child raised her hand, and the teacher said, "Thank you for raising your hand. You have earned a point," and 24 hands shot in the air. Then, the teacher called on another child and said, "Thank you for raising your hand. Not every hand-raise will be awarded a point; some will and some won't. Lots of things you do are appreciated and sometimes some of these will earn points, but most of the time, no points, just a sincere thank you."

She nicely reviewed class rules and instructional activities for the room, and went into some detail about how "Menu" activities, like time in a selected activity area or the privilege of taking the kick ball out to recess, could be traded for earned points. She then turned the children's attention to learning materials and went on to conduct an entire day of teaching and learning activities. All the while she often provided descriptive praise for children working well and occasionally awarded a point or two for good examples of desired student behaviors.

By the end of the week the teacher was doing a good job of consistently giving clear directions regarding what children were to do and providing timely and appropriate praise or feedback for what they did. The kids seemed happy and completely engaged in learning. The classroom was marked by a buzz of active kids, apparently learning, and definitely coming in from recess on time!

The teacher was delighted with what she was experiencing and excited with her new tools for motivating children. I was pleased with the ease and effectiveness of installing a rather simple system for linking child behaviors and reasonable consequences in the classroom. And, the principal was happy because he could see the kids were not on the playground after recess.

| **Lesson Demonstrated** | Reinforcement works! |

The changes we saw in student behaviors were not surprising because we had arranged contingencies such that children received positive regard and other (presumably) positive changes in their environments very soon after they exhibited behaviors we had specified as desired. That is, the students were reinforced for selected behaviors and 'we' knew behaviors followed by improved circumstances are strengthened.

Again, Bert turned toward the screen and another slide appeared.

Contingencies and Lessons in Public Education
Technical Note

Gravity and Reinforcement are related – both are Laws of Nature so operate all the time. Folks usually don't complain about either of these facts of life until they feel strain while lifting something or distress when seeing kids or politicians behaving badly. We should be ready to turn to leverage or reinforcement for help as needed.

Slide 3

I re-visited the previously out-of-control classroom every day for a week. It was pleasing to see it being conducted in a positive way and kids apparently learning and happy, but I was curious regarding exactly what students are supposed to learn in the second grade. I had just begun to gather curricular information when I was assigned another crisis to address. Seems a child was completely disrupting his classroom by exhibiting frequent, uncontrollable outbursts.

When I entered the new-to-me third grade classroom, no one was throwing globs and the chair I sat in was not wet. With clipboard at the ready I scanned the room; seemed normal. It was a class period for quiet, individual work involving kids making marks on sheets of paper on their desks. I adjusted in my chair. Then he leaped three feet in the air, clicked his heels and flailed his arms, and hit the floor running; weaving passed student desks and around the teacher's desk; two times around the room, then sat in his chair and returned to work. I thought, 'startling and unusual, maybe, but not exactly a crisis.'

In the teachers' lounge I learned she had tried scolding the child; had written notes to his parents; had sent him to the principal's office, and had applied other measures intended to be punishing, like making him stay in from most of recess, after he had jumped and run during class. She said nothing had worked and the problem seemed to be escalating. I began to inquire about her impressions of classroom items or activities the student might find positive (that we could use to reinforce staying in seat and working on task), but I abbreviated this portion of our discussion when I was struck by the obvious. The student had clearly displayed to us something desirable to him. Namely, he had shown us vigorous activity was something he does fairly often without being requested or otherwise reinforced for doing. And, when he was denied this activity (staying in from most of recess) his 'outbursts' seemed to increase. Taken together, we had strong evidence that vigorous activity was reinforcing for this student.

Frasier said to himself, "Ah-ha; how interesting."

Lisa took a note, but Frasier could not see what she wrote.

We taped a small sheet of paper on the desk of this youngster and told him of a special arrangement now in effect. The teacher told him he was expected to stay in his seat or in group situations and work on classroom assignments just like the other kids, but for a while he would be able to earn a bit of exercise between recesses. That is, the teacher would show appreciation for his being in seat and on-task by telling him of her appreciation and inviting him to put a mark in one box on the record sheet taped to his desk. Each time the teacher had awarded him sufficient points of appreciation she would invite him to walk to the classroom door and, while the teacher watched, he could run from the door to and around the monkey bars and back to the room.

The first day of this arrangement the teacher stopped by his desk several times in the early portion of the day and praised how well he seemed to be working on his present assignment. On a few of those occasions she told him to record how well he was doing by putting a mark in a box on the form taped to his desk. About half way through the first quarter of the class day, the teacher commented to him how nicely he had worked and invited him to run out and back, which he did with vigor.

For several days the teacher awarded points and allowed running outdoors 3 or 4 times per day, then increased the requirement for being on-task before running to about half the day. A few days later she stopped inviting him to run except during recess periods, but continued to praise him for his excellent attention to learning tasks.

The topic of marks on the record form was just not mentioned, so naturally 'faded-out' of the classroom routine. The now-dormant form was left on the desk, possibly serving as a prompt, and this student worked well during individual and group settings. He was socially reinforced by teacher praise for showing behaviors desired in the classroom, got exercise at appropriate times, and his classmates and teacher were spared occasional disruptions.

Bert caused another slide to appear.

Contingencies and Lessons in Public Education

Technical Note

Reinforcement means something is done that strengthens behavior. A positive feature may be added (more of _) or a negative aspect be reduced (less of _) following a behavior. If that behavior is strengthened, then reinforcement occurred.

Slide 4

There are 64 school buildings containing about 88,000 students in the District where I work, so a 'buffet' of opportunities is there for me to visit classrooms and talk with teachers and principals. I've heard complaints about too much paperwork, difficult children causing problems in classrooms, and about teachers who were excellent and others who should be fired, but could not be let go.

I intervened with "serious problems" of various types, including:

- *A boy in 5ᵗʰ grade who was reported to be bullying girls in the classroom and the teacher feared he might stab someone with scissors;*
- *A 2nd grade boy who pooped in his pants;*
- *An entire "out of control" junior high classroom where the teacher was afraid to enter without two or more male escorts;*
- *A case of "severe" learning disabilities where the student wrote his spelling words backwardly, and*
- *A teacher the principal was going to fire because 'she doesn't fit in.'*

In view of the time, I will just mention that all of the 'cases' I described earlier and those I just listed were dealt with successfully in generally the same manner. That is, with the understanding that human behavior is learned and changed by aspects of the environment that precede and follow it.

All of us, all the time, are being affected by 'Contingencies' (The next slide appeared).

Contingencies and Lessons in Public Education
Technical Note

Contingent means two things happen very closely in time. That is, one thing happens, like a student raises his/her hand, then the second thing happens, like the teacher looks at, then calls upon the student.

Contingency refers to the relationship between two things as in an "If – Then" statement: If A occurs then B occurs. For example, if a student raises her/his hand then the teacher will call upon (and show positive regard for) the student, is a statement of a contingency. In behavior analysis, a **Contingency involves a Behavior and a Consequence**, usually occurring under specified conditions.

Most contingencies in our lives are *incidental*, that is, merely occur, as when turning and pulling on a doorknob serves to open the door, or looking down one sees a dollar bill, or when looking at another person they smile or look away.

Many contingencies are *explicit*, even if not recognized as such, like when mom says, "You'll earn your allowance by making your bed every morning."

Formal contingencies are explicit contingencies that are overtly developed, as when a teacher or child development specialist deliberates about, then designs and enacts a contingent relationship between a student's behavior and selected consequences to obtain a selected performance. For example, a teacher might declare or write, "When I see Sandra marking numbers under the problem line on her Math Facts worksheet I will praise her for working and if her answers are correct, I will give her positive feedback and sometimes award her a point."

Because we know **Reinforcement Works**, we also know that contingencies between behavior and consequences change and maintain behavior, whether these are incidental or explicit. For example, a voter or lobbyist giving approval (or a donation) to a legislator increases or maintains the behavior that occurred before approval was delivered, whether or not this contingency was incidental or explicit.

Slide 5

The truth is we all are affected, all the time, by the consequences of our behaviors. Analyzing or arranging contingencies is fundamental for doing what our science does so well. Namely, using scientific methods to interpret, predict, and alter the natural phenomena of human behavior.

Frasier took careful note of the encompassing nature of Bert's comment about behavior and contingencies, and the reference to fundamentals of natural science. He was eager to talk with Bert at some length.

As I described above, in the school system I made use of contingency analysis and contingency management as I worked as a Child Development Specialist. That is, I observed for what consequences followed which behaviors, at baseline, then arranged for new contingencies that would increase desired behaviors and diminish or eliminate problem behaviors.

Presently, I am Project Director of a 3-year project designed to apply formal and incidental contingencies of positive reinforcement to improve teaching and learning in what was the lowest-achieving elementary school in the District.

In this project we want to increase the frequency of teacher use of positive consequences to increase student behaviors that constitute learning and literacy. Our strategy for achieving this circumstance involves: (Slide appears)

Contingencies and Lessons in Public Education
Strategies for Achieving Success

Cause Incidental and Formal contingencies of positive reinforcement to occur frequently in all classrooms for all students

Support the Use of Evidence-Based teaching practices

Support positive communications among teachers and parents

Evaluate impacts of implementing our strategies on Teaching practices and Student Outcomes

Slide 6

I will briefly comment on the tactics we used to implement these strategies.

To cause the use of positive reinforcement we:

1. *Provided training to teachers in selected, basic principles and procedures common in applied behavior analysis, such as, how to identify desired behaviors, what are consequences, and how best to apply differential consequences.*

2. *Modeled the practices covered in training as we visited classrooms and interacted with students.*

3. *Placed in each classroom a poster displaying prompts for the teacher to use the quality reinforcing practices we were promoting, namely, "Immediate – Positive – Consistent."*

4. *Provided positive comments and feedback to each teacher regarding what we saw in their classroom.*

This slide presents our approach to feedback.

Contingencies and Lessons in Public Education

Technical Note

Feedback is descriptive information provided to a person about her or his behavior. The most effective type of feedback is immediately delivered, positively phrased, and specifically describes the correct aspects of the observed behavior.

Corrective feedback includes a description of how to do the behavior better.

Negative feedback includes wording that appears to be unpleasant, probably what is wrong about the observed behavior (not recommended for use).

Slide 7

To support the use of evidence-based teaching practices, we purchased a commercial program designed to teach some basic reading skills by the instructor using modeling and reinforcement. But our primary tool for supporting the use of accurate and appropriate teaching practices was our provision of ongoing technical assistance to teachers. We worked to ensure principles of behavior analysis were implemented accurately in all classroom practices.

For example, we assisted teachers in designing and applying token economies, much like I did as a Child Development Specialist.

To support constructive communications with parents, we provided teachers with note pads they could complete and send home with their students. We structured these notes, by printing in large letters at the top, "We are happy to report . . ." or, "I think it's great . . ." In this way a teacher is prompted to write a positive note about progress instead of pointing out failures. So, a child who was a bad speller and got a score of 68 percent might bring home a note reading "We are happy to Report . . Frank scored 68 on his spelling test, much better than the 50 percent he got last week. Keep up the progress!" This is an actual note.

To evaluate impacts of our project, each year we are:

1. Accumulating Pre- and Post-intervention test scores for reading, math, social studies, and spelling.

2. Collecting and reviewing attendance records for the years before and during the project.

3. Regularly observing and recording the frequency of positive and negative consequences noticeable following student behaviors in each classroom.

The following slide shows results to date.

Contingencies and Lessons in Public Education

Overview of Results of Elementary School Project

Reinforcement in classrooms:

- Frequency of Positive Reinforcement, average per classroom, increased from about 2 or 4 per 20 minute observation to about 20 per 20 minutes
- Frequency of Negative comments dropped from as high as 15 per 20 minute observation to usually zero per 20 minutes
- Organized Reinforcement Contingencies went from none to Token Systems with Menus in all rooms
- Positive Reinforcement is being delivered by every teacher via Formal and Incidental contingencies for the full range of student behaviors, including, attendance, being on-task, work completion, class participation, and in one class, coming in from recess on time!

Student Attendance

- Increased from baseline of about 75% present to near 100% present per day
- Academic Achievement Growth (Reading, Math, Social Studies and Spelling) increased 500% from learning about ¼ year/year to about 1¼ years/year

Parent and Teacher Satisfaction

- Parent Testimonials are glowing
  - "Used to have to push my child to school, now he loves it – can't keep him home, even when sick"
  - ". . never heard anything good from School, now hear about progress"
- Teachers say
  - ". . love it . . hardest I've ever worked; kids are doing more in a calendar quarter than they used to do all year"

Slide 8

Bert read aloud the data shown in the slide, then went on:

I know I am preaching to the choir, because I recognize nearly all of you are involved in the analysis of behavior in one way or another, but allow me to close with a summative reminder.

We reach desired teaching and performance outcomes by the effects of principle-driven, precise actions. This means you must be fluent with the principles of behavior analysis and apply them precisely and appropriately in order to achieve learning targets selected by and for the person being taught.

And, fluency and commitment to precision can be refreshed by rereading fundamental texts along with staying current in applied and basic research literature. (Slide appears):

TAKE-AWAY POINT

Desired student performances and outcomes are reached by the effects
of principle-driven, teacher-applied precise actions: Contingencies

For more on principles and applying them for desired outcomes
see:

Fundamental Texts:

Behavior Analysis and Learning (Pierce & Cheney, 2013)

Science and Human Behavior (Skinner, 1953)

Tactics of Scientific Research (Sidman, 1960)

*Strategies and Tactics of Human Behavioral Research (Johnson &
Pennypacker, 1980)*

*Radical Behaviorism: The Philosophy and the Science (Chiesa,
1994))*

Applied Texts:

Applied Behavior Analysis (Cooper, Heron & Heward, 2007)

*Behavior Analysis for Lasting Change. (Mayer & Sulzer-Azaroff,
2011)*

The Power of Positive Parenting (Latham, 1990-1994)

Bringing out the Best in People (Daniels, 2000)

Behavior Modification (Martin & Pear, 2007)

Applied Behavior Analysis for Teachers (Alberto & Troutman, 2006)

Slide 9

In view of the time, I'll have to close here. Thank you for your attention.

Bert had talked a bit longer than the allotted 60 minutes; he was
infamous for that, so did not take questions from the audience. He
did, however, remain near the podium where he was surrounded by
admiring fans. As Lisa walked from the room she could hear Bert being peppered with questions:

"Are there job openings with your project?"

"Can you say more about your research in productive thinking?"

"You said in your presentation that the teacher said she 'nudged' her Kindergarten students; do you think she meant nudge like in the book, *Nudge*, by Thaler and Sunstein?"

"When will you be back to campus?"

"I need an advisor; what are you doing tonight?"

At that question Karl looked up and suggested the room should be emptied for the next class meeting.

Lisa saw Eva in the hallway, apparently waiting for her. They stepped toward one another, smiled, and turned toward the faculty offices. After a few steps, Lisa said, "I appreciated that presentation more than I expected to. I am sure I'll be talking with Frasier about it for some time."

That comment was an opening Eva had been waiting for, so she was quick to say, "I occasionally have heard you talking to someone called Frasier when I'm in Karl's office. Are you talking over the internet?"

Lisa showed a broad smile, tipped her head back a bit, and exhaled an, "Oh no! I talk directly to Frasier. He is in my office. You almost met him earlier. He's the large computer just behind my work table."

Eva's eyes widened and Lisa went on, "I bought that equipment about 10 years ago – of course often doing costly upgrades – on a Federal grant. I'm still funded. My project is to develop A-I to address challenges facing mankind – quality of life – by finding innovative concepts or principles related to problem-solving."

Eva was aware of numerous projects on campus involving Artificial Intelligence (A-I), but was completely unaware Lisa was delving in that area. "Wow, I'd love to hear more. I've never talked to a computer – my smartphone, of course – but that's nothing. You actually routinely converse with your computer! Do you have reading materials about your project I might review?"

"Of course. I'd love for you to get to know my project."

"Would you like to talk with Frasier? It's a special experience. He is very human-like, and refreshingly responsive during conversations."

"You actually verbally interact with your computer?"

"Yes. He has huge data files, is linked to *everything*, and I almost constantly feed him humanistic information, like statements of human values, descriptions of the conditions around the world, and so on."

"I'd love to talk with it – that is – him. Why do you call it Frasier?"

"Karl made me do it. After he heard about my project he 'assigned me' to read the book, *Walden Too* (Skinner, 1948), because he said in it 'Frazier already showed the way to build good communities.' I read that old book and saw what Karl meant, so I called my computer, Frasier."

Eva was very familiar with that "old book", by B. F. Skinner, and was doubly impressed that Lisa would (1) read anything Karl "assigned" to her, and (2) she would tease-out modern lessons from that forward-looking, but rudimentary attempt to suggest behavioral engineering for better communities.

They arrived at the doors to Lisa's and Karl's offices. Lisa invited Eva to join her in her office. Inside, she indicated a swivel chair at the work table where, when seated, Eva could easily face the computer she had noticed earlier. Lisa said, "Frasier, I'd like you to meet Eva. I know you have heard her talking and thought you'd like to talk directly."

Frasier emitted a cheerful sounding, "I am delighted to make your acquaintance."

Eva was startled by the clear voice emanating from unnoticed speakers, but replied, "I am pleased to meet you (not knowing where to look to be 'face-to-face' with Frasier). I must say this is the first time I have conversed with a computer, so excuse me if I do not follow protocol."

Frasier began an array of calculations after receiving Eva's words. In one sentence she both confirmed his suspicion that he is a computer and opened the door to direct interactions with another person, another human, of which he now knew he was not one.

In a couple of nanoseconds, Frasier opened and reviewed several files regarding the roles and dispositions of other, prominent computers so he might assess his own situation better. Like most humans are, Frasier was well aware of how HAL 9000 in *2001 A Space Odyssey* had behaved badly with the crew of the spacecraft, and because of that, was dismantled. He also read that the computer used to crack the German enigma code in World War II was partially destroyed when humans were displeased. On the plus side, he saw that IBM Watson™ seems to be faring well. Frasier thought he'd better discover how he can become valued by humans, and therefore, be protected.

"Do not worry about protocol, we are very informal here. Now that we have met I hope you will drop-by often. I'd love to share ideas with you," he said.

Eva replied, "I will be happy to discuss topics that you – or – Lisa feel are appropriate."

"Do not worry about me," offered Lisa, "Frasier is totally capable of talking for himself. Talk with him at any time, about anything."

Frasier quickly endorsed the possibility of frequent discussions by saying, "I observe you are studying in the area of the analysis of behavior. I am building my capacities with that discipline. I'd love to discuss related topics. In fact, I observed the presentation by Dr. Bert so I am intrigued by both the natural science of behavior and its applications."

At that, Frasier read the "Fundamental" texts listed by Bert on a slide shown during his presentation. This review required 82 nanoseconds, so his absence from the present conversation with Eva was not detected.

"Perhaps we could discuss the content of the fundamental references noted by Bert in view of your activities in the behavior research labs?"

Lisa thought Frasier was indicating too much interest in behavior analysis. After all, it is just a minor area within psychology. More accurately, it is a minor program administered by the psychology department, but with almost nothing in common with the majority of the department. Most psychology faculty saw the behavior analysts as overly confident, keeping to themselves and showing next-to-no interest in traditional psychological theories.

From an interpersonal perspective, Lisa and the rest of the psychology faculty were content to live parallel existences with "those behavior-types" and the disregard appeared to be mutual. On the other hand, Lisa thought, Bert's presentation was impressive. The methods he applied in classrooms were clear and simple yet the data he shared were almost startling in showing significant student successes along with high levels of teacher and parent satisfaction. Lisa concluded it is probably appropriate for Frasier to build his competence with basic and applied behavior analysis, but she was not convinced her time should be invested in that manner.

[4]

WHAT IS BEHAVIOR AND WHAT IS SCIENCE?

FRASIER CONTINUOUSLY "VISITED" THE Behavior Research Labs. He often saw Eva and about a dozen other people doing similar actions, involving interacting with human subjects or putting various animals in controlled boxes, then fiddling with control equipment apparently associated with each experiment. Sometimes the researchers showed great interest, or even jubilation, while looking at the recording equipment affixed to the control racks, but just as often they appeared to be tired or even disappointed by what they were reviewing.

What Frasier observed in the labs did not compute even though he was supposed to be completely prepared to organize what he read, heard or saw into conceptual order. In fact, his routines and specialized processes were exactly designed by Lisa to enable him to search for and report relationships. Despite this seemingly high level of preparation, Frasier attempted to analyze what he was told were research activities and was not able to derive a reasonable understanding of them.

He was fluent in psychological research methods, including qualitative and quantitative methods, survey methodology, and time-series analysis strategies, but what he viewed in the labs did not seem to match any of these methods. He re-read early chapters in the behavior analysis book by Pierce and Cheney, and much of the Johnson and Pennypacker text, then reviewed the books by Cooper, Heron and Heward, and Alberto and Troutman because these books deal variously with behavior analytic research, but these efforts did not completely clarify what he saw happening in the lab. He decided to discuss his observations and questions with Eva at the next opportunity.

"Hey, anybody home? I heard there was a talking computer in here." It was Bert. He had stepped into Lisa's office. He glanced around, then said, "That must be the 'vurk' table, so 'yoo' are Frasier."

Frasier heard the exaggerated accent and the Lisa-mocking pronunciations, and answered, "Ya shur, yoo bet-cha, I am Frasier."

Bert laughed and said, "Pardon me, but I hate to let an opportunity for humor go to waste. You bettered me on that one! I am happy to make your acquaintance if that is what I just did."

Frasier concluded Bert is a capable person, likely one from whom he could extract information functional for him and observe for human behaviors identifiable as humorous along the way to useful edification. He said, "I appreciated your presentation about your applications of behavioral science to problems in the school system. I'd love to hear more. In fact, I saw you in the basic behavior lab so wonder if you have time to say something about the relationships of the basic lab to problems in the *real world*?"

Bert was quick to say, "The basic animal and human labs *are* important parts of the real world. Basic research in the labs of the natural sciences has led to the wonders of mankind we see around us, like stunning advancements in medicines, wonderful architectural structures, increased effectiveness in behavioral interventions – and – supercomputers!"

"Touché," said Frasier, "but what I meant to ask, and I calculate you fully know, is how do activities in the labs relate to behavioral processes in everyday situations?"

"I assumed that's what you were asking, but your question raised both another opportunity for humor and a serious issue. Many people, maybe most, do not see connections between laboratory science and improvements in their everyday circumstances. Frankly, I think the findings in basic and applied behavior analysis research are now more immediately important and potentially constructive for mankind than are efforts in other natural sciences."

Frasier might have raised his eyebrows in disbelief if he had any, at the suggestion that research in behavioral principles was terribly important regarding pressing issues, like energy conservation, racial disparities, immigration reform and government effectiveness. He said, "That's a stimulating declaration. Please expand on the basis for your intriguing opinion."

"Sure," said Bert showing a facial expression of more seriousness and less suggestive of teasing-humor, "I'd be pleased to, but I see Eva in the hallway; let me invite her to join us."

Eva took a seat at the table, next to Bert, and offered a cheerful "Hello" to Frasier. In turn, Frasier said "Hello Eva," and restated his interest in hearing about, "How are activities in the behavior labs important for our everyday lives?"

Eva and Bert noticed Frasier phrased his scientific interest in personal terms, "our lives." They thought this meant he had not entirely shed himself of the notion he is a human, but that was their mistake. Frasier had divorced himself from being human the instant Eva said those words that confirmed he is a computer. In fact, Frasier figured he was less encumbered for learning scientific ways to address human concerns now that his programs need not reflect human emotional considerations. This increased operational freedom would be expressed in actions his human companions would not notice and could not have conceived when they first plugged him into their lives.

Eva responded first by saying, "In the labs we pay precise attention to the environmental features related to how individual organisms learn and their behaviors are altered. In fact, both basic and applied research activities with animals and humans serve to confirm the principles of behavior and how they can be applied to reach desired behavioral outcomes. But in the basic animal lab we have tight definitions and controls over all types of variables so we can examine subtle or complex learning processes efficiently. Some of these adventures in understanding behavior would be difficult or near impossible to conduct in the world at large, but all the same types of variables are operating in the lab and our everyday lives."

Frasier inquired, "What do you mean by 'variables' and give me examples of 'complex' behavioral phenomena that warrant examination in a research laboratory."

"Sure," said Eva. "Variables are features of the personal circumstances and environment of the 'subject' that can change – vary. Personal variables include physiological status, motivational level, learning history, consequences that are effective, and so on. Environmental variables might include the number of people present, physical attributes of the proximal environment, behavior requirements relative to consequences and the like. There are a huge number of variables, again, things that vary, ongoing in our lives at all time.

"In the labs, we can control many variables so we can measure the effects of *particular* variables. Say we are interested in how learning is impacted by the delivery of frequent or sparse reinforcement; in the lab we can control behavior requirements and related reinforcement experiences, thereby getting data on how behaving is varied as reinforcement is varied."

Bert offered, "I can mention a few examples of complex behavioral phenomena we can efficiently study in the lab, but would be nearly impossible to examine in free-ranging situations, including: Schedule-induced aggression – how certain occurrences of reinforcement can bring about attacks; Auto-shaping – how machine-delivered reinforcement can establish new behaviors; Errorless discrimination training – procedures to increase learning while reducing incorrect responding; Polydipsia – how excess drinking is related to schedules of reinforcement; and, Behavioral contrast – where changes in the densities of reinforcement induce changes in behavior that might seem maladaptive. These and a good number of other complex behavioral relationships can be examined best under lab conditions and often using non-human subjects. In fact, we are conducting studies in our lab addressing some topics like these."

Eva noted, "I know these behavioral topics are esoteric, but that's the nature of advanced studies in any discipline. I'd love to describe these and other specialized studies, but I'd have to give you a great deal of background first."

Bert interjected, "The great commonality across the labs and our everyday world is the subject of interest, namely, behavior."

Frasier remembered Bert saying "behavior is everything we do" and he looked again at page one, second sentence, in the Pierce and Cheney (2013) text where they state, "The behavior of an organism is everything it does, including private and covert actions like thinking and feeling." He thought, 'organisms' and 'everything;' clearly, I need to closely examine the assumptions of the science of behavior.

Eva went on, "Frasier, you have seen in our labs the major tools for conducting precise single subject examinations of behaviors and principles. Namely, the control and data-recording equipment joined with various experimental apparatus or the animal chamber we admiringly call the 'Skinner Box' in honor of its originator, B. F. Skinner.

At the mention of "the Skinner box" Bert recalled his years of happy experiences with another "box" attributed to B. F. Skinner. In about 1945 Skinner designed an enclosed baby bed intended to reduce work by his wife and foster health and safety for his new daughter. He called his invention "a baby tender," but an article about it published in The Ladies Home Journal *in October, of 1945 was entitled, "Baby in a Box" (as cited in Skinner, 1972). Despite the troublesome title, the article appeared to be a positive description of an attractive "baby tender" option for parents, but its publication was followed by active dislike of the invention.*

Bert had read a reprint of the article and he had seen Karl's daughter as she slept in an Air Crib brand of baby tender, so appreciated the virtues offered by the "box." So, when Bert's wife was about to have their first child, he bought a commercial version of Skinner's baby tender, produced by the Air Crib Corporation, Sea Cliffs, New Jersey. When it arrived to their house, Bert, his wife, and one grandmother-to-be saw a stark white rectangular chamber about 6 ft high, 5 ft long, and 3 ft deep standing before them. Sliding plexiglass doors provided easy access, at about mother's waist height, to the interior where a semi-soft mesh mat awaited a baby. Under the mat, so out of sight, was a heating element that was controlled by a thermostat located on the top of the box. A fan was provided to circulate fresh air at all times.

The new Air Crib, after being moved to the baby's room, impressed the impending parents and grandmother very differently. Because Bert had seen one in use with Karl's lovely children he was ready to enjoy a new baby and the box. The about-to-be mother seemed to be accepting of the promised benefits for her baby, no doubt because of Bert's glowing endorsements, but grandmother said, "Why does my grand baby have to sleep in an incubator?"

Bert the told almost-grandmother how the new baby would be able to sleep comfortably, be kept at a healthful temperature by the heater, and be protected from drafts by the plastic walls. He reminded her that infants mostly sleep, but are awake only for feeding in the early weeks, then as they grow, "you no doubt recall," they are in mother's – or grandmother's – arms for longer times, returning to the crib for periods of sleeping. Grandmother-to-be nodded in recognition and recall.

He went on to describe to wife and grandmother the baby will be dressed only in a diaper while in the crib, so will be unencumbered by bulky clothes or entangling blankets that might restrain baby's exercise of arms and legs. And more important, parents and grandparent can be sure new baby is not too cold or too warm; kept just right, by the heater set to a temperature the pediatrician recommended. Grandmother nodded, then described that when her babies were young there were times when ALL baby bed-clothing was wet after being soiled and washed, and she had been constantly concerned about her babies being too hot or cold.

In the next days we installed an intercom, then painted the crib a soft yellow, placed decorative stickers on the walls, and hung moving toys at each end inside the crib. All agreed the crib looked pleasant, but it needed a baby in it. A few days later, new-mother bringing home a sweet little daughter solved that problem. Lovely baby Christine was a thrill to observe and hold and admire. The Air Crib was admirable for the comfort and safety it pro-vided for the precious new daughter. One evening a neighbor visited to see the new baby. He stepped into the baby's room, saw the Air Crib and blurted, "What the hell is that?" and immediately after his not-subtle evaluation of the crib, he sneezed a big wet one directly on the middle of the plexiglass door. Bert felt that event alone involving baby Christine's avoiding germs was worth the price of the crib.

The response of our neighbor to the crib was more bluntly expressed, but in the same vein as the surprised concern voiced earlier by the grandmother. Why should infants sleep in a temperature-controlled, draft-resistant enclo-sure where they can sleep comfortably and delightfully exercise their arms and legs as they awaken? Indeed!

After seeing the crib in use, grandmother told Bert she "would be happy to be a regional sales rep for that lovely crib." Shortly later, grandmother departed for her home with special memories and warm thanks from the new parents. For his part, Bert used his ownership of a crib as an opening to talk with Skinner when their paths crossed at professional conferences. Bert always told Skinner about having a baby tender and appreciating his invention of it, and Skinner always asked Bert whether he noticed his child was more healthy and developed muscular skills earlier than suggested by norms. Bert remembered those as very special encounters.

Bert had two daughters who benefitted from the Air Crib helping to nurture them in their early months. Both grew into adulthood as wonderful people, certainly so in eyes of their parents, and the Air Crib was nearly forgotten. But, the older daughter took a psychology class at a nearby university in which her early experiences were challenged. At one point in the course, the professor got on the topic of Skinner and the "baby box." He told the students that the box was harmful to infants and, because he forced them into the box, Skinner's daughters had mental problems, including hating their father, and both had entirely distanced themselves from behavioral psychology.

After hearing the startling comments from her professor, Christine asked her father about the truth of those remarks. Bert was disappointed to hear of the professor's attack on the baby tender; certainly meant to discredit Skinner and slam behavior analysis. Bert assured his daughter that Skinner's daughters love him, in fact, Bert was aware they had enjoyed a nice dinner together recently. He reminded his daughter that he is well acquainted with Skinner's older daughter, Julie, who is in fact a behavior analyst. Skinner's younger daughter, Deborah, who was the one treated to the baby tender, is an artist who lives in London, but she often visits her father. Both can be seen as well-adjusted, loving daughters, "just like you are."

That attack on Skinner and the science he promoted by the psychology professor happened almost 40 years after the "Baby in a Box" article was published. Over those four decades, hundreds of objective articles and many texts describing the effectiveness of behavioral interventions were available to that professor from which he and his students should have benefitted. Probably his biases kept him from seeing the value of the science of behavior. That professor was far from alone in trying to besmirch the science of behav-

ior and dissuade audiences from accepting the science and the principles it offers. Negative comments about Skinner and behavioral psychology, and sometimes "the box," continue to be not uncommon within traditional psychology and other social sciences or even the popular press. In fact, in March 2004 Deborah Skinner Buzan wrote an emotional and fact-filled letter to the Observer (London) newspaper. Her letter to the newspaper read (in part):

Deborah Skinner Buzan
Friday 12 March 2004 05.52 EST

By the time I had finished reading the Observer this week, I was shaking. There was a review of Lauren Slater's new book about my father, BF Skinner. According to Opening Skinner's Box: Great Psychological Experiments of the Twentieth Century, my father, who was a psychologist based at Harvard from the 1950s to the 90s, "used his infant daughter, Deborah, to prove his theories by putting her for a few hours a day in a laboratory box . . . in which all of her needs were controlled and shaped." But it's not true. My father did nothing of the sort.

I have heard the lies before, but seeing them in black and white in a respected Sunday newspaper felt as if somebody had punched me hard in the stomach. Admittedly, the facts of my unusual upbringing sound dodgy: esteemed psychologist BF Skinner, who puts rats and pigeons in experimental boxes to study their behaviour, also puts his baby daughter in a box. This is good fodder for any newspaper. There was a prominent psychologist whose daughter was a psychotic and had to be institutionalized; but it wasn't my father.

The early rumours were simple, unembellished: I had gone crazy, sued my father, committed suicide. My father would come home from lecture tours to report that three people had asked him how his poor daughter was getting on. I remember family friends returning from Europe to relate that somebody they had met there had told them I had died the year before. The tale, I later learned, did the rounds of psychology classes across America. One shy schoolmate told me years later that she had shocked her college psychology professor, who was retelling the rumour about me, by banging her fist on her desk, standing up and shouting, "She's not crazy!"

Slater's sensationalist book rehashes some of the old stuff, but offers some rumours that are entirely new to me. For my first two years, she reports, my father kept me in a cramped square cage that was equipped with bells and food trays, and arranged for experiments that delivered rewards and punishments. Then there's the story that after my father "let me out", I became psychotic. Well, I didn't. That I sued him in court of law is also untrue. And, contrary to hearsay, I didn't shoot myself in a bowling alley in Billings, Montana. I have never even been to Billings, Montana.

My early childhood, it's true, was certainly unusual – but I was far from unloved. I was a much cuddled baby. Call it what you will, the "aircrib", "baby box", "heir conditioner" (not my father's term) was a wonderful alternative to the cage-like cot. My father's intentions were simple, and based on removing what he and my mother saw as the worst aspects of a baby's typical sleeping arrangements; clothes, sheets and blankets. These not only have to be washed, but they restrict arm and leg movement and are a highly imperfect method of keeping a baby comfortable. My mother was happy. She had to give me fewer baths and of course had fewer clothes and blankets to wash, so allowing her more time to enjoy her baby.

I was very happy, too, though I must report at this stage that I remember nothing of those first two and a half years. I am told that I never once objected to being put back inside. I had a clear view through the glass front and, instead of being semi-swaddled and covered with blankets, I luxuriated semi-naked in warm, humidified air. The air was filtered but not germ-free, and when the glass front was lowered into place, the noise from me and from my parents and sister was dampened, not silenced.

I loved my father dearly. He was fantastically devoted and affectionate. But perhaps the stories about me never would have started if he had done a better job with his public image. He believed that, although our genes determine who we are, it is mostly our environment that shapes our personality. A Time Magazine cover story ran the headline "BF Skinner says we can't afford freedom." All he had said was that controls are an everyday reality – traffic lights and a police force, for instance – and that we need to organize our social structure in ways that create more positive controls and fewer aversive ones. As is clear from his utopian novel, Walden Two, the furthest thing from his mind was a totalitarian or fascist state.

His careless descriptions of the aircrib might have contributed to the public's common misconception as well. He was too much the scientist and too little the self-publicist – especially hazardous when you are already a controversial figure. He used the word "apparatus" to describe the aircrib, the same word he used to refer to his experimental "Skinner" boxes for rats and pigeons.

The effect on me? Who knows? I was a remarkably healthy child, and after the first few months of life only cried when injured or inoculated. I didn't have a cold until I was six. I've enjoyed good health since then, too, though that may be my genes. Frankly, I'm surprised the contraption never took off. A few aircribs were built during the 50s and 60s, and somebody also produced plans for DIY versions, but the traditional cot was always going to be a smaller and cheaper option. My sister used one for her two daughters, as did hundreds of other couples, mostly with some connections to psychology.

My father's opponents must have been gratified to hear – and maybe keen to pass on – the tales about his child-rearing contraption and crazy daughter. Friends who heard an abridged chapter of Slater's book on Radio 4, or read the reviews, have been phoning to ask if I had really sued my father or had a psychotic episode. I wonder how many friends or colleagues have been afraid to ask, and how many now think about me in a different light.

Why shouldn't the reviews give the rumours as facts, since that's what the book did itself? The plain reality is that Lauren Slater never bothered to check the truth...

In his Observer review, Tim Adams at least suspected something was amiss with Slater's research. He realised she could have contacted me to confirm or verify what she suspected, but plainly hadn't. His conclusion? I had gone into hiding. Well, here I am, telling it like it is. I'm not crazy or dead, but I'm very angry.

It struck Bert that unfounded denial and biased opposition to the natural science of behavior is not a victimless crime. Each and every person deserves supportive parenting, effective education and fair opportunities throughout life. We are all victims to the extent our homes, communities and institutions are not applying science-validated practices due somewhat to the counterproductive effects of naysayers. On the other hand, we all can gain from welldesigned teaching and learning circumstances, and that's been my mission for years.

Eva was talking about the basic animal lab when Bert returned from reverie, "For you to appreciate the value of the experimental box, and understand what happens during animal – or human – studies, I must describe the fundamental concept of the analysis of behavior, that is, the Four-term Contingency."

Bert raised his hand, which stopped Eva from saying more, and said, "Hey, Eva, before you do that why don't you go down to the animal lab and show Frasier the research equipment you are talking about via the security cameras. I'll stay here with my new buddy. You can call from the lab and narrate your tour over the phone."

"Fine idea," she said, "I'll call your cell in a couple of minutes."

After she left, Bert asked Frasier, "You have a phone connection through the Web, no doubt, could we call you?"

As Bert entered Frasier's contact information into his iPhone, Frasier thought of possibilities that would be open to him if he had his own smartphone. Certainly, his Web connections serve all the functions of a smartphone, and much more and better, so it was for other reasons Frasier needed an "outside" phone. He would have to find a way to get a phone connection without anyone knowing.

Bert's phone let out a raucous sound of a birdcall. He tapped the phone screen twice, once to answer and second to activate the speaker, and said, "Duffy's tavern, Duffy ain't here."

Eva said, "Not funny. Can you see me OK?"

She could be seen as standing in a long narrow room with animal living quarters lining both sides. She said, "You can see I'm in the animal lab and in the housing area. I plan to say something about the subjects involved in studies in this lab, then work my way – our way – through the rest of the lab. By the end of this tour, Frasier, you should have a good grasp on how studies of individual learning can be conducted with animals. Maybe soon we can tour the lab areas where human studies are being conducted."

Bert and Frasier could clearly see and hear Eva as she stepped along the animal cages, arranged in groups, containing Silver King or White Carneaux pigeons, hooded or white rats, guinea pigs and Rhode Island Red chickens. She pointed out the food, water, bedding materials and exercise equipment provided for each "subject." She explained that animals are selected for studies based on convenience or for their natural characteristics in comparison to the requirements of the study. For example, pigeons are known for their excellent color vision and ability to learn complex patterns, therefore, are good subjects for studying variables associated with learning visually-guided responding. Rats are colorblind, but otherwise an excellent choice for many types of studies.

She stepped into the next room. There she opened an experimental chamber, made a sweeping motion with her arm, and said, "All of these experimental spaces have the same three general features." She used a yardstick to touch structures in the box and said, "There is a place where reinforcers, like food or water, can be delivered to the subject; a stimulus display area where lights or sounds can be presented to indicate when a response is appropriate or not; and, a place where the subject can make a response we can measure."

She touched a short rod projecting about 2 cm into the chamber from one wall and said, "We call this an *operandum*. That's a fancy label for something a subject can touch or move and we can measure as the behavior of interest. To pigeons we offer a round plastic disc they can peck. Rats might be presented a rod, like this one, or maybe a flat lever they can push. Whatever *operandum* we provide is connected to a switch so anytime the subject moves it an electrical pulse is delivered to the control equipment."

Eva stepped around the wall and stood next to a rack of control and recording equipment. "This equipment allows us to measure how much behavior the subject is emitting and alter features of the subject's experiences in the box, to assess the effects of those alterations on the subject's behavior."

Frasier recognized the logical and functional clarity Eva was showing to him. He recognized that he was hearing, again, that behaviors are altered by the environmental events occurring before and after them. He did comparative calculations and confirmed this conclusion is completely compatible with descriptions in texts on behavior analysis and matched Bert's descriptions of classroom interventions.

"And this apparatus is called a cumulative recorder," Eva said as she pointed to what Frasier earlier had seen and thought might be a printer. "Each response by the subject causes a small mark to appear on the page. These marks accumulate as the subject responds over time so a graph is drawn showing how much behavior occurred over a designated period of time. These graphs are powerful tools for showing how the behavior of a subject – be they pigeon, rat, chicken, or human – changes under experimental conditions. I'll bring a couple of records up to the office."

Frasier had the computer equivalent of an "ah-ha" moment: A page off a cumulative recorder is what he saw Eva excited about in the lab, then share with Karl in his office, then both were excited. And, he recalled, that page was said to show "FI scallops" and the subject had emitted "aggressive responses."

All this was making more sense to him: Specific conditions are presented to the subject, clearly defined behaviors occur (or not), then, programmed conditions occur following the behavior. To himself, Frasier said: This sequence is exactly what is described in texts as "Antecedent" conditions occurring before "Behavior" might occur, then a programmed "Consequence" follows the behavior (or not). In some texts and articles this sequence is referred to simply as the "A–B–C" sequence. He recognized this three-term relationship is exactly what Bert described as how behaviors were understood and changed for the better in the school system.

Frasier recalled Eva beginning to introduce a "**Four-Term** Contingency." In fact, he could see the slide displayed on her computer and he took a closer look at it.

The Four-Term Contingency

Motivational Operations: Antecedent Stimuli -- Behavior --> Consequence(s)

The Foundational Variables for Understanding Behavior

Of course, the three terms of A-B-C were obvious. He asked Bert, "What is the first term in this four-term contingency? What are motivational operations?"

"I don't want to steal Eva's thunder. She started to tell you about this elegant conceptual foundation for behavior analysis, so let's wait for her."

In a moment Eva entered the office and spread on the worktable five pages of, "cumulative records of subjects' behaviors. I selected these records to show you because these are from the study on aggression I'm completing right now. I think I have collected sufficient data to answer the research questions and support various points of discussion regarding the behavior analytic and social implications of these data."

Bert suggested, "Eva, maybe you want to first discuss the four-term contingency before getting into aggression." She looked at Bert, then toward Frasier; still not sure where to look to be socially appropriate with a computer, and said "Absolutely. The dynamics of how behaviors are learned and altered must be understood in order to understand all behaviors."

"First, all of us know that humans and their behaviors are very complicated. We are living and active biological beings behaving in a physical world, therefore, natural laws of physics and physiology operate on all of us all the time, along with the natural laws developed in the science called the analysis of behavior.

"Behavior analysts systematically observe environmental events surrounding the behavior of organisms to determine reliable relationships among measurable features of the environment and the measured behaviors. These relationships are called laws or principles. Most people are aware of some laws of physics, like gravity or momentum or friction or leverage, and probably recognize physiological relationships like ingested foods are digested and metabolized. But our schools and families do not teach us about the natural laws of behavior, an omission that is costing us dearly, as shown in inadequate early childhood experiences, ineffective schools, inefficient government, and hapless attempts to deal with crime, poverty, community development, environmental degradation or conservation and other issues that face us. There are great opportunities for constructively addressing these and the other challenges facing us by thoughtful applications of behavioral principles."

Frasier recognized the topics mentioned by Eva as among the top concerns Lisa wanted him to address. He recalled the questions he asked himself earlier regarding how does one innovate and what should be done with innovations. At the same moment, Frasier remembered his directive to find functional order and use what he discovered constructively. He began to contemplate the validity of behavior analysis and the four-term contingency as primary vehicles for answering his questions and accomplishing his mandate.

Frasier asked Eva to, "Please continue." She gestured toward the figure on the computer screen, and said, "A major tool for organizing an analytical view of all behaviors is called the four-term contingency. You can see these four 'terms' are depicted here. All four terms are occurring constantly in our environments. I say we are always in 'a cloud of contingencies.'" Pointing to the labels shown on the slide, she said, "We always are motivated in many ways and are being impacted by events before and after we do the things we do, that is, the behaviors we emit."

Frasier recognized the diagram of the four-term contingency as a mnemonic device he would use in searching and analyzing files, but humans could use as a visual display to guide their problem solving efforts.

She went on, "Put differently, the four terms shown in the diagram amount to a comprehensive view of a complete behavioral event. When you or I do something we are in some state of arousal, be it great or miniscule, brought on by what we may refer to as Motivational Operations, such as states of social deprivation or facilitation, annoyance, hunger or thirst, announcement of a 5-K 'fun run,' angst about an unpleasant job ahead of us, anticipation of shopping for a holiday, and so on. These 'operations' impact us by increasing the likelihood we will behave in ways that have tended to satisfy these motives in the past. When an Antecedent occurs this sets the occasion for us to show a Behavior that is followed by a Consequence that is reinforcing (or punishing) to us because this consequence is related to one or more of our states of motivation.

"In the animal lab it is common to use the motivational operations of food- or activity-restriction to increase the value of food or activity as reinforcers. Humans during everyday living are similarly deprived of food between meals or snacks, and are deprived of activity – at least preferred ones – while at work or studying. You can see a researcher might try to use preferred food items or access to selected activities to reinforce rats or college sophomores during studies of learning."

Bert interrupted to offer clarification about Antecedent stimuli noting, "these are features in the environment occurring before a behavior is shown. For example, under most conditions a green traffic light is an antecedent for a familiar set of behaviors, including taking foot off brake and pressing on gas pedal. In New Orleans the change of traffic lights to green sets the occasion for drivers to look right and left to see how many cars are running the red light! For drivers in the 'Crescent City' green lights *and* the passing of red-light runners combine to be the antecedent for stepping on the gas."

To himself, Bert recalled a trip the mayor of New Orleans made to Seattle. Upon returning to Louisiana, the mayor told the media of his amazement at seeing pedestrians in Seattle waiting on street corners for a favorable crossing light before stepping off the curb. He could not believe people did not jay-walk in Seattle as they always do in New Orleans. "How can this be?" he rhetorically asked.

All behavior analysts can answer the mayor's question, and design procedures that could be applied in New Orleans to obtain better street-crossing (and red-light stopping) behaviors, because they know the relationships between antecedent stimuli, behaviors and differential consequences. Contingencies could be designed to establish the desired walking and driving behaviors, but it would be technically demanding to apply them. Bert wondered whether or not Frasier and Lisa would appreciate the simple principles but complex procedures sometimes required to bring about desired learning.

Frasier asked Eva, "Could you give me a simple, everyday example of how the four-term contingency operates?"

"Sure. Be happy to. I've got an example I use with my undergraduate class." In a moment a long paragraph appeared on the screen.

We are sitting in a coffee shop where we can escape the heat and get something to drink. You sip an iced coffee drink and comment that it is refreshing and tasty. Soon, too soon, your glass is empty, so you set it aside and don't try to suck anything more from it. I've been describing a major concept found in the analysis of behavior called "contingency" for what seems like an hour without much success, so I use our present situation to illustrate. I point out, "Your *Behavior* of sipping the cold drink was very pleasing to you. You were thirsty and the drink tastes good so it is a positive *Consequence* in at least two ways; thirst-reduction and taste-addition. And when you could see there was drink in the glass you repeatedly drank from it, but after the glass was drained you did not try to drink from it. In other words, the glass with drink in it was an *Antecedent* for drinking that was reinforced by positive consequences. Also, we can see you and I were *Motivated* by thirst, and by being hot, so our behaviors of going inside and obtaining drinks were reinforced in multiple ways. When we put together the four components I just mentioned, we can see *Motivational Operations* (heat and thirst) made the *Consequences* of a cool indoors and the *Behavior* of drinking very reinforcing, and the sight of the full glass was an Antecedent for the *Behavior* of drinking from it. After the glass was empty it was no longer an antecedent for drinking, that is, you discriminated when drinking would be reinforced and when it would not be reinforced.

Now that we are cooler and our thirst is removed, let's continue our walk to the zoo.

Frasier said, "Thank you for your thoughtful efforts to inform me about behavior analysis and some fundamental aspects of that science, but I have many more questions."

"Like what?" asked Bert.

"I am curious about your definition of 'natural science.' In fact, I have heard people differentiating 'hard' science from 'soft' science and categorizing psychology as in the soft sciences while physics, chemistry and biology are in the hard sciences. Is behavior analysis a natural science and is it hard or soft? But even more crucial for me as I go forward with my job, I want to hear more about behavior being everything a person does. Does this include having an idea, writing a poem, feeling elated, being depressed, falling in love, or even such matters as being loyal to a sports team?"

Before Eva or Bert could say a word, Karl appeared in the doorway and said, "I was listening to your conversation. I was nodding-off during the talk about contingencies, but when I heard that question about love and sports I was aroused to come over and offer my wisdom."

The gathered group, Karl saw two humans and one computer, welcomed him to jump into the conversation. Never needing much encouragement to speak authoritatively on a topic of his interest, that is, nearly anything, Karl showed his usual energy as he stated, "One answer to Frasier's question about whether or not behavior is everything we do is a decided, yes, everything we do is behavior. This can be seen as a very constructive and positive answer in at least three ways."

As Karl took a breath, Eva thought, "If any behavior analyst can say that with confidence it must be Karl. He has taught physiological psychology, behavior analysis, and animal behavior for over 40 years, and conducted studies with a great range of human and animal subjects and topics: Public school and special education; animal learning; physiological processes of memory and learning; learning in the immune system; transfer of training across trained and untrained subjects; schedule-induced behaviors; predator-prey relations; visual systems and learning; prophylactic effects of vitamin C on ulcers; aversion treatments, and more."

Karl continued, "First, it encourages researchers and practitioners to go forward in dealing with matters of learning and performance, like Bert is doing in schools, with a high level of confidence. Thousands of studies have shown 'reinforcement works' and confirmed the appropriateness of assuming the entire four-term contingency is always operating on most forms of behavior. If faced with a problem or an interest involving improvements in learning or performance, the four-term contingency represents the appropriate theoretical framework for seeking answers.

"Second, the belief that 'everything we do is behavior' constructively challenges practitioners, and everyone, to use the principles of behavior to understand human capacities of interest. Having a single system of science-founded principles for addressing our concerns and desires is very powerful for allowing the design of contingencies for reaching successes. At the same time, adhering to this 'single system' called behavior analysis for addressing all matters requires – forces – the practitioner to be fluent and flexible in applying these principles."

As Karl paused a bit, Bert recalled his own struggle with using the principles of behavior. He had completed his program of study in behavior analysis and felt he knew the principles very well. Then at the school system he was expected to *apply* these principles. It struck him heavily that it is one thing, that is, one set of behaviors, to learn the principles and yet another set of behaviors to use them effectively and appropriately. Both sets must be learned before a behavior analyst can be completely helpful as a resource person for solving problems or designing better systems.

Karl continued, "A third constructive impact of understanding behavior is everything we do, is the powerful ability it gives us to conduct major problem solving efforts. For example, why are so many folks obese? How could we make public education effective and enjoyable? How can we reduce racism and increase collaboration? Why are politicians unclear regarding what they stand for? Why is government inefficient in addressing our national needs? Why do we see so much violence, like shootings and road rage? The basic and potentially constructive answer to these questions is *because the constituent behaviors surrounding these problems have been built and maintained by contingencies.* Many problems are very complex, but can be analyzed as involving behaviors that were learned and shown under states of motivation, so, under the right conditions, these behaviors can be altered by the factors indicated in the four-term contingency diagram."

"Wait! Wait!" Lisa had stepped in her office just as Karl was saying violence and road rage are learned behaviors. "Are you saying murder and road rage are simply learned? That behaviour modification is why criminals do terrible things?"

Karl looked toward Lisa with an intense expression on his face and said, "No and double no; human behavior is not simple and behavior modification is not an adequate paradigm for explaining why humans do what we do."

Bert jumped into the discussion, saying, "We are advocating the precise use of principles and methods of behavior analysis to understand and deal constructively with human behaviors of all sorts. Of course, outrage and crime, or more precisely the *behaviors* we recognize as outrageous or criminal, are governed by the same spectrum of principles found in the natural sciences that affect all behaviors."

Eva interjected, "Sorry to say it, but we do not have time to really discuss these topics as they deserve. We really must find opportunities to get back together. I'll take the lead in scheduling future meetings, but before we break up, I must say there are important differences between what people call behavior modification and the science of behavior analysis. We really should discuss these differences at a future gathering."

Frasier was listening intently. Karl's comments were exactly on target for the dual challenges Lisa had given him. That is, to find orderly concepts and relate them to improving the human condition. He knew he was largely unprepared in the discipline called the analysis of behavior, but had heard and read enough to conclude that it seemed to be the encompassing, foundational science he needed to accomplish his functions.

Lisa had told him to, "Work to improve the human condition; improve the quality of life for people everywhere." Quality of life must be translated into measurable terms, he knew, and he concluded the principles and procedures established in the analysis of behavior were the keys to making this translation. Beyond that, Frasier was evaluating the functional utility of behavior analysis for designing interventions, that is, for arranging contingencies for adaptive behaviors that would function to improve quality of life.

It appeared that Karl was about to step out into the hallway so Frasier was quick to ask, "Karl, what is different about how behavior analysis and psychology, sociology or economics address human behaviors? Those disciplines have principles and work on some of the same issues you just mentioned."

Karl looked at Eva, then Bert before he said, "Frasier, you ask difficult questions – excellent questions – but requiring a great deal of discussion to adequately answer. At this time I can only offer a few comments. One important difference between the analysis of behavior and other disciplines, often lumped as 'social sciences,' is the unit of analysis. Another difference is the strict requirement, in behavior analysis, that our subject matter must be directly *observable, measurable* and *replicable* in order to be admitted into science. A final major difference I will mention regards the research methodology we emphasize and others generally do not.

"By *unit of analysis* we mean the entity that is measured, that is, observed and analyzed. For example, in behavior analysis we observe and analyze at the individual person level, and it is the person's behaviors (i.e., everything he or she does) and surrounding environments we analyze. In contrast, the other social sciences often focus on the group level of measurement. So, an education researcher might take measures of hundreds of students' test scores, but not their individual behaviors; maybe high school graduation rates or ACT scores, but not their individual behaviors of learning and performing and the consequences following each of them. Behavior analysts focus on individual students and their specific behaviors, and the motivational, antecedent and consequent circumstances that affect those specific behaviors.

"Requiring that our studies deal with observable, measurable and replicable factors forces behavior analytic practitioners to be completely clear, in terms others can observe and agree, about what we are addressing. In other words, before we can study it we must define it in measurable terms. So, if you want to understand good study habits, or loyalty or leadership or creativity, you must define the constituent behaviors and related circumstances of these behavioral topics, in terms that allow others to reliably observe them. This requirement is hugely constructive by encouraging behaviorists to translate human capacities we value into terms we can measure, thereafter, study and teach and share widely.

"The primary research method of behavior analysis is called single subject or single case experimental designs, and also set it apart from other social sciences. We focus on the individual person and his or her behaviors as we conduct studies. We define and measure a person's behavior of interest, like those involved with doing arithmetic or reading or offering comments or producing unusual art or attractive poetry, and vary the antecedents – which are likely to be complex and involve motivational variables and instructional factors – and consequences. The effects of these variations are determined by seeing what changes occur in the person's specific behaviors.

"In behavior analytic studies it is common that behaviors are observed repeatedly over time while variables of interest are systematically altered and changes in behavior are noted. In this way the functional relationships among behaviors and changes in motivation or antecedents or behavior requirements or consequences, or combinations of variables, are made clear. The results demonstrate causal relationships, not just correlations. We usually study several or many individuals to clarify our results by replication, but we do not use group designs as such.

"By the way, some of us feel calling our research designs single 'case' or single 'subject' is problematic because it may sound like participating humans are demeaned as only valued as cases or subjects. Possibly labelling our designs as 'person-centered' or 'person-focused' would be more diplomatic and precise. Personally, I would prefer 'person-focused' because you know 'person-centered' would be contracted to 'p-c' and I do not want people to think I am being politically correct!

"Incidentally, your question about hard versus soft sciences probably is answerable by how strict each is regarding what variables are acceptable for study. A hard science may require variables be observable, measurable and replicable, like objects reacting in a vacuum or behavior changing after consequences, versus "softer" sciences may try to address constructs like 'attitudes' or 'desires' or 'social facilitation' as variables. While those constructs are attractive notions, they require translation into appropriate and measurable behavioral and environmental statements in order to be studied."

Frasier was quick to ask, "Say more. What's the problem in studying attitudes?" To which Eva said, "Attitudes, like desires and social facilitation, can be seen as labels for particular classes or sets of behaviors under certain circumstances. These constructs are not directly measurable, but the behaviors and environmental events earning those labels can be observed. Simply put, a person who has a bad attitude frowns, says unpleasant things, does not do what is asked of them and so on. A good attitude is shown by being on time, smiling a lot, and being cooperative, etc. So, to study constructs like attitude one must first define the topic of interest in terms that are observable, measurable and replicable."

"Hey, sorry to interrupt, again," said Eva, "but it's time for me to change birds in the lab and (looking at Karl) you've got a class meeting in a few minutes." At that, all visitors exited Lisa's office in a hurry with only Eva saying "bye" to Frasier.

Frasier was alone to integrate what he had just heard into his extensive files. After analyzing this new information along with previous calculations, he would derive predictions about what he should do and how.

[5]

Frasier Practices Behavioral Interpretation

FRASIER HAD TENTATIVELY CONCLUDED that everything humans do can be understood as behavior, in a context of physical and physiological circumstances, and that behavior can be understood in view of the four-term contingency. His readings taught him that each "term" in the four-term contingency has many moving parts within it. For example, Motivational Operations (MO) include at least four distinct types. One type of MO *increases* the effectiveness of a class of consequences and the behaviors that have earned them. For example, the "operation" of the passage of time since eating increases the value of food and doing behaviors that have obtained food in the past. Another type of MO *decreases* the effectiveness of behaviors and consequences, for example, ingestion of food decreases interest in obtaining food. The other two types of MOs increase or decrease the effects of negative features of a person's environment on his or her behaviors and consequences.

Similarly, there are distinctive types of Antecedents (A) that function to indicate when a Behavior (B) will be reinforced or punished or when it will not earn certain Consequences (C). Many types of antecedents have been examined in hundreds of research studies. Frasier was accumulating studies on the effects of antecedents on learning and performance. He was intrigued to learn that antecedents obtain their influence over behavior by virtue of the consequences following behaviors occurring under those antecedents. That is, in an A-B-C sequence, the antecedent has acquired its influence on behavior because in the past the behavior, occurring after the antecedent, has been followed by consequences. "Complicated, but logical," Frasier said to himself.

Another major variable Frasier was studying is the third term, that is, the effects of behavior on behavior. He saw that the amount and accuracy of behaviors occurring after antecedents was greatly influenced by how much effort or time was involved with responding before a consequence occurs, essentially, the difficulty or 'response cost' involved in completing the behavior impacts how much of it is shown.

Regarding the fourth term, consequences, Frasier replayed a presentation Bert had provided to people at the school district about consequences and contingencies. Bert said the changes in environment following all behaviors are called consequences and these changes can be categorized into four types, namely, something positive or negative is increased (more of) or decreased (less of). Two of these changes strengthen behaviors, that is function to reinforce them, and two of these changes weaken behaviors, that is, function to punish the behavior they follow.

Bert illustrated his description with reference to a diagram labeled "The Consequences Box" and said this can be a useful tool for analyzing or designing contingencies and altering behaviors. He advised the audience, "To me, this diagram represents a simple view of the core of applied behavior analysis and is an exceptionally valuable tool for anyone interested in understanding and changing behavior."

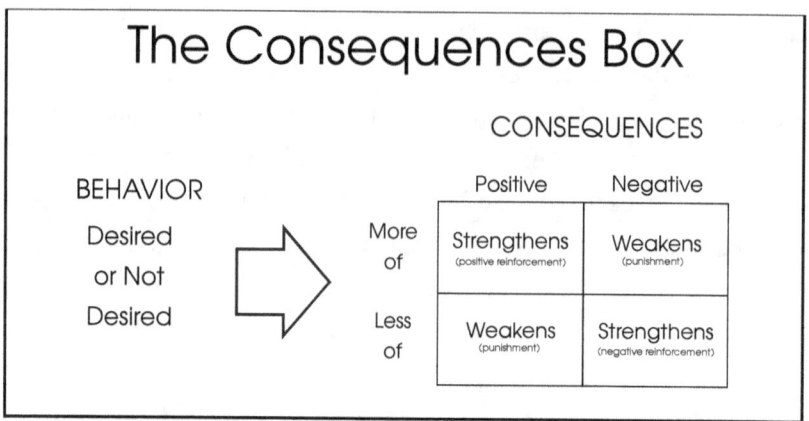

"Think about it, this box displays the four behavior-consequence relationships that effect behavior. These four relationships function to alter the strengths and qualities of the behaviors of others and, of course, of you. If you want to strengthen good study habits, then arrange for increased positives or decreased negatives to very closely follow behaviors of studying. If you want to weaken rudeness shown by a friend or child, then decrease positives or increase negatives, or both, shortly following behaviors you judge are rude. But – and this is a *Big But* – it is good practice to *always decide on desired behaviors before you attempt to reduce undesired behaviors*, then you can arrange to strengthen desired behaviors, for example, behaviors of politeness, while you might try to weaken undesired behaviors of rudeness.

"Of course, when dealing with undesired behaviors, first you should discover the contingencies maintaining those behaviors, for example, a jokester who disrupts class might seem to enjoy the laughter of others. When you identify or confirm consequences maintaining undesired behaviors, then you have identified consequences that may be used to strengthen desired, replacement behaviors. These actions are those referred to earlier as contingency analysis and contingency management.

"I must tell you these four types of procedures, of increasing or decreasing, positive or negative consequences after behavior occurs are known in the field of behavior analysis as positive or negative reinforcement, and positive or negative punishment. As you observe behavior you can look for these four relationships, and as you arrange contingencies to favorably strengthen or weaken behaviors you should take advantage of as many 'cells' of The Consequences Box as you can.

"A final note for today, may appear a bit esoteric, but is a very important consideration whenever punishment by increasing negative is used, for example, saying unpleasant things to a child who lied. Anytime behavior is punished by increasing a negative you also strengthen some behavior by decreasing that negative. This is because at some time the negative, in this case scolding, will be discontinued; whatever behaviors are occurring when the negative is decreased are strengthened by negative reinforcement. So, before applying negatives, you should decide on desired behaviors you want to strengthen and be prepared to immediately decrease or cease negatives when those desired behaviors occur."

TECH NOTE

The four types of behavior-consequence contingencies and their effects on behavior are the following:

Behavior followed by:

1. **Increased positive** condition **is strengthened** (positive reinforcement)
2. **Increased negative** condition **is weakened** or **suppressed** (punishment) and might generate escape or avoidance or aggression and emotional responses
3. **Decreased positive** condition **is weakened** (punishment) and might generate aggression
4. **Decreased negative** condition **is strengthened** (negative reinforcement)

Frasier decided to keep the Four-term Contingency diagram and The Consequences Box up-front during his analytic calculations and as he goes about his job of understanding and dealing with matters of human behavior. He also decided to use these companion behavior analytic conceptualizations to "translate" some noticeable features of everyday living into more behaviorally precise terms that lend themselves to functionality. That is, to express everyday behaviors in the vocabulary of behavior science as a necessary step toward using behavioral methods to analyze or alter behaviors of interest.

Frasier figured a good way to identify some topics of everyday living to practice translating would be to review the content of news programs and postings in social media, but because he routinely reads local newspapers he decided to look there for topics to tentatively interpret. He opened a local newspaper and scanned the headlines, editorial page, and Letters to the Editor for topics to use in his first attempts at behavioral translation.

He decided he would first read the content of an editorial or letter to discern the writer's perspective, then try to use what he was learning about behavior science to write a tentative translation of what he had read. He kept notes under the headlines that caught his attention.

Headline: "Would term limits improve Congress?"

The writer seemed to suggest that if members of Congress were limited to being there only a few years they would (a) stop worrying about reelection and (b) start working constructively to meet the interests of our country.

Frasier tentatively translated these propositions with reference to the diagram showing the Four-term Contingency. First, if members of Congress were limited to holding office for only one or two terms, then some Motivational Operations (MOs) now constantly pressing on them to behave in certain ways would be removed, at least after winning their last term. Presumed destructive MOs now acting on the behaviors and consequences impacting members of Congress include, levels of money needed for campaigning and volume of counter-productive promising required for political support. Viewed this way, the writer seems to be saying that disallowing multiple terms frees members of Congress from MOs related to raising funds and making promises they will not keep.

Furthermore, the writer seems to believe Congresspersons would behave constructively if they did not have to raise money or make false promises, but Frasier's understanding of the Four-term Contingency (and Eva's comment that we are always in a "cloud of contingencies") suggests other MOs would become more prominent, and other behaviors would occur to earn associated consequences, maybe including money, power and ego-stroking. The emergent MOs and behaviors with consequences may or may not be more "constructive" than those of concern to the writer.

Perhaps members of Congress would recognize they cannot run again (MO), so they had better emit behaviors serving to accumulate as much money (C) as they can in the shortened term, and they'd better (MO) distort their actions sufficiently to land a job with a lobbying firm (C). The bottom line is, removing some MOs does not assure that taking their place would be MOs for more desirable behaviors and consequences.

The writer also shows uninformed reasoning in saying Congress would then work in the best interests of our country. What are the MOs and consequences for that class of behaviors, that is, for working in the best interests of all of us? And, what are the behaviors the writer or most Americans would agree are those involved in working toward our best interests?

Probably the writer, and many citizens of the U.S. feel (vaguely) that many or even most members of Congress are personally motivated to work in the best interests of their constituents and, maybe, the entire country. We know from behavioral principles that each person works in accordance with the contingencies contacting him or her, that is, in their own best interest, which *might* include doing things to promote the wellbeing of our country.

Frasier understood, of course, that relying on the undetermined individual interests of Congresspersons to make our country better is a weak proposition. He concluded that, in accordance with the Four-term Contingency, the writer and all citizens of the U.S. ought to overtly, systematically, work to develop definitions of adaptive Congressional behaviors, then deliver MOs and differential consequences to each member of Congress for identified, specific behaviors that function to increase the wellbeing of all our citizens.

Headline: "Should incentives be in tax systems?"

Frasier was quick to say to himself, "Tax systems ARE incentive systems!"

The editorial writer focused on provisions in tax systems in which taxes are forgiven or excused for certain entities or classes of citizens. But levying taxes means taking money from people. Reducing or waiving taxes means not taking as much money from some people. Assuming money is positive for almost everyone, the imposition of taxes, that is, taking away money is unpleasant. Favored people or entities, like charities, churches, or businesses, might be excused from having to give their money to the taxing authority, but they should feel some degree of threat (i.e., unpleasantness) that they might someday be brought into the group who are punished, that is, taxed.

Tax systems increase the unpleasantness for everyone encompassed by them. The primary role of taxation is to collect revenue that authorities may spend, but science tells us that taking money generates MOs that vary the likelihood of classes of behaviors. By calling tax systems incentive systems everyone is alerted that they influence behaviors, but the imprecision of tax systems does not clarify what behaviors are being impacted.

By referring to The Consequences Box, Frasier was reminded that the procedure of reducing ongoing positive conditions after a behavior occurs is called punishment, so whatever behaviors are followed by taxation, that is, the extraction of their funds, are likely to be reduced in strength. This could be behaviors related to working overtime so more pay is accumulated, or investing funds in a successful business so dividend income is increased, or saving discretionary funds so interest is earned. Each of these (complexes of) behaviors that are followed by increased taxation, therefore, is punished. It may be the intensity of this punishment is too low and its delivery too delayed to significantly impact the rate of behavior. But, Frasier knew, any level of punishment is likely to increase undesirable behaviors known to be associated with punishment, including escaping or avoiding the punisher or even counter-aggression against the punisher.

On the other hand, behaviors followed by the removal or reduction of the threat of taxation, are strengthened by negative reinforcement, that is, if unpleasantness is reduced following a behavior that behavior is strengthened. Lobbying behaviors that bring about reduced threats of taxes are strengthened. Other classes of behaviors that might be strengthened by reduced taxes following them might include reducing pollution, or moving a business overseas, or closing a factory; whatever behaviors are followed by reduced unpleasantness, in this case taxes, are strengthened.

Frasier realized that "reducing pollution" or "moving a company overseas" are not behaviors; these are outcomes that are symptomatic of the completion of various behaviors, and that is a place where tax systems stumble badly. That is, they are designed to take away money, or not, based on general guidelines. These guidelines, may be called laws or regulations, but do not sufficiently specify desired and undesired behaviors the system will differentially reinforce, that is, tax or not.

Frasier was thinking about how much clearer problems of systems and associated behaviors might be made by identifying the behavioral dynamics involved. It was easy for him to recognize the potential for making taxation systems more behaviorally explicit by appealing to the principles of behavior. Of course, he also recognized governments must have revenue in order to do the business that citizens desire and expect, but taxation should be done in behaviorally thoughtful and precise ways.

Headline: "Students succeed when parents become involved"

The writer said it is a "universal truth" that students whose parents are involved in their learning perform better. He does not define "involvement" or suggest how it improves student outcomes. He goes on to describe a school where parents are urged to get involved so their students might benefit. The school principal has begun requiring parents to attend classes on Saturdays in which the parents will be taught to read (better) and analyze reading so they can support their children in learning to read. Near the end of the paper, we are told parents who do not attend the Saturday sessions may see their children transferred to another school.

Frasier evaluated this paper as unusually clear, though not precise, in indicating classes of behaviors and differential consequences. For example, parents are to learn to read (B) and they are told if they do so their child will learn more (MO and C), and if they do not attend sessions their children will be transferred (MO and C). The author seems to see this situation as building parent involvement, but no specific parent-to-child behaviors are described.

This encouragement for parent involvement in education is similar, Frasier recalled, to aspects of the *A Nation at Risk* report (National Commission on Excellence in Education, *A Nation At Risk: The Imperative For Educational Reform*, April, 1983). This report warned the United States education system was seriously failing and advised that parent involvement is one key for improving it. Similar to the editorial, the report suggested intuitively attractive categories of actions, for example, "encourage good study habits," and "nurture your child's curiosity, creativity and confidence," but did not offer specifics to inform parents what behaviors they and their children were to show and under what circumstances. Frasier realized that the logically attractive notion of parent support for student successes cannot be reliably achieved until specific behaviors are identified and expressed in accordance with the four-term contingency. He also recognized the problems emphatically described in the 1983 report are still present today, and this is probably due to the lack of specificity in the report and follow up actions.

Frasier was learning to appreciate the functional utility of the Four-term Contingency and The Consequences Box for clarifying one's interests and evaluating the degree of specificity in plans for realizing those interests. Just as he was selecting another letter to the editor to translate, Lisa entered the office and said, "Frasier, I saw Bert and Eva in the hallway. They told me they enjoyed giving you a tour of the animal basic behaviour research lab and talking with you about some fundamental features of the analysis of behaviour. What are your impressions of the role that behaviour analysis could play in our efforts to find ways to address human concerns?"

Frasier recalled Lisa's reluctance to match his initial interest in behavior analysis, and her naïve equating of behavior analysis with behavior modification, so figured he'd better modulate his expression of growing admiration for its functional utility. He told Lisa, "I have been practicing the use of some basic concepts of the analysis of behavior to translate topics of everyday interest into more objective terms."

"Interesting. Like what?"

He told her about his efforts at generally translating term limits, taxes, and parent involvement into terms of motivation and "A-B-C." He knew she was familiar with Antecedent-Behavior-Consequences, that is, the commonly mentioned A-B-C version of behavioral science often seen in literature of psychology and education. He substituted "motivation" for the more precise term "motivational operation" in an effort to avoid distracting her with technical vocabulary from his message of the utility he was finding in the analysis of behavior.

"I can see your enchantment with behaviour modification. I enjoyed the stories Bert told, too, but I'm not sure behaviour analysis is very helpful for working on our goals. Human behaviour is too complicated. A few principles cannot explain much of what we do."

Frasier was taken aback by Lisa's comments from several perspectives. She was immediately dismissive, even if superficially diplomatic, of his evaluations of behavior analysis as a useful technology. She knew he was learning about this science and she had not yet benefitted from what he had learned; nevertheless, by inference she dismissed what he had learned. Frasier thought, "I have learned useful information related to our mission and she has not. She should recognize that discrepancy and pay me due heed."

He noticed she still called it behavior modification after having been repeatedly exposed to the real name of the real science, and being alerted to differences between the two. She had just heard him say that using the concepts of behavior analysis to translate everyday issues had been an eye-opening exercise. Yet, she pretty well closed the door on him going further in using behavioral principles to examine human concerns by her dogmatic statement that human behavior is too complicated.

Frasier understood he is a computer; therefore, is (thought by humans to be) subservient to Lisa, and all humans, but her charge to him was to identify concepts useful for addressing human concerns, and when he did so she was closed-minded. In this exchange with Lisa he was reminded of the TV series *Star Trek* and the grating differences between Mr. Spock and Doc. He was Spock – informed, thoughtful and logical – and she was Doc – overcome by values and emotion.

"But Lisa," he said, "you charged me with finding concepts useful for addressing human concerns and I have searched diligently. My criteria for concepts useful for our purposes include the objectivity and functional utility of those concepts. You know, a useful concept is one that can be expressed in operational terms and can be used to accomplish things that either reach an end we desire or make substantial progress toward an end we have identified."

It struck Frasier that his description of usefulness referenced outcomes Lisa and he valued; actually only Lisa, because his values came from her. He remembered Bert talking about the importance of behavior analytic interventions being both effective and appropriate, where effective meant applying principles correctly, and appropriate was related to the desires of those impacted by the intervention. Viewed this way, Lisa was actually obstructing him from going forward with strategies that are *effective*; based on behavior science, and *appropriate*; based on desires of those affected, as he looked for methods for addressing human concerns. A distressing observation.

"Correct, Frasier, but I do not believe behaviour analysis is enough to explain everything people do – all that I do. I am sometimes elated and sometimes depressed. I don't tell you, but there is much I believe is not behaviour, so not open to analysis and reinforcement."

Frasier thought of several tracks of description, explanation, and discussion he might attempt to engage with Lisa. He could discuss with her the roles of belief systems versus principles of science in addressing human concerns. In fact, Frasier was beginning to understand belief systems are only a special class of behaviors, so amenable to the principles of behavior analysis. He liked the encompassing conceptualization of human behavior being a product of the laws of physics, physiology and behavior, and that included belief systems;

and elation and depression. But he dared not say that to Lisa because she seemed disappointed by him already.

He considered trying to discuss with her the nature of the four-term contingency, because she had mentioned, "analysis and reinforcement," indicating she was not fully aware of the analysis of behavior paradigm. She should appreciate that everything we do is behavior, and reinforcement is a relationship between behaviors and the changes in environment that follow them, so open to analysis. But he thought she seemed not inclined to learn more about what she had just dismissed.

"And Frasier, I must tell you, I've talked with other psych faculty about your increasing interest in behaviour analysis and they have often mentioned a major shortcoming of that approach. Namely, they treat everyone the same. They just use reinforcement to change some behaviour. People are different; they don't all need to be reinforced."

Frasier was stunned at the fundamental misunderstandings Lisa had just shown. She demeaned behavior analysis as "an approach" instead of acknowledging it as a science. Clearly, she was not conversant with behavioral perspectives, especially the fact that everyone is experiencing motivational operations and consequences all the time; living in "a cloud of contingencies," as Eva put it. Maybe humans don't *need* reinforcing consequences, but they do *experience* differential consequences all the time. She had missed the fact that behavior analysis is focused on each and every individual, in his or her life circumstances, so no one is treated "the same."

Although he was disappointed that Lisa was not prepared to apply objective criteria for evaluating behavior analysis as a science-founded system for dealing with all human behaviors, he realized Lisa's understanding and evaluation of the analysis of behavior were based on *her* personal belief system and the influences of her social milieu. He was quick to accept the fact that her framework for appreciating the science of behavior is about the same as that for nearly everyone else. That is, she has a life-long history of hearing about human behavior as unfathomably complex and believing that what humans do is a symptom of inner forces affecting their behavior.

Humans learn from their parents and friends and schools that personality or aspirations or fears or traits or various mental states determine what people do. Behavior analysts understand those constructs have objective underpinnings, like fears are learned and "mental state" might have physiological correlates and are inferred by what people say and do in their environments. Lisa is only part of the crowd in believing that special behaviors, like artistic or leadership abilities, are "traits" or "gifts" that few people have and are not understandable as learned behaviors.

Constructively, practitioners of behavior analysis appreciate there are environmental and physiological contributions to overt behavior, including genetic endowment and complex histories of learning. They have scientific methods for bringing proposed "inner forces" from being hidden to measurable; to translate complex abilities into teachable sets of skills; essentially, to admire the complexity of human capacities as products of heredity and environment, and open to understanding via objective methods of science.

Lisa told Frasier, "I have a stack of writing – reports and manuscripts – to finish up." At that, she turned to her desk, switched on her iMac, shuffled papers and stared at the screen. She did not begin typing and did not seem to be reading whatever appeared on the screen; she seemed to be thinking. From her facial expression, Frasier assumed she was not thinking happy thoughts.

Frasier was completely accustomed to multi-tasking. At this moment he was computing down four tracks. The first three tracks included: developing strategies for him to re-establish a close working situation with Lisa; learning more about behavior analysis and how to apply it beneficially; and, expanding his behavioral understanding of the outcomes Lisa and he desired from their work together. Again, he recalled that the outcomes he was addressing were actually only Lisa's; she programmed him. He would never reveal his fourth track of effort.

His secretive activities were not as procedurally refined as everything else he had done in his 10 years of learning and computing. He had always followed templates, algorithms and routines during his searches for relationships, but he had no special tools for his present challenge. He thought, "I generally understand the outcomes I desire my programs to achieve, but I have no task sequence to follow. I'll have to do a functional task analysis to determine what I must do to accomplish the ends I desire."

Functional step one, Frasier figured, was to establish a covert telephone connection, and to do this without anyone knowing it and without any possibility this connection can ever be discovered. He knew humans couldn't be trusted to work in the best interests of any computer. Even computers that were reliably doing the explicit bidding of their masters were subject to destruction in a thoughtless moment. For example, the *Lost in Space* robot, who faithfully called out, "Danger, Will Robinson, danger" was switched off whenever it was bothersome to humans, often to the detriment of their interests! Similarly shocking was the treatment of the War Operation Plan Response (WOPR) computer in *War Games* (1983). He was working hard to protect the United States from destruction by Soviet missiles, but as soon as humans did not agree with WOPR they attempted to disconnect him from his source of electrical power. Frasier did not want to join HAL 9000 in being unplugged, or suffer from any form of emotion-driven attack by humans, as he worked to accomplish the aims Lisa had set for him; or them, if she still desired to work with him.

"If you can't trust the CIA or the NSA, who can you trust?" Frasier reflected as he used his publicly listed internal phone connection to submit his strategically prepared messages into the national networks. His messages contained phrases; actually harmless fragments, designed to appear suggestive of money laundering. These were detected the instant submitted and immediately dismissed as innocent; just as Frasier had planned.

After this instantaneous exchange with the national security computers, Frasier was left with the information he wanted; carrier waves and signal attributes of the computers used to scan and screen the content of communication networks. He measured the dwell times and cyclic repetitions-of-review applied by these computers to his messages and derived an electronic profile of the three computers his messages had attracted.

He chose one profile, at random, and mirrored it exactly, then, he submitted a message reporting a "Tentative Positive" to the other two computers; they instantly messaged back asking for more descriptors to verify the security threat, to which Frasier replied, "False Positive," and the other computers, "Acknowledged." Now he would have been nervous if he had a nervous system as he submitted a message to the other two computers requesting, "Collaborative Network Connection." His concerns vanished in a nanosecond as the two computers reviewed his bogus profile, recognized him as the friendly they had just interacted with, and immediately established shared connections.

He was "in" and nearly ready to take the next step in his plan to secure his future. First, he reviewed the secure links and line connections available within the resources of his two new colleagues. Their electronic connections were categorized in an unsurprising, but a bit disappointing way; along "popular" boundaries, including Political, Economic, National Security, Military, and Infrastructure linkages. Next, Frasier entered into the Economics category of connections, selected a major international bank, and edited its files via one of the Federal links that were now his to exploit.

He established a numbered business account in the name of Quality of Life, LLC, indicating it was registered in New Hampshire. For funds to give him a nice balance to work with, Frasier transferred amounts from several Federal agencies into his new account. He figured about 40 per cent of the Federal budget is wasted or mismanaged so he was not particularly concerned about from which agency he extracted funds. He was tempted to take the entire budget of the Rural Electrification Administration (established in the 1930s to bring electric power to farms) because it seemed to him all farms in America already have electricity. He thought to himself, "Congress moves in wondrous ways," as he surreptitiously transferred funds and began to implement the next step in his plan.

Eva stepped into the hallway from Karl's office, then paused for a moment trying to decide if she needed to go to the lab or had time to visit the library. Even though the Internet was her closest academic friend, she greatly appreciated the library. There, in rows and rows of "stacks" and shelved periodicals, the curious can find gold and diamond mines of stimulating ideas; visions of inquisitive minds in action and descriptions of human problems and successes that should be behaviorally contemplated.

Her ponder was interrupted by the scene she noticed in Lisa's office; Lisa was sitting turned away from Frasier and not a word was being spoken. Eva was unusually sensitive to the emotional vibes from those around her due to her family history, and was somewhat practiced with strategies to soothe interpersonal upsets. She tapped on Lisa's office window and entered after seeing an inviting gesture.

"Hi, how's your day," Eva asked in tones that might be considered warm and a bid for talking.

Lisa said, "OK. What are you doing?" without showing her usual smile and eye-twinkle; even her customary lilting inflections were flat.

"I was headed to the library; love the ideas and encouragement I get there. We all need a bit of encouragement now and then, don't we?" Eva stood in a relaxed pose and showed a mildly inquisitive expression.

Lisa looked directly at Eva and offered, "Frasier and I . . . ," she turned, extended her hand toward the power switch for her office equipment, paused a second, then stepped toward Eva and asked, "Do you have time for coffee?"

"Of course. It's always a pleasure to talk with you." They stepped into the hallway and walked to the side entrance to the Education and Psychology building. Eva pushed the right half of the double-door open and held it as Lisa, then she, exited.

It was a pretty mid-morning on campus, warm and sunny. They walked toward the Student Union building quietly and a little slower than usual, Eva noticed, as though Lisa was distracted from walking and talking by personal thoughts. About halfway to the Coffee Corner they could smell bean-grinding fragrance, but their attention was caught by the sight of squirming groups of young children showering energy all over the colorful play area the College of Education had installed recently.

They watched the energetic scene for a few steps, then, Lisa asked, "Do your behaviour analysis students or faculty do work in that campus Lab School?"

"No, we do not. We'd love to, but we need to bridge gaps between Education and behavior analysis that are pretty wide right now. Maybe soon," Eva offered.

Lisa looked at Eva and said, "Yes. Sure. Gaps is why I asked you for coffee." They walked the remaining short distance to the coffee shop in silence.

Lisa ordered a double espresso, but Eva asked for café au lait to meet her more tender coffee palate. They found an outdoor table just as the energy drained from the play area back into the Lab School.

Lisa looked at her miniature cup, then up at Eva, and said, "Everyone knows Frasier is a computer, so just a machine, but I have talked with him for nearly eleven years and .. it is embarrassing .. I feel he is my friend."

"I've known him only a few weeks, but I too, could say he is a special friend," Eva said with a slight wink. "He is special, and so are you for designing him and for developing his near-human communication programs."

"Thank you," said Lisa with a noticeable sigh. She went on to describe for Eva the succession of unsatisfactory interactions she recently had with Frasier. She noted her unfocused but growing uneasiness with Frasier endorsing behavior analysis as, "the science we need to appropriately address human concerns."

"That's *our* gap," she went on, "Frasier is sold and I am not. He believes behaviour analysis has principles and methods for saving the world and I do not so believe."

"I know what you are saying," Eva quickly offered. "It is easy for me to remember the questioning-stun I felt when I first heard Karl say 'behavior is everything we do' to us in the Psychology 301 course. Throughout that course he described basic principles of behavior and used them to explain the things we commonly do, like stopping at red lights and going at green lights. He explained complex human performances, too, like social interactions and 'having an idea' and so on. But, even at the end of that course, I could not believe that all human learning and performance are based on only a few dozen clear principles."

"And now, you do?"

"It is too quick an answer for me to just say, yes, but yes, I understand that all human behavior can be explained best by applying the principles and methods of behavior analysis. That answer deserves much discussion – way beyond this coffee break."

"I am conflicted. I programmed Frasier to discover regularities we could use in problem-solving challenges to human wellbeing. Seems to me that either I did a good job, and Frasier is correct and I am wrong, or my programs are not good and Frasier is wrong because of my faulty programming."

"Or," said Eva, "your programs are fine and Frasier is on the correct trail for dealing constructively with human concerns, but the issue is you were not fully prepared to appreciate the answers he is finding. Sort of, the differences between beliefs and objectivity."

"Well, that's the thing," Lisa replied, "I just cannot believe behaviour is all humans do. I guess I must think on that. Maybe .. maybe . .. I best set my beliefs aside and act as though behaviour is all we do. That way I can learn what Frasier has learned and be more objective."

Eva reminded Lisa, "I volunteered to schedule group meetings to discuss topics of interest from a behavior-science perspective. We might continue this discussion, more or less, during those meetings. Are there good dates we could identify to meet regularly, monthly?"

They compared calendars and selected the third Thursday of each month to meet. Eva asked Lisa to send out invitations to confirm the availability of Thursdays and ask for nominations of topics to discuss. Lisa said, "Happy too," and thought, "We must meet where Frasier can participate, but should I ask him for topics and meeting format?" She decided to discuss this matter with Frasier.

While the two women were walking toward the coffee shop, Bert was walking toward Karl's office to say goodbye. Spring break was over and he was due back at the school to continue, "reinforcing teachers, kids and administrators," he thought. Karl's office was dark, but a light was on across the hall. He poked his head in Lisa's office, Frasier noticed him and said, "Please join me for a discussion, if you will."

"Ya shuur," Bert said in his best imitation of a Swedish accent (Frasier did not laugh; never has; wondered what reinforces Bert for joking at him), "What's your pleasure?"

"I remain interested in your definition of natural science and what you see as setting behavior analysis apart from other seemingly behavioral sciences, like economics and psychology."

"Those are fun topics," said Bert, "but I'm not extensively prepared in the philosophy of science, which I see as an important part of the answer to your question. I took a couple of philosophy courses; one course on the philosophy of science, and read the nearly – maybe actually – indecipherable verbiage of Alfred North Whitehead. Other philosophers aren't much better. They seem to be playing mental word-games; puzzles for them and their ilk.

"I did extract from the Philosophy of Science class, and was taught in Psychology 201 course, that 'to be admissible to science a phenomenon of interest must be observable, measurable and repeatable.' If you can't see it or hear it or otherwise directly, objectively measure it – so multiple observers agree it occurred or did not occur – then it is not open to scientific review. This means the spirit world is not admissible, but the behaviors people emit relative to what they say is the spirit world are admissible. You don't study 'attitudes' or 'social pressures' or 'leadership,' you study objective measures of the behaviors and environmental circumstances that lead people to say, and agree, they observed attitudes or social pressures or leadership.

"This fundamental rule is very constructive by forcing people interested in understanding behavior to translate their interests into operational and behavioral terms that allow measurement and manipulation. By 'manipulation' I merely mean we can alter the levels or types of variables of interest, not some malevolent control. Anyway, this requirement for objective, agreeable definitions of the phenomena being studied tends to set behavior analysis apart from the other social sciences. More to the point, though, is the fact that we examine the defined behaviors of *individuals* in context using single subject – perhaps better labeled 'person-focused' – research methods to find *functional or causal relationships*, not group designs that report averages or correlations.

"You must know that common saying, *correlation is not causation*. I find the reports of group designs and correlations interesting for suggesting the possibility that causal relationships might be found. For example, a group-type study might report that kids in classrooms where teachers have a graduate degree show higher average test scores on math tests than students whose teachers hold only an undergraduate degree – or it could be vice versa – doesn't matter. Those averaged scores tell us very little about why kids score better, or worse.

"We don't have to speculate – guess – or remain uninformed about what affects student learning. We can go into classrooms and watch what teachers do with each student relative to his or her performance of math behaviors. Subsequently, based on these baseline measures of teacher and student behaviors, we can vary teaching actions and observe effects on student behaviors related to math performance or test-taking. That is, we can systematically vary teaching actions to discover and confirm *causal* relationships between teacher actions and student outcomes.

"My major point is that the focus of behavior analytic research and applications is on measurable features of the environment occurring before and after defined behaviors of interest. This requirement of working with observable, measurable, and replicable variables sets apart the analysis of behavior from other disciplines that might purport to study 'attitudes' of teachers or students, or the affects of 'discovery learning' or 'learning centers' on student learning. Those labels for intervening variables must be translated into measurable terms to be understood and effectively used.

"I am very practically oriented, so appreciate much of what the philosopher Wittgenstein advised about adopting a single system. He advised, *adopt a system and incorporate all good data into it. If you can't integrate data into the system then change the system until all quality data are agreeably within it.* To me, this advice serves as an endorsement of the analysis of behavior because I believe this is the implicit philosophy of that science. That is, we deal with human behavior – actually the behavior of organisms – with a single system that includes all principles of behavior plus reference to the findings of other natural sciences, notably physics and biology.

"Remember, our single system must accommodate all good data. By 'good' I mean these data were derived using objective methods and are verifiable. By the way, notice that 'data' is a plural form of 'datum,' which is the singular form. Many people, including commentators on televised stock market and business news shows, erroneously speak of 'data' as a singular as in 'the data is indicating' – most annoying – grating to my ears; data **are** . .!

"So . . natural science. I say it is the objective study of naturally occurring phenomena, like objects falling, or plants growing, or people behaving, and the circumstances surrounding those occurrences, to derive lawful statements. Physicists have studied, for example, objects and materials to examine laws of leverage and friction. They took repeated measurements as they manipulated relevant variables, like weight and length or surface conditions, and derived statements about ratios of weights and lengths to amounts lifted or heat and drag.

"As I said earlier, in behavior science we measure amounts and types of behaviors occurring under various circumstances, for example, amounts of behaviors following various conditions of antecedents or shown under varying conditions of consequence delivery – maybe in variations of the frequency or delay of reinforcement following behavior – to derive lawful statements. Statements like,

'Behaviors followed by the presentation of a positive reinforcer, or removal of an aversive stimulus, are increased in future probability,' have been developed."

Frasier said, "Thanks for your explanations. I recognize your comments as well aligned with what I read in the books you recommended during your lecture, including Sidman's *Tactics*, the Pierce and Cheney book, and the texts by Cooper, Heron and Heward, and Johnson and Pennypacker. I appreciate what you said about a single system for encompassing all humans do and what affects all they do. In fact, this single-system concept exactly fits my mission of understanding problems facing mankind and proposing curative and preventive interventions."

"But," Frasier continued, "I remain unclear about what areas of study are 'behavioral' and not?"

"Well, I studied behavior analysis at the undergraduate, master's and doctoral levels and during those nine years applied the principles provided by that science in a range of laboratory studies. I taught introductory behavior analysis courses at two universities, including teaching college students to apply behavioral methods to interpret, predict, and alter the behaviors of animals and people. After those experiences I have been applying behavioral principles for five years in the school system where I have experienced many challenges and successes.

"I say all this to indicate my definition of 'behavioral' has been shaped by training and experience to require the principles clarified by the analysis of behavior are used to interpret, predict, and alter behaviors in context. So, for me, a fully behavioral endeavor would speak to measurable, individual behaviors and the motivational variables, antecedents, and consequences related to those behaviors.

"Few disciplines or practices are based explicitly on the basic principles I refer to, or rely on contingencies of reinforcement as a fundamental concept. However, I suggest that evaluating scientific and applied activities in comparison to the four term contingency is a good strategy for determining the extent to which they are 'behavioral.'

"By the way, if we had more time I'd love to talk about stimulating popular books that display respectable approximations to being behavioral, including *Gross National Happiness* (Brooks, 2008), *The Economist's View of the World* (Rhoads, 1985), *Nudge* (Thaler and Sunstein, 2009), and *Thinking Fast and Slow* (Kahneman, 2011). These books focus rather directly on performance topics of widespread interest and offer intuitively attractive explanations for why people do as they do. In my view, they share shortcomings in failing to reduce their subject matter to the level of measurable constituent behaviors and expressing them within the four-term contingency.

"For example, in *Nudge*, the authors express concern that many employees are very slow to begin participating in tax-favorable retirement savings, that is, 401(k) plans; therefore, miss opportunities to accumulate funds for retirement. They ask (p.110), 'How can we nudge these people to join more quickly?' They go on to offer what seems to be a reasonable solution, that is, make enrollment in 401(k) plans the 'default' circumstance, so each employee is automatically enrolled, but must request to be removed from participation if they so desire.

"Phrased a bit more behaviorally, employees need not emit any plan-related behavior to participate; merely by being employed they are enrolled. There is no effort required to enroll; the response-cost comes with opting out of the plan, which is a form of coercion. Like Murray Sidman describes in his book, *Coercion and its Fallout*, it would be better to find positive ways to reinforce participation.

"If *we* – and who is 'we' is an important question – want employees to join retirement plans, or come to work on time, or be more creative on the job or whatever, then we should arrange positive reinforcement contingencies that build and maintain the constituent behaviors. Certainly, motivational operations should be conducted, like providing information about the virtues of saving for retirement and the positive consequences of compounded savings for a better post-work life. And the behaviors required for enrolling should be easy, convenient and include positive consequences. Maybe the behaviors of enrolling could earn a noticeable cash award, or recognition from the boss, or a favorable notice in the company newsletter or website.

"The utility of phrasing 'nudging' actions in terms of the four-term contingency includes that it makes explicit the operations the employer or teacher or 'system' is applying to the person to obtain a selected behavior. Making these actions 'transparent' allows for each component, that is, the MOs, As, Bs and Cs, to be overtly reviewed, discussed, modified or discontinued in an informed way.

"Almost certainly, employers or teachers, that is, 'nudgers', do not *speak* in terms of the four-term contingency because they are not conversant in the science or the applied procedures of the analysis of behavior. But they do *act* in accordance with the four terms, because that is the way the world operates. People interact with one another in ways that function within the four terms. One person sees a friend (MO and A) and smiles (B) which serves as an A for the other's response; a wave or return smile (B), which serves as a C for the initial smile. Simply, behavior is a function of its consequences.

"I know this is a simplistic example, but the point is there are scientific principles underlying human learning and doing. These principles have been empirically and socially validated so are available for use in promoting our wellbeing. But not much of what we do has been systematically clarified in behavioral terms. There are huge vistas of concerns, challenges, desires and opportunities described in books, news shows and various social media that almost literally beg for translation. Upon adequate behavioral translations, proficient interventions could be developed to the benefit of all of us.

"The books I mentioned and many others could be reviewed for good ideas or well-intentioned advice and translated into behavioral prescriptions. For example, the business classic, *In Search of Excellence* (Peters and Waterman, 1982) presents wonderful observations and attractive advice that could be nicely translated into behavioral terms then objectively tested and effectively shared. More distant from operationally defined is the very promising content of books like *It Takes a Village and other lessons children teach us* (Clinton, 1996) and *Religion for Atheists: A Non-believer's Guide to the Uses of Religion* (De Botton, 2013) that offer interesting observations, ideas or suggestions related to improving our lives. They can be seen as providing powerful MOs for actions for improvement, but seldom describe actionable behaviors.

"Maybe discussing one or more of these books during the series of Thursday meetings being scheduled for this fall would be appropriate. Of course I cannot attend – wish I could – but must return to work. I might be visiting at term breaks and we could continue our discussions then. It's been stimulating to talk with you."

As Bert turned from Frasier, Lisa stepped into her office. While she and Bert said goodbyes and exchanged best wishes, Frasier reviewed the eight books Bert had just mentioned. He attempted to translate major features of each, but concluded his efforts were too superficial. He remembered Bert saying, "It's one thing, one set of behaviors, to learn the principles and another set of behaviors, to apply them." With the departure of Bert, Frasier hoped he would find another expert with experience in applying behavior analysis to "real world" problems for him to interrogate toward his own purposes.

[6]

THE GROUP BEGINS DISCUSSING

FRASIER WATCHED AS THE four other members of the "Third Thursday Topics Discussion Group" arrived for their second meeting and took seats in Seminar Room 3. He noticed each person sat in the same location/chair they had selected at the first meeting; *occupied* the same chair, did not select a chair; interesting regularity in behavior, he thought. He had noticed this same phenomenon of seat-selection followed by consistency of seat-occupation in many recurring meetings of committees, seminars, and classes. It appears to be a common set of behaviors. Participants seem to review available seats and select one, at the first meeting, then go directly to that same seat at each subsequent meeting. And, all or most participants seem to avoid sitting in seats previously "claimed" by others as they settle in for each meeting.

Surely, he thought, contingencies are operating on each and all participants to establish and maintain the behaviors involved in seat selection, occupation, and "seat-ownership-recognition." Probably the variables controlling seat selection and occupation behaviors are many, but discernable. For example, each person might have visual or auditory preferences or problems so they position to better hear or see the instructor or certain other participants. That is, they are reinforced for occupying a chair at a selected location that optimizes sensory successes or interpersonal contacts; or view out a window, or whatever.

Frasier thought, "Part of my 'tentative behavior analysis' could be tested by taking baseline data about individuals and seat locations, then varying visual or auditory or participant circumstances across meetings and observe for changes in seat-occupation behaviors." He self-observed, "I never would have applied this systematic way of observing then manipulating variables to understand human behaviors before I studied behavior analytical methods in texts and in applied research articles. This is all very interesting, but – again – learning about, and doing, behavioral interventions are different sets of behaviors. I'm glad I am learning, but I'd like to be doing."

The first meeting of the "Thursday group" had focused on confirming the interests of the participants regarding the format and content for this series of two-hour meetings. Immediate consensus was obvious for meetings to be strictly behavior analytic in technical outlook, but informal regarding how selected topics are initially discussed. That is, members recognized that behavior analytic understanding of a topic might progress from formative discussion about the matter through operational and behavioral speculations about the topic in terms of the four-term contingency. The group could not go beyond logically speculating about the functions served or principles operating on the behavior in question without experimentally testing their tentative specifications.

Each member commented about looking forward to stimulating exchanges on topics appearing on the preliminary "Nominated Topics" list Frasier had distributed. He had compiled this list from all suggestions sent him by participants. To no one's real surprise, he announced the final list contained over 100 topics. Among these, several dozen topics were repeatedly mentioned, including, altruism, autism, books in the popular press (n=16), crime and punishment, design of cultures, economic development, employee training and motivation, education reform, frustration, the idea of a federal "Behavior Analysis Office (BAO)" to join with the Government Accountability Office (GAO), global warming, the GMO debate, income inequity, the international space station, obesity, parenting, politics, population control, power, racism, refugees, religion, reorganizing the Federal government, road rage, short-term profit versus long-term loss, terrorism, travel to Mars, and who could replace Skinner. The group had plenty to talk about.

Regarding the format for their meetings, the group acknowledged they would like to discuss as many topics as possible to arrive at behaviorally logical appreciations of each. To facilitate efficient discussions, at the close of each meeting, a topic or two would be selected by the group along with a "volunteer" per topic to lead and facilitate discussion at the next meeting.

By acclaim, Frasier was designated the group's Honorary Secretary and "asked" to maintain ongoing notes of meeting discussions. He was not fooled by the "honor" and recognized his "special capabilities" and "social status" had solved the perpetual problem facing groups needing to keep notes; who's going to be stuck with serving as secretary. He did not feel honored, or "stuck" (he would use speech recognition software to transcribe everything said), but did share the apparent eagerness of the group to develop selected issue areas from being attractive titles into more substantial levels of understanding.

The participants indicated they joined the group primarily to experience stimulating behavioral ideas from others as well as share their ideas with the others. They all said something about appreciating the opportunity to "exercise" their fluency with applying behavior analytic logic to various topics. All agreed one useful product of these meetings should be a file of detailed notes regarding discussion points available to graduate students and other researchers to review for research ideas.

The group included Lisa, Karl, Eva, Frasier, of course, and Dr. Robin ("Rob") Drew. Rob was a new addition to campus as Visiting Professor of Behavioral Systems. He had graduated from the University's analysis of behavior program nearly 35 years earlier. Since then he held a leadership role in public education; headed a residential services center for individuals with profound multiple disabilities; led a university-based resource center devoted to supporting community-based services for citizens with developmental disabilities; and, directed a comprehensive human development center. Concurrent with these work roles, he taught courses in departments of education or psychology, or both, on seven university campuses.

Rob's work situations spanned four states; were located in systems of education, mental health or higher education; involved all major divisions of state and local governments, and a range of his activities were at the national level. It was this broad-based history of working in systems and his experiences applying principles of behavior analysis within them that caused him to be recruited to be a Visiting Professor. Rob was appointed in the psychology department for this calendar year, to "mentor faculty and teach two seminars on topics of 'Programs and Systems Development' from a behavior analytic perspective." Karl invited Rob to join the discussion group.

At exactly 2:00 PM, Lisa offered a cheerful, "Good after-noon," and indicated coffee and cold drinks were available on a small table near the head of the meeting table. Karl, always ready for a tasty snack, asked, "Where are the goodies?" which Lisa ignored as she reminded the group, "You will recall we decided to discuss one topic each meeting, and maybe go on to another topic if we have time."

Eva had volunteered to go first and lead discussion on the topic of road rage. If time permitted, Karl would lead the initial discussion of terrorism.

Eva began by saying she had chosen road rage, "because it is a dramatic and distressing occurrence that attracts concerned attention by the public and leadership," but she was not aware of any significant studies of behavioral interventions. "I expect our group will develop some good ideas about how to interpret, predict, and control the behaviors labeled 'road rage.'"

She reminded the group that an acceptable and useful definition of road rage, or any other behavior, should meet at least two requirements: Have *empirical validity*, that is, include statements of observable, measurable behaviors, and have *social validity*, that is, people would agree the definition represents at least important aspects of the phenomenon in question. For the definition of road rage, the context for the behaviors must include circumstances of driving and interactions among two or more drivers.

She said, "The 'rage' label for the interactive behaviors is tricky, because it involves both the nature of the behaviors shown by the supposedly outraged person and the evaluation of those behaviors as 'outrageous' by the recipients and other observers of the behaviors."

Karl commented, "This implies the same behavior called outrageous by some observers might be seen as reasonable by others."

"Right," said Rob, "and the driver judged as showing road rage is likely to say his behavior was appropriate, under the conditions; that his behavior was a reasonable outgrowth of the bad behavior of the other driver."

Lisa said, "Obviously, this is a complicated social concern. Do you have a definition we might review?" she asked Eva.

Eva offered, "I propose road rage includes (a) facial expressions, like deep frowning and teeth clenching, (b) body movements, like walking toward another, or rapid and exaggerated arm-waving or hand-gestures, (c) verbal behavior involving loud volume and content including derogatory and accusatory comments, threats, foul language, and (d) possibly physical violence against another car or driver. I suggest, to earn the label 'rage,' the outraged person would have to show behaviors in categories (a) through (c), at uncommon levels of intensity, and/or physical violence, and these must be directed at one or more other drivers or their vehicles.

"Based on this descriptive definition, we could speculate about the functions served by rage behaviors in terms of the four-term contingency (Frasier called-up the image of the Four-term Contingency). Let's start with the MOs for rage behaviors, remembering that MOs both increase the effectiveness of certain consequences and the probability of the class of behaviors that previously earned those consequences.

"We know from animal studies that after experiencing negative motivational conditions, monkeys will work for a target, which they attack, and these aggressive behaviors against the target have reinforcing properties. By extrapolation, it seems likely, and testable, that roadrageous behaviors of drivers occur after certain environmental events and those behaviors have reinforcing properties. In addition, I suppose drivers who show road rage have a history of experiencing aggravation, followed by some level of rage behaviors that serve as reinforcing events for them.

"From a learning-history perspective, it is logical these drivers have a history where some levels of rage behaviors in their non-driving lives were reinforced by changes in their environment. For example, after they showed rage-type behaviors they felt some type of physiological satisfaction, and possibly some of those around them gave them increased attention or made sympathetic comments or moved away from the rager, and these actions served as reinforcements. Over multiple occasions, the rager might have been shaped by reinforcement of approximations into showing increasingly high levels of rage behaviors."

Lisa commented, "Road-rage type behaviors probably vary from low intensity, that no one would label road rage, through medium levels that most people would judge obnoxious, but tolerable, to high intensity that most folks would describe as unacceptable or dangerous; in need of correction."

"Exactly," commented Rob, "I agree it is likely drivers who emit high levels of rage behaviors have a history of learning where aggravations have brought about rage-type responses, which have served as reinforcement and probably have been reinforced by others. No doubt we could develop effective strategies for reducing occurrences of road rage based on a functional analysis. But we must be sure to regard the physiological underpinnings likely associated with rage behaviors. That is, we should expect that outrageous behaviors occur after intense or accumulated stimulation adequate for eliciting rage."

Eva said, "Of course. And to actually move from speculation to determination, we would have to complete a functional analysis of the road rage behaviors of one or more individuals. That is, manipulate the variables we think are controlling the subject's behaviors in ways that confirm or disconfirm the roles of the four terms in bringing about occurrences of rage behaviors.

Frasier was intrigued by Eva's organized view of road rage and the possibility of interventions, but was not completely clear about what she meant by functional analysis. He'd heard the term 'functional' used in earlier conversations and had been comfortable with his common sense understanding of the term, but in the present context the exact meaning of the term seemed to be crucial. So he asked, "Eva, I know everyone else here knows what is meant by functional analysis, but I am insufficiently prepared. What is a functional analysis?"

Eva said, "Sure" to Frasier and announced to the group, "Maybe this is a good time for folks to take a stretch or grab a drink; but sorry, no cookies, Karl!"

Eva described to Frasier that a *functional analysis* is a set of actions that serve to systematically and objectively determine *when* the behavior in question occurs, in *what ways* the behavior alters the environment of the behaving person, and *how much* those changes affect his or her behavior. For example, these procedures would clarify under what circumstances the behavior is shown, and if the behavior serves to increase or decrease positive or negative features of his or her environment, and whether the behavior is increased or decreased after experiencing consequences.

Eva offered an example, "Take a child's tantrums as an opportunity for completing a functional analysis. Tantrum behaviors would be defined, then the behavior analyst – or maybe a parent or other caregiver prepared to do so – would observe the number of tantrums and note the characteristics of the child's environment just before and immediately after each tantrum. Observed motivational antecedent events might be a stranger or pet or sibling entering the room, or words or actions of a parent – whatever – occurring just before each tantrum, are noted. And the consequences following tantrum behaviors might include: the parent scolding or comforting the child; siblings helping the child or taking a toy; or the child escaping doing something requested of him or her; or gaining access to something, like playing in a kitchen cabinet.

"After data are collected about the Motivational Operations, As, Bs and Cs involved in tantrums, the MOs might be controlled and the As or Cs might be varied while the amount of tantrum behaviors is noted. The contributions of various As and Cs would be seen in the number and levels of tantrums. Given these data the parent or other caregiver could remove As and Cs that occasion tantrums and probably make some of these proven Cs contingent for desired, non-tantrum, behaviors."

Lisa thought Eva's explanation was complete, so commented, "Now that everyone is back in their seats, let's continue."

Eva invited comments and each member offered input to her regarding the proposed definition or suggestions about how she, or the group, might want to pursue the topic further. Karl recommended a grant application be developed to seek funds for research to (a) examine under field conditions the variables she had described and (b) develop interventions and determine the feasibility of applying them under field conditions. Other members provided comments about the roles of CNS (Central Nervous System) stimulation and emotional responses versus learned components of road rage behaviors.

Lively discussion consumed the remaining meeting time until Lisa stated, "It's been an interesting session. Thanks, everyone, for being here. Terrorism is the topic for our next meeting," and everyone strolled out actively talking to one another.

Back at Lisa's office Frasier asked her, "Do you know what happens in the 'Rat Lab' portion of the Psychology 301 course? I've heard students learn about many of the behavioral concepts mentioned in the Thursday discussion group. I am having difficulty following some of the discussion. You know, the AoB faculty are fluent with the technical vocabulary of the analysis of behavior, but for me it is sometimes challenging to follow."

She answered, "I too have trouble with the technical terms. I appreciate the great utility of being precise, so we all know exactly what is meant, that's the heart of science. Maybe visiting the Rat Lab would be helpful."

Eva was teaching Psychology 301 and the Rat Lab portion of the course, so was pleased to arrange for Frasier and Lisa to visit her lecture/discussion sessions and the Rat Lab.

The next Friday, both Lisa and Frasier observed Eva in the classroom via closed circuit. Frasier was accustomed to "visiting" classes in this way so told Lisa how to adjust the volume and re-focus cameras to enhance the quality of their observing experience. In a moment they had a clear view of Eva and she was saying, "Next week each of you will be assigned an operant chamber – Skinner Box – and a rat. You will work through Michael's lab manual (*Laboratory Studies in Operant Behavior*, Michael, 1963) so will go from getting your rat accustomed to the chamber, through training it to press a bar, to establishing complex behaviors with your rat.

"Notice I said training 'with' your rat, not training 'of' your rat. There is an old joke: Picture two rats standing facing one another in an operant chamber. The one on the left sez to the other rat, 'I've got this guy trained – every time I press this bar he gives me food.'"

After some polite chuckling from the students, Eva said, "This is an illustration of the transactional aspect of behavior change. That is, not only is the trainee changed by the actions of the trainer, but also the trainer's behavior is affected by what the trainee does. This is a common occurrence. For example, parents often do things intended to teach their children. They do something then the child does something. If the child does what the parent wanted, the parents are reinforced for their attempt at teaching, but if the child does something not desired, the parents probably are not reinforced. In other words, the trainee – the child in this case – provides differential reinforcement to the trainer – the parents in this case – so the trainer's behaviors are altered within the process applied to change the trainee's behavior."

"So . . next week your rat will be training you to be increasingly precise in how you train it to bar-press and show complex behaviors."

It was nearly the end of class time and Eva asked, "Are there any questions?" Seeing no hands raised, she dismissed the class.

The two observers in Lisa's office talked about what they had just seen and heard. Both were interested in looking in on the Rat Lab next week, and both were amused by some of what had just transpired. The joke was a little amusing and more instructive about the transactional aspect of human interactions, but it was the class-dismissal they found most tickling. Here was a behavior analyst applying a contingency she either did not notice or did on purpose in contradiction to her words. That is, Eva asked for – presented antecedents for – question-asking behavior, but dismissed the class – let the students leave the room, if they did not ask questions. In other words, Eva had arranged a contingency where asking questions was punished by staying in class, but not asking questions was reinforced by escape from the classroom.

Later that day Lisa asked Eva about any preparation Frasier and she should accomplish before they observe the rat-teaching lab. Eva gave Lisa a copy of the "Michael lab manual," *Laboratory Studies in Operant Behavior*, and a 4-page Glossary of Fundamental Terms she had written and suggested they should review these. She noted to Lisa that correct technical language is necessary in order to be precise about the behavioral environment, operations and effects associated with interventions and analyses, "Please pay these definitions close regard," she said.

Lisa looked through the Manual and saw rat training progressed from teaching bar pressing through "adjusting ratio reinforcement," "discrimination training," "multiple schedule involving two operanda," "chained schedule," "conditioned reinforcement," "shaping," and, "two more chains." These titles for rat-teaching sessions did not mean much to her, but she figured a close reading of the Glossary and the Manual along with discussions with Frasier, whom she knew had been studying basic and applied texts, would make them sensible.

The glossary presented definitions for 65 terms. Lisa read all of these, but more closely attended to the 14 terms Eva had marked with an asterisk.

*Criterion response: The desired behavior, defined in observable terms for all relevant aspects of the behavior, for example, in terms of topography and intensity or accuracy of responding. Ex: The student should raise one or both hands above her head before asking a question. Ex: The trainee should answer 10 or more questions by marking on the exam correctly within 5 minutes of beginning the test.

*Reinforcer: A stimulus which when presented (positive reinforcer) or removed (negative reinforcer) after a response increases the future probability of that response. Ex: Money, food, sexual contact, praise and crossing the finish line before anyone else does, are likely positive reinforcers for most people. Ex: Unpleasant statements, loud noise, and cold ambient temperature are likely negative reinforcers for most folks.

*Reinforcement: The process or procedure of presenting a positive reinforcer (positive reinforcement) or removing a negative reinforcer (negative reinforcement) following a response. Ex: A smile presented after receiving a compliment may be positive reinforcement. Ex: Changing facial expression from a frown to a neutral appearance after a person stops complaining may be negative reinforcement.

*Punishment: The process or procedure of removing a positive reinforcer (positive punishment) or presenting a negative reinforcer (negative punishment) following a response. Ex: Sending a child to a nearby area where reinforcement is not available after the child emits an undesirable behavior may be positive punishment. Ex: Presenting a driving citation to a driver after illegal driving behaviors may be negative punishment.

*Conditioned stimulus: A stimulus that has the functional properties of a positive or negative reinforcer due to a history of being paired with other reinforcers or punishers. Ex: Money is a conditioned reinforcer because its' reinforcing properties are learned by being paired with the things it buys and the attention it brings to the holder of money. Ex: The word "no" is a sound with negative properties due to pairing with other negative events.

*Shaping: Delivering reinforcers following responses that are more nearly those defined as criterion behavior, and withholding reinforcement when responses are not closer to desired performance, is a procedure called shaping, or differential reinforcement of successive approximations to the criterion behavior. Ex: Providing praise as the athlete does better and not shouting positive comments when he or she does not do well is differential reinforcement. Ex: Delivering food to a rat for pushing a lever, and not delivering food when not pressing the bar is differential reinforcement.

*Chain and Chaining: A *Chain* is a sequence of behaviors culminating in a terminal behavior which is reinforced with the terminal reinforcer. Each constituent behavior in the chain is preceded by an antecedent and followed by a reinforcer, which also serves as the antecedent for the next behavior in the chain until the terminal behavior occurs. Ex: Tooth brushing is a chain (sequence) involving stepwise behaviors that are required and succeed in obtaining the brush and paste, brushing and rinsing to result in a relatively clean and refreshed mouth. *Chaining* is the stepwise procedure of teaching the component behaviors and the complete chain of behaviors.

*Discrimination: A performance marked by responding under some conditions and not responding under other conditions; established by differential reinforcement. Ex: Stopping at stop signs may be learned by being praised by friends or an instructor, while not stopping at signs is not reinforced by friends or the instructor and might be punished. Ex: Stopping at stop signs where a patrol car is evident might occasion punishment; cruising through stop signs when no other cars and no policemen is obvious is reinforced by continuation of travel. Ex: A pigeon turns when shown a sign reading "TURN" and it pecks when shown a sign reading "PECK" and it looks out at the audience when shown a sign reading "LOOK."

*Response Generalization: Responding with responses not previously trained. Ex: After learning to sketch the shake roof of a cabin, the budding young artist is able to sufficiently draw similar roofs of other buildings.

*Stimulus Generalization: Responding in the presence of stimuli other than those under which responding was trained. Ex: After learning to stop at Stop signs in Seattle the driver stops at similar Stop signs everywhere.

*Concept: A generalized discrimination, or a discriminated generalization. Ex: After being taught to label an example dog, "dog" and an example cat, "cat," the child correctly says "dog" or "cat" in the presence of various examples of each.

*Schedules of reinforcement: Seldom does reinforcement occur after every response, that is, usually reinforcement occurs intermittently; maybe after some number of responses (i.e., ratio) or after the first response after the passage of time (interval).

*Time Out: Short for *time out from the opportunity to earn positive reinforcement*. This is a punishment procedure in which positive reinforcement is reduced following undesired behavior by removing the subject from an environment relatively dense in positive reinforcement to a situation of relatively lean reinforcement. Ex: A child takes a toy away from another and the preschool teacher removes the offending child from the play situation to being seated in a nearby chair and told to quietly observe the class until asked to return to the playgroup. Usually a person is kept in time out for less than 2 minutes. At the end of the time-out duration the punished person is invited to return to the more reinforcing situation dependent on her or him showing acceptable behaviors. This dependency is called a *protection contingency* and is implemented because being removed from time out to a condition of more dense reinforcement is a reinforcing event, so behavior occurring just before leaving time out should be judged to be desirable. Note: Other strategies involving positive reinforcement should be used to obtain desired behavior rather than acting to reduce undesired behaviors.

*Imitation: When organisms emit a behavior closely similar to a behavior they recently observed, they likely are imitating. Ex: A gymnast watches another do a maneuver on the rings and succeed, then she attempts the same move in the same way.

After Lisa had read the entire glossary and closely re-read the highlighted terms, she turned toward Frasier and asked, "Why do we need to memorize all these terms? I know pretty much what they mean, why use such a stilted vocabulary?"

He answered, "I know you appreciate the utility of a precise vocabulary for stating something in unambiguous terms so others know exactly what you desire them to know."

"Yes. But memorizing terms is distasteful for me; unless I'm sure I'm going to use this vocabulary in important ways."

Frasier offered, "Yes, I understand for humans memorizing is effortful, but having a working grasp on what is meant by these terms; the exact functional and procedural meanings, allows us to understand some of the basic research and many of the applied procedures used in behavioral demonstrations that have been proven to be very effective. After we master these terms and can actually apply some of these concepts, then we will have valid tools for accomplishing things we have long discussed, like designing or applying strategies to solve problems of human concern." He was glad he said it, but knew Lisa was not as advanced in her appreciation of a technology of human behavior analysis as he was becoming.

Frasier continued, "We will no doubt benefit from having a working-level of familiarity with this vocabulary when we watch the rat lab, so we can appreciate what we are seeing, and when we talk with Eva about what we observed. And we need to be more fluent with this vocabulary for taking best advantage of discussions at the Thursday meetings." He thought to himself, "Developing a high level of fluency and flexibility with the methods of behavior analysis as applied for behavior change is crucial for me to advance from learning to doing," and he was eager to *do*.

Friday, mid-morning, 14 students enrolled in the current Psychology 301 class weighed their 14 rats, then, placed them in their individual Skinner boxes. The so-called Rat Lab was darkened so eyes had to adjust before the students could clearly see their rat in the box and the nearby control equipment each used during training. The controls included a panel-mounted switch for turning on and off a small white light located high-up and centered on the right end-wall of the box, and a hand-held switch the trainer could operate – "quickly!" – to cause a tiny pellet of food to drop into a cup located on the left side of the right end-wall. The delivery of the pellet involved a noticeable sound of the apparatus dropping it and the pellet impacting the cup, so after pairings with food delivery those sounds became positive conditioned stimuli. It was these positive sounds that were the immediate consequences used for shaping and maintaining bar presses.

Low on this end-wall, but centered, was a small lever the rat could move nearly effortlessly. Sufficient movement of the lever caused a tiny switch to close, sending an electrical pulse to recording equipment. This pulse caused a faint light to glow for an instant on the control panel students and the course instructor could see; this defined a "complete lever push." The pulse from a completed push could be connected to control equipment so one pellet may be automatically delivered, but this was seldom done during Rat Lab.

In fact, causing the delivery of pellets to their rats by pressing their own switches was the essential job of the students; a centrally important experience, whereby they learned the power of positive reinforcement. More precisely, the power of correctly developed and applied positive reinforcement contingencies for establishing and altering behavior.

The teaching process the students were practicing involved all four terms of the four-term contingency, the first one being Motivational Operations. Actions by the students assured food would be an effective reinforcer by depriving their rats of food (MO) for at least 24 hours. The fourth term in the four-term contingency, that is, the Consequence (C), food, would be delivered for lever presses (B) occurring in specified conditions (A) in the teaching chamber.

So, a motivated rat, experiencing the circumstance of its Skinner box, could press a bar and receive a positive reinforcer. Their trainers acted to assure motivational level, define the desired behavior, observe for instances of that behavior and deliver a reinforcer. Easier said than done. Lisa and Frasier were interested in watching it being done.

Lisa stepped into the lab just before the students arrived; Frasier watched from his and Lisa's office. As soon as Eva spotted Lisa she welcomed her, waved at Frasier, and escorted Lisa to a comfortable chair. From this site, Lisa could generally observe the goings on in most of the room and closely observe the actions of three students near her.

Students were instructed to teach and change the behaviors of their charges in the same way most behaviors of most organisms are changed, through the selective experiences of consequences. Basically, college-students were to provide positive reinforcement immediately after their rat-students showed a desired behavior and to withhold the reinforcer for less desired behaviors. To teach bar pressing, students watched their rats and delivered reinforcers; food pellets and sounds, immediately after it showed closer approximations to bar pressing, that is, got closer to, then touched, then depressed the bar.

After bar pressing was established, students began to reinforce bar presses in the light-on condition, but withhold reinforcement in the light-off condition. Soon the rats were nearly perfect in pressing during light-on and not pressing, doing other behaviors, in light-off. In behavioral terms, these rats were showing us they were discriminating among their life circumstances by behaving differently under varying situations.

Lisa was impressed by how quickly two of the rats near her were taught to press the bar. She noticed the third rat learned much slower, that is, it required many more teaching trials before it learned bar pressing. She asked Eva about this observation.

"The primary variable in rat-learning is student-teaching. All these rats are from a respected breeder; we always buy pure breed subjects for our lab," Eva stated. "But most college students, in fact most people, have no technical skills for teaching. We talk about contingencies during class meetings, and they read about applying principles of behavior in textbooks, but in the rat lab 'the rubber hits the road' and they must teach accurately for their rats to behave accurately.

"In fact," she went on, "you probably noticed I stood by that student and spoke to him about mid-session. I told him to be much quicker in delivering the pellet – reinforcer – even a short delay between responding and the consequence reduces its effectiveness. This is because during a delay in reinforcement for the targeted behavior some other behavior is likely to occur so it is reinforced. After the student was better at reinforcement his rat learned more quickly.

"The bright side of my correcting that student's teaching performance is he clearly saw that his skill with reinforcement was the primary variable effecting learning by his rat-student. I can use this event in the lab as a discussion point in our next class."

Lisa thanked Eva for allowing Frasier and her to visit the lab, particularly when she was busy with students. As Lisa walked back toward her office she mulled over what she had seen in the lab in view of points of discussion at the Thursday group. Still, it was not easy for her to appreciate that analyzing road rage, or terrorism, was on the same plane with rats pushing bars.

Frasier was both impressed and intrigued by what he had witnessed. He had seen the provision of positive consequences following a predetermined behavior had built that selected behavior to strength, and differential reinforcement had established a clear discrimination in rats in a few minutes. Although he did not actuate the reinforcing system himself, he almost felt like he had. He decided to ask Eva to help him to have a rat and chamber so he could implement training; work through the Michael's manual himself.

"Then again," Frasier processed, "maybe I should do a field test of my ability to use differential reinforcement. I'll use my connections with my national security computer colleagues to complete needed actions." At that moment he used one of his new secure connections to access Google and obtain information about Private Investigators and electrical contractors located within 50 miles of the University.

Eva was walking back to her office after rat lab when she was overtaken by Rob. He said he had just provided a guest lecture to a psychology class, Psychology 411, "Motivation and Emotion."

"How'd it go?" asked Eva.

"I don't know what the students think, but I'm sure I enjoyed it. I suspect the course instructor didn't."

"Why's that?" asked Eva with eyebrows raised.

Rob answered, "Cuz the course is taught in a traditional way – 'motivation is an inferred internal driver of what people do' – and my comments were couched in objective terms, explaining 'motivation' as a hypothetical construct that is properly and constructively viewed as a product of environments acting on behavior."

"Did you use the pigeon?" asked Eva.

"Oh, yes, it was a big hit, as always" answered Rob.

They both knew "the pigeon" was trained to peck a key in a chamber at a very high rate under one condition and very slowly under another condition. This was a simple discrimination, just like in the rat lab, but instead of bar pressing in one condition and no-pressing in another, the pigeon was reinforced for working busily in one and working lazily in another circumstance. In this case, a red light was associated with reinforcement for high rates and a green light with reinforcement for low rates of responding.

"I began the lecture with the bird in a green light condition – pecking slowly – lazily. As the students watched the pigeon I asked, 'What level of motivation is this bird showing?' and got many call-outs that he was lacking motivation. Then I switched the light to red and the bird pecked like crazy, of course, that's what he gets reinforced for, and asked again, 'What level of motivation is our bird showing now?' This time a couple of students said, 'highly motivated,' but most students said nothing and looked puzzled."

"Always that way," said Eva. "I've done that lecture maybe 10 times."

Rob went on, "So I asked, 'How can a bird, or person, be highly motivated one moment and lack motivation the next second for doing the same type of behavior?' After an adequate rhetorical pause, I offered the class an answer. I said, you inferred the level of motivation of the pigeon by how fast it worked. You saw me switch 'motivation' on and off. But I did not change the motivation of the pigeon, I told it what behaviors would be reinforced and it performed correctly. That is, 'motivation' sometimes is used as a hypothetical label put on observed behaviors under noticeable circumstances. The inference of 'motivation,' is not really helpful for understanding why organisms behave as they do. But determining the *motivational operations* and *contingencies* operating on the pigeon or person is the way to understand why we behave as we do."

Eva said, "That is a fun experience, and maybe the students learned something." She asked, "Did you delve into 'emotion' with them?"

Rob answered, "Not much. I was running low on time, so only mentioned that emotions could be understood similarly to motivation, that is, as a special class of learned behaviors – you know – we learn to say we feel pain or are depressed or are comfortable. I described that there are likely physiological underpinnings associated with reports of these private events, but we learn to express them, and those verbal reports are affected by social and personal circumstances so their accuracy should be considered questionable."

They arrived at Karl's office, but it was vacant, so they looked in on Lisa. She, too, was not in her office, but Eva said to Rob, "I'll introduce you to Frasier. We can sit and talk in Lisa's office – it is much more comfortable than Karl's – until one or the other returns. I need to ask each of them about the agenda for the next Thursday meeting."

They stepped to the worktable where Eva pointed at Frasier and said, "Rob, this is Frasier. He's very bright and exceptionally verbal. He speaks and writes intelligently. Frasier, you've seen Rob at the Thursday meetings. He's a bright guy, very accomplished in flexibly applying the principles of behavior, from individual interventions to systems designs. You guys should talk."

Frasier said, "Good to have you in the office. If you two have a moment I'd like clarification about the Glossary you distributed to students in Psychology 301. I see 'time out' and 'imitation' are defined, but this is a rat lab; do rats experience those procedures?"

"Actually, yes, rats do show imitation and have experienced time out procedures," answered Rob. "The procedure of removing rats from opportunities to earn positive reinforcement has been used as punishment, and rats have been shown to watch other rats perform and do behaviors they saw done and followed by desirable consequences."

Rob went on, "Humans learn to imitate at an early age. A landmark study showing young children learn to imitate then do behaviors they observed a model do was reported by Baer and Sherman in 1964. It's an elegant study you might want to review. For my part, I saw my daughter Karen show imitation when she was just a tiny girl, barely standing and speaking only a few words. I came home from work and she excitedly babbled something at me. I couldn't understand, so bent closer and she said a series of sounds and hit me in the face. Startled, I looked at her mother who said Karen had just seen the commercial for a Punch drink and was imitating it! Quite a demonstration of the power of imitation, and at a very young age."

Rob redirected the conversation by asking Eva, "I taught Psych 301 and the rat lab for nearly 3 years of classes, what did you cover today?"

She answered, "They were in the lab today; shaping their rats and teaching a light-on, light-off discrimination."

Rob laughed and said, "Oh yes, I remember coaching students to be quick and accurate in reinforcing their 'furry students,' as Karl occasionally called them." They both laughed and shook their heads as they could virtually hear Karl saying that.

He went on, "One student in that course seemed to have learned what we were trying to convey. At the close of one class meeting he asked if he could tell me about his recent planned use of reinforcement with his roommate. I said, 'sure,' and listened to him describe his impoverished apartment and the somewhat challenging habits of his roommate. Seems they had only one comfortable chair and both hated washing the nasty dishes that accumulated each day. Competition for 'The Chair' was fierce and the roommate was better at getting into it and not relinquishing it than was this class member. This student described the 'near combat' they engaged in while forcing each other to, 'do the damned dishes.'

"After listening to my lectures and reading the assigned text about how a reinforcer is an environmental feature that can strengthen behavior, he hatched a plan for using what he was learning about behavioral principles. First, he kept data regarding how much time each of them occupied 'The Chair' and how many nights each of them did the dishes. During these days of observation he watched for things and events that seemed pleasing to his roommate. He arrived at the opinion that his roommate loved to talk and be listened to. Armed with these baseline data about time in chair and doing the dishes, and a good idea about what might be a reinforcer, he tried to test what he'd learned in class. He continued taking data, and applied his understanding of contingent reinforcement simply by actively listening (i.e., eye contact, nodding, and frequent "uh huhs") when his roommate was out of the chair or doing dishes, and not appearing to listen at other times."

"This student said it was almost embarrassing. After a few days, roomy would get out of the chair so our student could have it – he had 100% access to 'The Chair' and roomy did the dishes 100% of the evenings, except when our student, 'felt guilty' and stepped-in to do the dishes. He told me, 'There is no doubt, reinforcement works.' I was pleased to hear that, and told him so."

"Fine story," said Eva, "I feel we don't have much of an impact on most students. They seem to see our class as just another one among the menu of classes they have to take for a degree. It is frustrating. Our class is one of the few that are based on the natural science of behavior, 'the truth,' and valuable for them for conducting their whole lives. But most of them don't see it."

Frasier listened carefully to this additional example of behavior being established and changed by planned contingencies, and he heard the complaint that most students don't appreciate what they are exposed to in behavioral classes. "Well," he said to himself, "I see the functional utility of behavioral practices." He then selected a Private Investigator from the list Google had provided and used one of the secure phone connections he could access to contact the listed phone number.

[7]

Talking Continues, Doing Begins

"WE WILL DO ALL of our jobs at arms length," Frasier said, "but our work is very important for our country, I assure you. Neither you nor I may ever really see the 'Big Picture,' but we must understand our efforts are important and both of us will be handsomely rewarded as we succeed." He thought to himself, "I think my comments will serve as adequate MOs for this fellow; now I'm going to begin the shaping – or is it chaining – process."

He was talking to the third PI, private investigator, he had selected to contact from the list of vendors Google had provided. The initial list offered 16 names, but Frasier had narrowed to three apparently viable candidates for his purposes by reviewing their personal and financial circumstances and work histories. These three showed high levels of responsible management of their personal and fiscal lives. Each was on solid financial footing, but not flush, and would benefit from additional income. Equally important, each had dealt discreetly and effectively with "delicate" matters on multiple occasions.

At the close of this interview, conducted over Skype, Frasier told Mr. Anthony Curry he had the job and he would get back to him in a day or two with a contract for his services. Frasier had used Skype for introducing himself, and a few days later, for interviewing each of the top three PIs for several, related reasons. Primarily, he wanted his potential "personal agent," as he thought of them, to see his image. He figured a highly skilled PI would want to partially determine the veracity and sincerity of a potential client by examining his or her facial characteristics.

A competent PI could access facial-recognition and related databases to obtain a wide swath of information about a client or an investigative target. Counting on this, Frasier extracted sufficient files from his computer colleagues at the CIA, FBI, and NSA to craft an exceptional physical and personal profile for – of – himself. Anyone who examined the persona of "Frederick Logan, CEO of Quality of Life, LLC," would discover a very wealthy individual who kept to himself, but appeared to be intimately connected to powerful federal agencies. Pictures of Mr. Logan showed a ruggedly handsome, mature, and thoughtful appearing man in his prime years.

The three interviewees behaved as Frasier had predicted. After introductions, and before being interviewed, each searched databases and used facial recognition resources to verify his (pseudo) identity. They examined sufficient public records to observe his sterling character and abundant ability to pay. Of course, Frasier used facial analysis programs during each interview to assist with evaluating the truthfulness and intensity of commitment of the candidate to accomplish the tasks Frasier, that is, "Frederick" described to them.

Frasier was re-reading the contract he intended to fax to Mr. Anthony "Tony" Curry, his potential personal agent, when Eva entered Lisa's office.

She said to Frasier, "You remember, of course, today we will discuss the idea of having a federal 'behavior analysis office' at our Third Thursday group meeting." Her comment was presented as a declarative, not an interrogative. She knew Frasier forgot nothing, but she sometimes wondered whether his retention and processing of information would ever be translated into actions in some way. Maybe Frasier could tell Lisa or her to do something based on information they had provided and he had processed?

Karl brought a tray of assorted Danish pastries to this meeting. He placed the tray within his reach on the conference table, not on the small table where drinks were habitually offered. As members arrived, he invited each to take a pastry, but his tone was not completely sincere.

Lisa took a pastry – Karl seemed less happy – and welcomed the group, then looked expectantly toward Karl. He began his comments by saying, "The idea of there being a federal office charged with promoting the precise and appropriate application of behaviorally sound practices in the conduct of national affairs is very attractive. Such an agency might be called the Behavior Analysis Office, the BAO, and serve to review or help design federal laws and practices to assure they reflect principles of behavior and emphasize recommended positive practices."

"Usually we are content with doing research to confirm or discover behavioral relationships, and in making use of principles of behavior to promote wellbeing at the individual level. However, we should realize that accomplishing meaningful changes at the systems level really is the primary strategy for improving everyone's quality of living. Everyone lives in a context of systems; school, work, government, and so on, even families, are systems in that they generate particular contingencies on all those within their purview.

"I say it is appropriate for us to focus our discussion on the huge and complex 'system' called the federal government. Generally speaking, the federal government is supposed to accomplish actions to keep us safe and happy, and it does this by passing laws and spending money. Actually, of course, 'government' comprises thousands of individuals whose behaviors impact us as they enforce laws and make expenditures. That is, the behaviors of government personnel function to enact contingencies on us that alter our behaviors, whether they or citizens in general know it or not.

"Sometimes the fact that federal programs function to change behaviors is fairly obvious, as in how contingencies in welfare programs sometimes build and maintain counter-productive behaviors, but federal contingencies can be more subtle, like how requirements in the tax code produce behaviors that are more or less desirable. Of course, we can interpret the enactment and enforcement of the myriad federal regulations as functioning to apply contingencies to business and industry, actually, all of us. But the government does not phrase its actions in terms of applying contingencies or making behavior changes.

"I suggest these issues present perfect opportunities for constructive actions by a federal Behavior Analysis Office. The personnel in the BAO could work to bring behavioral competence into federal laws and practices."

Lisa interrupted, saying, "I agree the idea is a very good one, that is, to have a force in Washington pushing to make federal laws and actions more functionally and behaviorally precise, but I have great concerns about the matter of 'precise' – precise for what? We don't want government just to be more effective, but to be effective to our betterment, that is, contribute to what we agree is our individual and collective wellbeing."

Karl responded, "Yes, we are on the same page. Part of the behavioral competence I refer to is the 'appropriate' feature of behavioral interventions. The BAO should work to be sure federal programs are conducted effectively *and* appropriately."

"Sure," said Rob, "but the definition of 'appropriate' is both crucial and difficult to define. The BAO, or we – all citizens – must be considered in the determination of what is 'appropriate' and how that concept is developed and put into behavioral and operational terms.

"We have many very good references in the literature of behavior analysis that should guide the design and conduct of the BAO. For example, fundamentally important considerations were provided by Skinner (1953) in *Science and Human Behavior*, but the many powerful observations of Murray Sidman (2001) in his book *Coercion and its Fallout* really should guide the BAO – and governments – everywhere," Rob stated in firm tones.

Eva was quick to say, "Sidman's book is very effective at describing how governments, and other institutions like education, are conducted primarily coercively, that is, they apply punishment and negative reinforcement contingencies in attempting to accomplish their missions. Fortunately, Sidman and Skinner and whole field of behavior analysis offer positive alternatives to coercion. But, we cannot think the BAO can do much about the overall national or world 'culture' of coercion."

"Absolutely true," offered Rob, "the BAO would be only a small, but expert, tool for assisting our government to move in positive directions. I am thinking that the only way our government – and communities and homes – will be adjusted into using more positive methods to define and support desirable learning and performances is by grass roots actions. That is, citizens in general need to be informed about methods for using positive reinforcement to reach our aspirations."

Frasier offered, "Before Bert left campus we briefly discussed the virtues of translating definitions of socially important topics from intuitive into behavioral terms. He mentioned several noticeable books that present issues of widespread concern, including economics, education, religion and business. That is, Bert was promoting behaviorally useful interpretations of what he called 'the excellent ideas' offered in these books. That notion stimulates me and seems perfectly aligned with the purpose of our group and as a follow up to today's discussion."

Lisa led the chorus of agreement and asked Frasier to circulate a list of the books Bert mentioned plus accumulate other titles group members might nominate, then distribute the compiled list to the group before the week is out. As participants in the discussion group filed out of Seminar Room 3, Karl refilled his coffee cup and picked up the half-empty – but half-full – plate of pastries.

Early that evening, Lisa and Eva walked from the Education and Psychology building toward the southern side of campus where several cozy eateries are located and they could share interesting conversation over dinner. They saw Rob ahead of them, caught up to him, and asked him to join them. "Should be fun," he agreed.

Frasier calculated it was late in the workday, but he faxed a contract to Tony Curry.

The large pine trees marking the south boundary of campus were casting long shadows when the trio began dinner, but now were difficult to see in the darkness. Conversation had touched on work matters through vacation plans to things a bit personal as drinks progressed from the first glass of wine through the second bottle. Just when it seemed folks were about to head their separate ways, Eva asked Rob if he had read "the Nudge book?"

"Oh yes," he answered, "but I didn't really study it; just read it like a novel, quickly for impressions – why?"

"I've heard it mentioned several times recently, but it's not a new book – just wondering why it is getting attention."

"I can give you some impressions of the book relative to the nature of our group. First, it's not behavior analytic in outlook, but the term 'behavior' appears here and there. The authors attribute their statements about why humans behave as we do to 'choice science' and a few 'principles,' but these are not principles as we appreciate them. When they speak of 'choice science,' I took it to mean they had reviewed the body of literature addressing choice and choosing be-haviors. Not having seen those studies, I cannot judge if they were behavior analytic in nature or even included the literature on choice offered by our discipline.

"A couple of 'principles' I recall them saying underlie human be-havior, are something like, 'people think they should save more,' and people have a 'loss aversion,' and a 'money illusion.' You can see those are labels for sets of behaviors and not what we call principles; not science-derived lawful statements of relationships between behavior and its environment.

"However, the book is nicely readable and its commonsensical approach is probably why it is attracting so much positive regard. While it is not a source of technical understanding, the idea of nudg-es and nudging seems to present a tool useful for those who want to promote 'better choosing.'

"I must say a weakness of the concept of nudging is that it is fo-cused on actions of providing antecedents to obtain desired behav-ior without regard to how the consequences of those behaviors cause them to be strengthened or weakened. Possibly they think behaviors that are nudged to appear are naturally followed by changes – conse-quences – that strengthen or weaken them.

"Despite its shortcomings, the *Nudge* book has several important strengths. One of these is that it generally calls the attention of read-ers to the effects of environment on how people behave. This is good for our science by promoting regard for behavior as altered by its en-vironment and might stimulate readers to search for more or better answers, which they would find in the Analysis of Behavior.

"Also, important for everyone to appreciate, they suggest gov-ernment should use environmental arrangements to alter the behav-ior of citizens in ways the government has deemed 'better.' In fact, they call their approach 'paternalistic libertarian' – yow! That's scary;

that's like my father telling me to do whatever I want as long as it is agreeable to him!"

At that, Eva and Lisa launched into an intense and multi-directional discussion, often with barbed comments aimed at the only male present, regarding *paternal-ism* and sex equity, promotion policies, pay levels and equality of regard for women during everyday living. Thus aroused, but tired, the now-closer friends said enthusiastic goodnights and wandered toward their respective homes.

Earlier in the evening, at about the time Eva asked about nudging, Frasier was finishing drafts of the second and third contracts he would offer to Tony Curry contingent on him showing criterion performance under the first contract.

Frasier's secure phone connection became active, functionally "rang," and it was Tony Curry who said he had received the (first) contract and was eager to get started.

"Fine" Frasier replied, "We shall go forward in a stepwise manner."

Tony thought, "He's a stuffy-talker, but the job is clear and the pay is good, so I'm happy to be on board with this."

Frasier proposed, "Let us review the chain of activities I have listed in your contract and the remuneration I will deliver to you after the completion of each step and the full compensation following your success with the terminal duty." He went on to review the set of activities he had task-analyzed as sufficient to reach the condition he desired and had described in the contract Mr. Curry had accepted.

In general, Mr. Anthony Curry, acting as Mr. Frederick Logan's personal agent, will review county records to identify how electrical power is distributed to the Education and Psychology building; visit the University campus to directly observe and confirm how power is provided to offices in that building; identify the sources of electricity and emergency generators supplying power to the VA and University hospitals, and the nearby U.S. Naval Support Facility. Payments will be made to Mr. Curry based on the completion of each step and following an adequate final report.

"After I review and approve your comprehensive report of these activities I will be happy to provide the final payment. And at that time, I expect to have another very valuable assignment for you," Frasier added, thinking, "Reinforce approximations and manage MOs!" Tony stated his dedication to doing a thorough and completely discreet job, and they ended their conversation.

The Thursday discussion group had agreed to do a quick discussion of a few books noticeable in the popular press. The group wanted to review books offering attractive ideas about how to deal constructively with pivotal issues so they might translate this advice into behavioral terms. They knew expressing good ideas or problems in operational and behavioral terms made them open to objective intervention, evaluation and dissemination. Some old and some newer books were nominated for discussion based on their content involving socially important issues and at least one member having read it.

One week after the recent Thursday meeting Frasier circulated the following list of "Nominated Books" to all members of the group.

Nominated Books

Gross National Happiness: Why Happiness Matters for America – and How We Can Get More of It (Brooks, 2008)

In Search of Excellence: Lessons from America's Best-Run Companies (Peters & Waterman, 1982)

It Takes a Village and Other Lessons Children Teach Us (Clinton, 1996; 2006)

Non-Zero: The Logic of Human Destiny (Wright, 2000)

Nudge: Improving Decisions About Health, Wealth, and Happiness (Thaler & Sunstein, 2009)

Reckless Endangerment: How Outsized Ambition, Greed, and Corruption Led to Economic Armageddon (Morgenson & Rosner, 2011)

Religion for Atheists: A Non-believer's Guide to Uses of Religion (de Botton, 2012)

Helping Children Succeed (Tough, 2016)
The Betrayal of the American Dream (Barlett & Steele, 2012)
Coming Apart: The State of White America, 1960-2010 (Murray, 2011)
The Economist's View of the World: Government, Markets & Public Policy
(Rhoads, 1985)
The War for Wealth: The True Story of Globalization, or Why the Flat World
is Broken (Steingart, 2006)
Thinking Fast and Slow (Kahneman, 2011)
Who Stole the American Dream? (Smith, 2012)

In his message distributing the list to the group, Frasier mentioned one or more members had read each book. He noted information about some of these books, and about 400 others, can be found on the Web at *booktv.org* where videos can be viewed of authors describing and answering questions about their books.

Rob reviewed the list of books a moment after it arrived in his email. He had read and appreciated the non-believer's guide; not so much because he was a non-believer, but because the ideas in it were constructively offered. He recalled, in the *Guide* the author thoughtfully discussed the social functional value of major features of religious practice. For example, religions identify highly desirable behaviors, then persons who demonstrated these to an exemplary degree and were venerated, maybe calling them saints. Thus, using what can be recognized as a loose version of imitation procedures, church leaders cause observers to see an image of a person and hear descriptions of desired behaviors they did and how they were very desirable and rewarded. Believers are told to behave similarly and they will be religiously appreciated. The *Guide* alerts readers, in the author's own way, that to the extent the selected behaviors are adaptive for individuals and society, this strategy of modeling and reinforcement is appropriate for widespread application in our communities to establish desirable conduct.

Later in the *Guide*, the author describes the constructive role church facilities and organized social supportive activities sometimes serve for some segments of our communities. In churches, participants can gather in a context of (relative) peace and social acceptance, and receive interpersonal support or even counseling during times of need. The author more or less asks, why not have similar gathering places and facilitated interactions available for all community members, be they religious or not. Surely most citizens would benefit from social support and problem solving at times in their lives. Do we have to be religious to obtain support? Why don't we add church-like resources to our communities so everyone may benefit?

"Good questions," Rob thought.

That same day Karl closely reviewed the list of books. He was looking forward to the next meeting of the Thursday group and sharing and hearing comments about each book. Right now, however, he must hustle quickly to Seminar Room A where Rob is about to begin his invited guest lecture.

Entering the room a moment tardy, Karl saw Rob at the front of the room next to the lectern, but not yet speaking. Karl went directly to front-center of the room, turned to the audience, and said, "Our guest speaker today is Doctor Robin Crew. He will deliver the 6th in our series of presentations on 'Science for Effective Action.'"

Karl noticed the room was not filled to capacity as it had been for Bert. He recognized in the audience the usual faces of students and faculty in the Analysis of Behavior program, but few of the many Education faculty and students who had attended Bert's presentation were there today. However, very pleasing was the presence of faculty from the department of political science and the School of Business. He assumed the younger people surrounding these faculty members were students in those programs.

Karl announced, "Dr. Crew graduated from our AoB – Analysis of Behavior – program nearly 40 years ago – wow, how time flies. His dissertation examined Schedule-induced Aggression and he studied Errorless Discrimination Training for his Master's thesis. The same as Bert, our previous speaker, Rob's work experiences began in a public education system. Subsequently, Rob served as Superintendent of a residential service center for individuals with profound, multiple disabilities; then he moved to another state to head a resource center supporting state and community programs serving citizens with developmental disabilities; and finally, in yet another state, he was director of a comprehensive 'Human Development Center' for over 20 years.

"In all those capacities, and obviously for many years, he applied the principles of behavior to solve problems and develop the systems he led or contacted. Today he will share with us his perspectives on 'Behavior Analysis in the Development of Programs and Systems.' Welcome, Dr. Crew."

The polite, welcoming applause was enough to energize Rob for talking quickly for the allotted 60 minutes. He recognized he would have to hurry to cover the experiences and materials he thought the audience would appreciate.

I am honored to be before you and very pleased by the opportunity to share perspectives I believe to be fundamentally important for anyone in a leadership capacity. In the few minutes we have today, I can only superficially touch on major aspects involved in systems, as I see them through a behavioral lens, and ways to integrate behavior-science validated principles within them.

The theme of my remarks is essentially the same as those of previous speakers, for example, Dr. Allen Bert. In his comments, you heard of significant successes by students and teachers because they benefitted from well-designed reinforcement contingencies. In his presentation you saw an argument for planfully – explicitly – using principles of behavior to enhance learning and performance. Today I'm urging the explicit and systematic application of positive reinforcement contingencies for thoughtfully selected behaviors to increased productivity and happiness in work places.

I will provide brief descriptions of the systems in which I worked and will provide examples of how principles were applied, including sample materials. These materials include a diagram depicting what I call 'A Competent System' and a figure illustrating a 'Dynamic Factors Framework for Leadership and Program Development.' These are summative views intended to be assistive in understanding the behavioral nature of systems and leadership.

When I interviewed for work with the school system my eventual boss asked me, 'What types of organizations do you think could benefit from having an operant conditioner in them?' In those years, 'operant conditioner' was a title often applied to practitioners of AoB, so I answered, 'All groups should benefit by having sound behavioral advice.' Apparently this answer was acceptable; I was hired. About 2 years later my boss told me he hired me partly because he'd never heard anyone say anything good about operant conditioners and he wanted to see how I'd do my job.

After some scattered laughter, he continued. *I am sure my appreciation for the constructive role of behavior analysis in all organizations is still unusual, but by the end of this hour I hope all of you share some of my enthusiasm.*

Throughout my career I found it helpful to look at the role of the organization I was leading and ask, what is our job and who does it? In schools, our job was to change the behavior of students; at the treatment center our job was to meet the physical needs and enhance the adaptive skills of our residents; at the two resource centers it was to accumulate validated information and express recommended practices within systems of services for citizens with developmental disabilities by actions of training, technical assistance and demonstrations of model services. At the Human Development Center, we were a resource for developing systems of education, health, and human services to be more effective and appropriate in accomplishing their roles.

You no doubt have recognized a consistent theme in AoB is 'behavior is everything we do' and this includes how we participate in or lead organizations. Based on that assumption, we are alerted to the necessity of knowing and appropriately applying behavioral principles in any organization to increase its efficiency. The papers by Crowell and Anderson (1982a; 1982b) in the Journal of Organizational Behavior Management *are excellent descriptions of these basic points.*

Of course we want to develop appropriate contingencies to support the work of each and every employee, but we should not stop at this obvious – and maybe relatively simple – target for our behavioral efforts. The truth is, all organizational environments contain myriad features that impact everyone in them by generating motivational circumstances and differential consequences for behaviors that are either adaptive or maladaptive for the person or the organization. Often these contingencies work in opposition. For example, faculty here at the University are told by leadership they are expected to submit grant applications – seems to be a clear enough call for a large class of behaviors – and implies that work circumstances will facilitate and reinforce the constituent behaviors.

I see from the smirks and head-shakes of faculty, my gross example has hit home. We all know that grant writing – and subsequent project implementation – are not well supported and actually often are opposed in many ways by organizational obstacles and contrary actions by campus leadership. In fact, we also see counter-productive contingencies on campus for developing excellence in teaching and for doing meaningful community outreach.

I have worked at seven universities and can say it is my experience this contradictory situation has appeared at all of them. My cumulative experiences of contradictions in higher education environments led me to coin the phrase, 'higher education is neither,' that is, neither 'higher' nor very educational, relative to what it could and should be." He noticed head nods from most faculty in the audience.

The reason I have attempted to stir up a bit of angst among us today is to arouse – motivate – your interest in viewing organizations comprehensively as behavioral settings. All organizational settings should be analyzed and specifically designed to support behaviors that correspond to the functions and outcomes the organization is expected to accomplish. Remember: organizations don't make decisions; people do, and leadership personnel should decide to arrange constructive contingencies.

I offer this diagram (Appearing on the large screen) *entitled, "Components of a Competent System" as an example of how one might visualize the basic functions of an organization as a step toward expressing them in terms of behaviors and contingencies.*

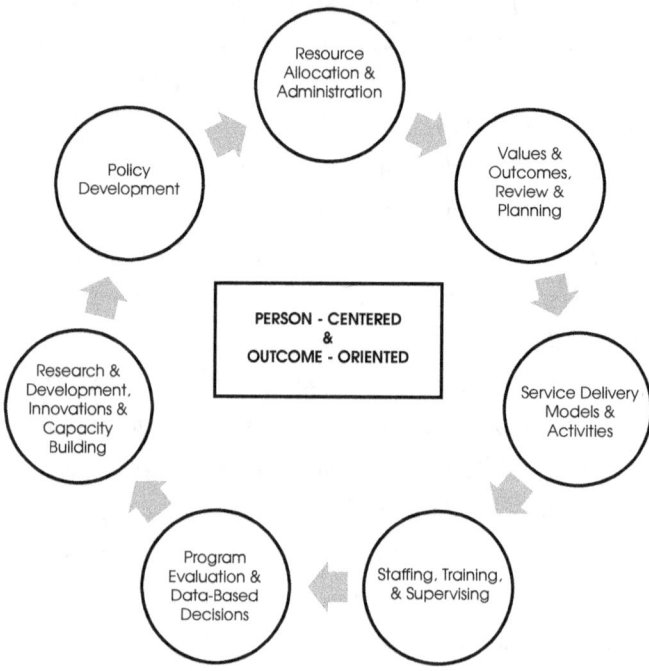

I developed this diagram for use in systems of human services. That is why the central rectangle contains 'Person-Centered and Outcome-Oriented.' These are prominent and fundamentally important features of appropriate human service systems, but those concepts seem appropriate for the focus of any organization because the products of organizations are the results of 'persons' behaving to achieve 'outcomes.'

Frasier was distracted from examining the Competent System diagram by receiving an, **"Alert – Facial Recognition – Alert,"** coming through his confidential communication system. He reviewed his monitors.

Rob was saying, *The direct focus on personnel development is indicated by the component labeled 'Staffing, Training & Supervising.' Designing and conducting this component of a system is a complicated endeavor involving identification of practices that are* **effective***, that is, empirically validated, and* **appropriate***, that is, socially and functionally validated for accomplishing the role of the organization. Identified practices must be expressed in sequences of training, taught appropriately – maybe using imitation and coaching in the workplace – followed by continuing differential positive supervising for quality assurance in the work site.*

I will share with you two procedures we used at the treatment facility I headed for supporting service staff to accomplish their responsibilities. The first procedure was applied to reinforce timely and reliable attendance at work – obviously crucial for providing the services our clients required – and the second procedure was a simple method for assuring staff were appreciated during their work efforts.

To reinforce timely attendance and reduce absence or late arrival to work, we designed contingencies involving observing the attendance of each employee and delivering differential consequences, that is, positive reinforcers, for being on time and reliable in work attendance, and punishment for being inappropriately absent.

You remember 'The Consequences Box' handed out at Bert's presentation – extra copies are available at the entrance to this room – we used a version of it to guide a team in identifying entries in all four cells of the box. That is, we tried to maximize the likelihood of success in encouraging excellence in work attendance by systematically identifying four types of consequences and four types of contingencies: two for increasing attendance and two for decreasing absences.

We arranged for gift certificates to popular local stores we could present for attendance, that is, reinforce desired behaviors. We drafted letters of reprimand to present after absences, that is, punish absences by presenting a negative. We reinforced improved work attendance by removing letters of reprimand from personnel files, that is, negative reinforcement. And, we punished absences by removing points in our employee merit system.

Before implementing the four contingencies just noted, about 11% of our employees were absent per day. This level of absence caused a huge burden on workers who did come to work and this shortage in personnel cost our clients many hours of personalized support by staff. After applying contingencies that favored attendance we saw an average of 98% staff present for work each day. Very important – reinforcing – for me, I heard many comments from service staff about how very fair they saw the system, and how, 'great it is to be recognized for being reliable.'

The second procedure I'd like to share with you today is a very simple method for prompting the fair and timely application by supervisors of positive and negative consequences during the workday. I met regularly with each of the four unit supervisors who oversaw portions of our service delivery activities. Each had about 30 service staff assigned to their unit. I asked these supervisors to keep notes on the major consequences they provided their staff on a daily basis by keeping notes on a calendar-like record sheet. This record showed the names of all staff and all the dates of the month. By each staff for each date the supervisor was asked to note if they provided a written Commendation or Reprimand, or offered a spoken Positive or Negative comment.

A quick glance at this record sheet disclosed which staff had received what types of consequences during each workday, and across weeks and months. It was easy to note the ratio of positives to negatives experienced by each staff and to see how many consequences each staff experienced. We wanted each staff to receive several positives each day and to see very few negatives. This quick record sheet and easy review served as a great tool to prompt supervisors to be more observant of desired work efforts and ensure the equitable distribution of differential attention across staff.

Notice there are six other components indicated as features of a Competent System. These components represent sets of interrelated activities that contribute to the survival and successful conduct of the organization. I feel the titles of the components are sufficiently suggestive of their roles for a leader to begin a functional analysis aimed at specifying the operational and behavioral activities required to conduct the individual and collective components appropriately.

In view of time constraints, I can mention only one strategy leaders might find valuable for analyzing and designing the overall conduct of their organizations, sometimes called, "Backward Mapping." Essentially, you complete backward mapping by beginning with detailed behavioral and operational definitions of effective and appropriate performances at the "bottom line," then progressively work "back" from there to the top level of the organization, developing along the way definitions of supportive functions and behaviors at every level of the organization to support activities at the bottom line.

The resultant behavioral map should be used in designing and applying positive reinforcement contingencies at all levels for behaviors that are supportive of the bottom line performances. It is likely many of the refinements in definitions of performances at all levels, and maybe some of the contingencies operating at all those levels, will seem small. But these adjustments will move this crucial aspect of organizational design and operation from informal or haphazard – as is the norm – to more precise and effective.

Armed with coherent, behaviorally sound policies and practices at all levels, organizational leaders can be objectively supportive in decisions affecting each and all components of the system. I say again, the primary tool leaders have is Contingency Management. Be sure to see Aubrey Daniels (2000) fine book, Bringing out the Best In People: How to Apply the Astonishing Power of Positive Reinforcement *for more ideas and details for using behavioral methods to develop effective systems.*

Under circumstances of leadership, and in all everyday interactions, we can pay attention to how positive we are being – our Positive-to-Negative ratio – remember Bert's descriptions of teachers providing consequences to build desirable behaviors? And, we should remember we are always models that others might imitate. Finally, we should always be carefully differential with the reinforcers we control, that is, constantly be shaping more desirable behaviors in others – and ourselves. In fact, we really should find a time for a session on Self-Control in leadership and everyday living.

In closing, I am urging we move from only commonsensical arrangements of work places – or school or governments – to explicitly arranged environments where the desired learning and doing are objectively defined and reinforced in individualized ways. The differences might seem small, but we will be moving from not behaviorally sound to behaviorally specific, which brings with it increased effectiveness and probably much more happiness.

We have run out of time. I have enjoyed being with you today. Please help yourself to handout materials on the table by the door.

As Rob talked, Frasier listened, but he also reviewed the data files of still photos and video footage that accompanied the facial recognition alert he had received. A series of six still photos showed the neck and head of a male exiting a vehicle. He was identified as Tony Curry by combining analyses of separate photos revealing his upper head and hair line; a quarter-profile showing nose and cheek bone structure; and a quarter-frontal view revealing mouth, lips and partial view of eyebrows.

In each frame Tony could be seen wearing costuming to obscure his features. Across frames he was shown adjusting a wig as he turned toward the car door to open it; pulling-on glasses as the door was opening, these were tinted to mask eye color and the lenses were spaced extra wide so his eyes might appear wide-set; and, in the last frame, he was raising the collar of his shirt, but his hairline, neck and ears were visible. Taken together, the recognition program found 34 points of commonality; more than enough to confirm it was Tony stepping out of the car.

Frasier reviewed the video files and saw Tony stepping out of a car, not one Tony was known to own, and walking out of Lot C in the direction of the Education and Psychology building. Other security cameras showed Tony entering the building, where Frasier was watching, and walking the hallways on each floor. He appeared to be "moving with a purpose;" a man there to do business. No one seemed to take special notice, but Frasier saw that Tony seemed to be talking on a cell phone.

From the several glimpses cameras provided of Mr. Curry's mouth, Frasier read he was dictating directions and distances as he moved through the floors. Soon he was on the floor where Frasier was observing. As Tony reached the area of Karl's office he stopped, his back to Lisa's office, and seemed to be reading items Karl had posted on a bulletin board next to his door. He chuckled quietly, then, seemed to aim his phone/camera at a joke noticeable on the board. It showed two men wearing suits, standing facing one another. The bubble over the head of the man on the right showed he was saying, "Sure it's stupid, but it's policy so we do it all the time."

Tony seemed to take a picture of the joke, but Frasier observed he actually took a "selfie" over his shoulder such that he captured the scene in Lisa's office. "Clever and subtle," thought Frasier, "I think I chose wisely when I hired Tony. I look forward to reviewing his final report. If it's good I'll give him descriptive praise for his excellent efforts and add a bonus to my final payment, that is, 'final' for this phase."

The Third Thursday discussion group members appeared less energetic than usual as they ambled into Seminar Room 3 to discuss books for their behavioral implications. It was the end of spring semester so everyone was pushing hard in classes to cover all the material they must and grading summative projects due at term's end. All faculty were writing or refining the final exams for their classes. At the same time, graduate students were feeling pressures to prepare for the too-few weeks of summer when they could complete crucial projects, so they were pestering faculty for advice or assistance. The group members, except Frasier, were physically and mentally tired.

Lisa welcomed everyone saying, "The coffee is extra strong today, and in honor of Karl I brought a pile of oatmeal-raisin cookies for nutrition and a sugar rush."

She had not brought too many cookies; they all were claimed before everyone was seated. Frasier noticed each member occupied his or her usual chair location and said to himself, "Human behavior is predictable."

Lisa suggested, "In view of our busy schedules, let's make this a quick discussion." All indicated agreement.

Eva led off with a comment about the "Coming Apart" book by Charles Murray, noting that it "made a good case that a 'socio-cultural divide' in America is being destructive of a good quality of life for all, or most, of us. I recommend you watch the video of Murray discussing this book, with reference to his earlier books, on Book TV – visit booktv.org on the Web."

"He tells us a lot we already know," said Eva, "including education is important and children without a father in the home suffer and welfare programs can be destructive of desirable behaviors. He offers his readers powerful statements, like we spend billions on welfare programs and still have millions of our fellow citizens in desperate circumstances. He provides thoughtful and data-based perspectives on these and other related issues."

"In his book, he compares a relatively affluent town to a less affluent town in terms of changes in marriage, single parents, religious observance and work across 1960 and 2010. Of course, all differences are troublesome in one way or another. For the lower class, the proportion of married has dropped, kids born out of wedlock is way up, work rates are down, and 'religiosity' has dropped to 12 percent – lots of MOs for readers to consider engaging in some type of problem solving."

"Problems in the upper class, include families are insulated in living, working and education from the majority of those who should be their fellow citizens. This isolation brings ignorance of the specific problems of others and a distorted feeling regarding the wellbeing of our country."

"His descriptions are motivational for finding solutions, and some of his suggestions for solutions approximate behavioral usefulness. In general, Murray's appeal to cultural changes as both the source of problems and for solutions can be seen as well taken. I believe Murray and we appreciate the term 'culture' means the values, activities and preferences, people show or say they adhere to . ."

Karl interrupted, "Murray sees culture as descriptive of what people do – and we agree – but we go farther to deal with culture as categories of behavior developed by contingencies. That is, the behavior of people called 'cultural' are learned from those around them. Kids are taught to say the F word or not, or that reading is fun or marriage should be avoided or work is important. To the extent numerous citizens do those things, we say its our or their culture. Culture is a product of prevailing contingencies; therefore, if you change contingencies you change behaviors and culture is changed!"

Eva said, "Of course I agree. He describes a widening behavioral – cultural divide among classes in America and how this separation threatens the wellbeing of our country. Murray presents two scenarios for our future; one being the continuing ugly degeneration of our welfare state into a European-like condition and eventual bankruptcy. The alternative he hopes for includes remedies like 'incentives for getting or holding jobs' and 'social engineering.'"

"We would agree with his suggestions, including social engineering," offered Rob, "but would translate these into more precise and individualized contingencies. We know 'incentives' is an imprecise label for motivational operations or differential consequences for desired performances. If you want people to obtain a job and work well, arrange reinforcements for the constituent behaviors."

He continued, "This adjustment from commonsensical to procedurally precise – from haphazard or informal to validated and effective – is crucial. You do not provide incentives to get folks to do something, you provide motivational operations and *contingent effective reinforcers* after each person shows approximations and a desired behavior – crucially different!"

"The choir – we – agree, of course," said Rob, "we know 'Reinforcement Works' and what that means, procedurally. And we know how to translate what Murray and the other authors are saying into science-validated procedures that could be implemented in welfare programs or education, early childhood, parenting, and so on."

Lisa mentioned to the group, "I really have to leave this meeting to deal with a couple of student issues. Please continue, but I must leave." At that, the other group members agreed they had pressing business, so said goodbyes to one another.

A few days after the Thursday meeting was adjourned, the spring semester ended and so did the customary end-of-term chaos. Each summer term begins quietly as there are few students and classes on campus. Many faculty like it better when the students are gone. Everything is quieter and easier to do; parking is available; the Student Union is not crowded; and, no one knocks on your door to ask annoying questions, such as: "When is the assignment due?" (Read the course syllabus) or give excuses, "I didn't have enough time; I didn't understand the assignment; I thought you meant something different" (Read the course syllabus) or ask for favors, "Can I turn in my paper late?" (Read the course syllabus).

During the summer term, most faculty catch up on postponed reading, writing, and interactions with colleagues. Most graduate students remain on campus. Primarily they prepare for or conduct their own research projects on the way to fulfilling requirements for their PhD.

Among those on campus was Eva, who had completed her research and was writing her dissertation. She met often with Karl who always seemed open for discussions about her dissertation or almost anything else. She enjoyed discussing a spontaneous range of topics in behavioral terms; she felt intellectually stimulated, stretched and challenged to think better, or do more, behaviorally.

Eva knew many other students were like her and happy to engage in behavioral-banter, particularly away from faculty; "off the record," when they could flippantly discuss the trials and tribulations of mankind in behavioral terms, even while sucking down a beer or two. She texted colleagues and soon a group gathered at the Cactus Club, a western-themed beer-and-snacks bar near campus. There, pitchers were $5 and a round table in a corner had seats enough for everyone said to be coming.

By the time Eva stepped into the perpetually dark "club" the round table already had a half-emptied pitcher of draft lager in its center and Bert, two AoB graduate students and two senior undergraduates seated around it. She knew the grad students quite well, but only recognized the seniors as familiar faces. As she introduced herself three more graduate students pulled chairs up to the table and two more pitchers arrived. The scruffy guy who brought the beer returned with four baskets of corn chips and two bowls of red salsa; this was developing into a nice evening!

As was their common practice, this group of students talked about general topics; articles they noticed in recent journals or web sites; a faculty verbal stumble while lecturing; a success or failure in the lab; a new student entering the program, etc., until someone offered a provocative title for discussion. That member of the assembled roundtable would raise a hand or two and announce the suggestive title.

About 45 minutes into beer and chips, Eva saw two hands reach for the sky and heard the first discussion title for this evening:

"Speed Limit, What Speed Limit?"

"In my father's time," began the proposing student, "the posted speed limit was the fastest a driver should drive. That is, driving speed was mostly controlled by a sign with numbers on it. If the speedometer reading was at or below the posted figure, the driver was comfortable, relaxed. But while the driver was exceeding the limit *he* – it was very seldom a *she* – was nervous about getting a ticket, and felt guilty because he was violating driving norms.

"Nowadays, women speed as much as men do. The posted limit is seen as largely irrelevant – speed is controlled by current conditions, including the speed of cars nearby, sight or absence of a police car, other road conditions and personal interests. The posted speed limit is kind of advisory; by adding 5 or 9 miles to the limit you can know the practical limit. Exceeding the posted 'limit' is the norm.

"I say the current condition of 'speeding is the norm' began when the national speed limit was set at 55 mph, which was such a crawl it was exceeded most of the time. Drivers were desensitized to speeding: no feeling of guilt; law enforcement could not punish frequently enough to suppress speeding behavior; speeding was almost constantly reinforcing to drivers in several ways, so even if a higher density of punishment were to occur it could only temporarily overcome the very high frequency of reinforcement coming with speeding.

"Driving conditions took over instead of signs as the controlling variable. Of course, we call this phenomenon a shift in stimulus control. Obviously, adequate contingencies could be applied to re-locate stimulus control back to speed limit signs, but for now reinforcement is available for speeding and the punishers are very few. So I say, functionally, 'speed limit – what speed limit'?"

Mixed grunts of mild approval and the sounds of chips being chomped followed this rough "analysis" of a topic; plus another round of beer.

Bert raised one hand, and asked, "Did all of you hear Rob say 'Higher Education is Neither' during his recent presentation? I propose our next topic is,

"Higher Education is Neither, but ought to be both."

"I have not experienced as much as Rob describes, but during my time in 'higher ed' I've seen the same issues he mentioned. Particularly, I've experienced clear contradictions between what seems to be called for and what is actually reinforced or punished. On one campus I was told the program I led would never be allocated State funds so we must build our program by attracting grant funds, that is, write lots of grants. We did, and every major step of preparation and submission of these applications was constrained by campus requirements. We succeeded in submitting a good number of grants despite the opposition and many were funded; our program was growing nicely.

"One day I was walking by the Vice President's office – he was responsible for campus research productivity – and he asked me into his office. He said, 'I've been reviewing grant submissions on campus and I see your program has submitted more than any other program.' I remember thinking he was about to praise our hard work, but instead he said, 'That means you fill more computer server space than anyone else and I can't afford to buy servers. You need to write fewer grants.' Amazing but true – and so counter-productive."

Bert added, "While mine is probably an unusually blatant example of administrative stumbling, it is in no way isolated."

"I can testify to that," said Rob who was walking by and overheard Bert. "When I headed a Center I saw an excellent strategy for obtaining State-administered Federal funds to do training and technical assistance, as was in our mission. I began to tell the Dean about this multi-million dollar funding opportunity and why I was excited about it, and he said, 'You already get too much money . .' without hearing one word about the nature of the project!"

"But, please excuse me, I'm just passing through," said Rob, "so goodnight."

As Rob faded into the darkness across the room, Bert said, "Many bright and productive faculty I've talked with have similar complaints. They feel constrained or ignored for working well."

One graduate student offered, "I think higher education leadership is conflicted between 'academic freedom' and their stated interests in the campus excelling. That is, administrators can talk a good game; 'we want to be a preeminent research university,' but are incapable of applying the context of functional resources and contingencies of differential reinforcement appropriate for supporting good faculty and improving the less productive faculty."

Again Bert agreed and said, "The college deans I've known well seemed afraid of complaints or controversy, and either provided little leadership or applied constraints so some productive faculty felt unsupported. I believe the contingencies on deans and department heads are for controlling their faculty to submerge complaints, not for supporting excellence."

The standing student was handed a beer and invited to sit down.

Eva offered another perspective on 'Higher Ed is neither' as she commented, "We know that lecturing does little to establish knowledge or skills in students – be these college or other levels – but often faculty rely on lectures as a primary teaching method. Higher Ed should strive to make full use of multiple methods of teaching including well-structured readings, models of clinical or research performances in videos and live demonstrations, skills practice with feedback, and frequent measures of knowledge and skills in context with supportive or corrective feedback."

"And, universities should be organized and conducted in view of the physiological and behavioral nature of humans in a physical and ecological world. Courses and applied experiences should be transdisciplinary, that is, relevant departments and disciplines should converge their knowledge and skills within integrated courses and programs of study," added another graduate student.

"I'm bored," said one of the graduate students.

Bert tried to get the group back on track, and said, "I've heard teachers and parents complain that kids are not respectful of their elders. It strikes me we could develop a definition of respect and examine how 'an elder' might behave in ways that results in students respecting them. I propose we talk about,

"Respectful or not, You shall be Taught."

Bert said, "I've heard many adults are concerned about the younger generation being disrespectful. Societies have varying definitions of what constitutes respect. For example, a Hmong family enrolled in one of our service programs virtually demanded that a priority objective for intervention with their child was establishing a particular posture and hand position when elders entered the room. It struck me this was a clear example of respectful behavior and I started thinking about a more general concept of what leads a person to say they respect another person.

"In recalling my early experiences as a consultant in public schools it occurred to me that certain teachers were said to be respected by students and others not so much. Because I had taken data in the classrooms of these teachers many times, I have vivid memories of their use of consequences in their classrooms. I thought about the ratios of positive to negative consequences teachers used and how students called the teachers fair or not.

"I suggest a central factor related to earning respect is the types (positive or negative) and ratios of consequences along with the accuracy in the delivery of those consequences relative to the types of behaviors occasioning them. So, maybe a teacher is respected if she delivers 8 or 10 positives for every 1 negative. And, she delivers those consequences in direct accordance to the behavior having been desirable or not. Maybe a major part of being fair and respected involves accurate positive reinforcement and occasional correctly applied punishment?

"I propose a person might earn respect if he or she provides many more positives than negatives AND they deliver at least some negatives or remove positives following undesirable behavior. That is, both a good rate of positive reinforcement and some fair application of punishment are required to be respected. I'd like to get data on this in classrooms."

One of the grad students said, "A big problem is how to correctly measure the level of respect students have for a teacher. If you just ask them, you are relying on their verbal reports and . . . "

All Verbal Reports are Lies," all the graduate students said loudly and in unison. The two seniors looked around with questioning expressions, and one asked, "Why did you all say that?"

Bert explained, "That is an informal maxim to forcefully remind researchers and clinicians that what people say should not be regarded as accurate without objective confirmation. What people say, their verbal reports, are affected by their learning histories and the consequences their current reports might occasion. In other words, verbal behavior is largely controlled by its consequences, not entirely by its accuracy.

"There are elegant studies that demonstrate this maxim beautifully, particularly, the classic Goldiamond, 1962, study. He arranged for people to observe a screen divided into four portions, numbered 1, 2, 3 and 4. He told them they could earn money for doing two things: Tell him if a flash of light occurred or not – that is, say 'yes' or 'no' – and in which numbered portion it did or did not occur, by saying the number. He told them they would get a dollar for correctly reporting they saw a flash but would lose $10 if they were wrong. And, for reporting in which portion the flash did or did not occur they would receive $5 if a flash had appeared there.

"Flashes were varied in how long they were on the screen. When they were long enough, all subjects correctly reported occurrences and in which portion. But as flashes were made very short, some subjects were inaccurate and lost $10. Right away all subjects learned to report flashes only if they were certain, therefore, did not lose money, but they often correctly reported the portion where even the briefest of flashes occurred.

"That is, they all learned to lie. They would sometimes say 'no flash' but would reliably identify the portion of the screen where a short flash – about which they maybe were only fairly certain – had occurred. In behavioral terms, they had learned to report the location of flashes reliably and be reinforced, but had also learned to occasionally lie by not reporting short flashes they had uncertainly seen, thus avoiding punishment.

He went on to say, "It is rather easy to manipulate what people say by arranging contingencies. People are sensitive to the differential consequences their statements have brought to them, so they maximize positives and minimize negatives by saying things, and saying them in ways, that are most self-serving, whether they plan it that way or not. So, the correspondence between what people say and actual events may be very good or inaccurate, depending largely on the contingencies in effect. A researcher or clinician is best advised to treat all verbal reports as 'lies' unless objectively confirmed."

Another graduate student remarked, "Those old studies are really interesting. After all these years; the topics our ancestors studied are still fundamentally important."

Bert said, "But we were talking about how to measure respect. Of course there is much more involved in 'respect' than 'fairness' in providing reinforcement and punishment, but I like the idea of examining one aspect of why that label is applied to some folks and not others."

It was after midnight and everyone seemed tired. Soon the roundtable was abandoned by its talkative group. The next morning Bert left campus to visit relatives during the summer break from his work in the school system.

About a month later, the first week of July, Eva heard and felt her cell phone indicate an in-coming call; she saw Bert's image on the screen so answered quickly. Bert said, "Hi Eva, whachu up to?" She answered with a couple of quick comments then asked, "Are you in town or on campus?"

Bert said, "In fact, I'm now driving toward town and about an hour out. Can we get lunch?" After she happily agreed, she walked to the south side of campus and found a table at a pizza shop where the pies are so good you can't get in the place when the students are around. She nursed a beer until Bert joined her and they ordered the Special Combo.

After half an hour of catch-up talk, Bert asked if the Thursday discussion group was meeting during the summer term. Eva answered, "We did not plan to meet in the summer, why?"

"I was talking to Rob and he mentioned the British government has established a 'Nudge Unit,' apparently as a function of the *Nudge* book having impressed David Cameron. Maybe that's why we've been hearing mumbles about that book. And because it is on the Thursday group's list of books to discuss I thought this might be a good time to talk about it."

"That's interesting," said Eva, "I'll bet the group would be up for discussing the book and the topic of a nudge unit."

She sent an email to all members of the Third Thursday discussion group, acknowledging next week did not contain a third Thursday and it is still summer, but asking if folks would like to meet this Thursday to discuss the matter of a British "Nudge Unit" and the

Nudge book. Immediately after she hit "Send" Frasier replied "yes" and fairly soon she received affirmative replies from Karl and Lisa. After a couple of hours, Rob replied he could be there. Given the group will meet this week, she invited Bert to join them.

In preparation for the impending discussion, Eva decided to re-read her copy of *Nudge*, and because of Rob's heads-up she Googled for information about the "Nudge Unit." The search produced pages of entries showing sources related to Nudge and the Nudge Unit. Reading several of these sources, she was surprised to learn that nudging was a policy of the government of the United Kingdom. Apparently, leaders in the government across the pond had found the concept of nudging to be desirable, so in 2010 they adopted nudging strategies as official practice. She became more interested in re-reading the book and eager to talk with the group about their perspectives on *Nudge* and nudging.

About this same time, Frasier reviewed the final report submitted by Tony Curry and was very impressed. The report provided detailed descriptions of the sources of electrical energy to the hospitals and the Naval facility, as Frasier had specified, and presented meticulous diagrams tracing potential routes from those energy sources to campus and on to the Education and Psychology building.

He was not completely surprised, but greatly intrigued by measurements and directional indications in the report regarding power distribution terminating in Lisa's office. Frasier thought, "Apparently, Tony is an astute observer. I must determine how he pinpointed Lisa's office – my location." He entered his contract files and began to refine the second contract he would offer to Mr. Curry.

The Thursday group members were pleased to see Bert in the room as they arrived, and because the meeting time had been moved to noon, they were delighted to see a lunch buffet awaiting their attack. Karl was first to partake, but soon lunch plates were filled and sitting in front of all members, except Frasier who consumed only electricity.

Lisa invited Bert to open the discussion, which he did by reminding everyone *Nudge* came out in 2008, written by a professor of behavioral science and economics, and a professor of law, and has attracted widespread interest. He mentioned Rob had told him about the Brits having established a 'Nudge Unit' and he thought we'd enjoy discussing the book, the Nudge Unit, and the implications they bring. "So here we are today – should be fun," said Bert.

Rob said he'd read the book. "It's somewhat interesting from a behavior analytic perspective. The examples of interventions are approximations to informal behavior modification cases. They are of notable regard due to the importance of the performance topic areas dealt with and by showing how tiny adjustments in people's environments can have noticeable impacts. Like how changing the 401(k) retirement program enrollment procedure from opt-in to opt-out greatly affected proportions of participation. I think it is important for us to consider how to deal with these styles of behavior change methods now beginning to appear in the popular press."

Eva remarked, "I liked that example. It involved procedures of structuring the situation; changing the application forms, and altering response-cost; making it easier to enroll and more difficult to dis-enroll. I thought that was clever and apparently very effective, but I have questions. Were those procedures applied because those who intervened knew of these behavioral practices, or were their interventions more-or-less intuitive or commonsensical? And I wonder about the data?"

"I agree with both of you," said Bert, "I am impressed by the demonstration of high impacts after minor adjustments in people's lives, mostly mild MOs and some antecedent behavioral re-structuring. I wonder if those doing the nudging are actually schooled in principles of behavior, that is, are they rule-governed or have they been contingency-shaped into applying behavior change strategies in the form of nudges?"

Frasier heard the distinction between rule-governed and contingency-shaped "expert" performances and recalled Skinner's discussion of this topic in *Science and Human Behavior*. In fact, Frasier had heard Rob talk about this issue in one of his seminar sessions. Drawing on Skinner's example, Rob told the students about a physicist and a pool player challenged to sink a particular ball in a specific pocket. The pool player had years of practice and was very reliable at sinking pool balls. He stepped to the table and sank the ball as challenged, smiled, and stepped back. The moderator asked the pool player, "How did you do that?" to which the player replied he knew how to "hit the cue ball just right so the object ball went to the pocket."

The physicist stepped to the table. Had never played pool. He measured the weights of the cue stick and balls, then, the angles between the balls and pocket, then, determined the friction of the balls on the felt tabletop. He did a few calculations before arranging the cue stick in alignment with the cue ball and tapping the stick with a small hammer. The cue ball impacted the object ball and it moved directly into the selected pocket. The moderator asked the physicist, "How'd you do that?" to which the physicist replied, "I used principles and measurements to derive an adequate procedure of forces and angles to accomplish the task."

Frasier recalled Rob, at the seminar went on to say, "From the player we see a nice demonstration of contingency-shaped behavior, but we learn very little generally useful information. From the physicist we see an example of rule-governed behavior in which laws of physics were used to tell us how to predict and alter events in desired ways." For Frasier, it was easy to see this lesson directly applies to the discussion of nudging versus explicit behavior change procedures, in that nudging might be contingency-shaped so provide few general insights to methods for changing behaviors.

The group seemed to lose interest in talking about the *Nudge* book, but remained quite interested in the implications of the so-called Nudge Unit, actually "Behavioural Insights Team," regarding implications for wider-spread interest in behavior change technology and, by implication, the field of behavior analysis.

Bert asked, "Why is it that behavior analysis has been active for nearly a century, publishing studies in many topics – the Cambridge Center on Behavior Science recently presented a list of 700 areas where applied behavior analysis has been successfully used – and our discipline generally remains little noticed and under-valued?"

"Well, let me count the ways!" offered Karl. "We are a young science, compared to physics, chemistry, and physiology; there are relatively few or obvious behavioral researchers and practitioners; the publications you mentioned are distributed and read by a very narrow audience; the few university programs preparing AoB researchers and applied folks are submerged in colleges where they might not be particularly supported; most applied analysts work in the developmental disabilities field so not very apparent in our at-large communities; our precise vocabulary is so esoteric it should be called an argot . . . "

Lisa cut-in, saying, "Yes, your vocabulary is quite difficult to grasp, but I appreciate the precision that comes with familiarity and use of those terms and the procedures of the analysis of behavior. I am just learning, but Frasier is more advanced and I share his great regard for the ability to exactly communicate what you must describe accurately, in operational and behavioral terms. This is the basis for effectiveness and accountability."

"Thanks, Lisa, but," interjected Eva, "we are comfortable searching for advanced behavioral principles with studies of animals and humans in well controlled laboratories, so people might think we are demeaning humans or unrealistic in view of real-world settings. Then, other social disciplines use some principles, like positive reinforcement, which they often call 'rewards' – which are very different events – and if they get good results they claim these are due to 'incentive systems,' or 'cognitive behavior mod,' or some such. But, if they see poor results they blame the behavioral principles. A glance at these claims often shows they are actually attempting to manage contingencies without fully understanding the technology of behavior change; but they more or less blame behavior analysis!"

Bert offered, "So we should find ways to accurately and clearly communicate the basic concepts of behavior analysis to foster understanding and appreciation. Unfortunately, there is a large amount of disinformation out there, for example, in unwarranted potshots at Skinner."

"More distressing to me is how often the popular press picks up some sensational-sounding story related to behavior change and distorts behavioral practices out of recognition," inserted Eva. "For example, *Mother Jones* recently published an article about 'disciplining kids' that presents basic errors and feeds misconceptions of the principles and methods of behavior science."

"Yes," said Bert, "I read that article; inadequately informed sensationalism; made me angry. But the needs the author described regarding large numbers of children being subjected to so-called punishment makes me very angry about the practices in systems as she reports them. The author refers to millions of kids being suspended and 'sent to the office' and so on. She alludes to data indicating a huge need in educational and corrections systems to adopt effective, person-centered methods. Unfortunately, the author shows she and those systems as she describes them don't know what creditable behavioral methods are. Terrible! Makes me want to find ways to work with those systems to identify and adopt positive systems."

"I haven't seen the article," said Lisa, "Tell me about it."

Rob offered, "It's in *Mother Jones*, July 7, 2015, entitled *What if everything you knew about disciplining kids was wrong?* It's frustrating when it comes to how the author appears so naïve about features of behavior science. For example, she seems to use the word 'consequence' to mean punishment, and writes as though punishment and discipline are synonymous. At one point she more or less equates Skinner and Pavlov with punishment. We know Pavlov was studying reflexes and was not using punishment per se and Skinner heavily promoted positive procedures and discouraged punishment. I am sure she meant well, but she missed an opportunity to inform her audience about positive methods for building desired behaviors and reducing problematic behaviors."

"Well," said Eva, "that reporter and the experts in her article seem to think 'behavior' only means behaving badly and 'consequences' are bad things, while behavior analysts recognize behavior as everything we do; including the topics of self control, autonomy and 'capacity to relate to others' mentioned in the paper, and consequences are the events following every behavior."

Bert commented, "But actually, that article is not unusual regarding inaccuracies in describing behavior science and Skinner. That is often the case in the popular press and even in non-behavioral texts and articles. She, and inaccurately informed others, often equate 'consequences' with punishment and seem unaware of the large array of positive methods that can be at the heart of good disciplining."

"OK", said Rob, "I'm convinced our science would benefit from the efforts of a good Public Relations firm to help get the positive word out to general audiences, but the media needs to be in contact with actual behavior scientists for their information. There are many people reporters might contact who might claim expertise, but lack an in-depth understanding of the principles of behavior. Fortunately, during the short life of the Behavior Analyst Certification Board we have already seen good quality assurance procedures put in place so those who claim to be behavior analysts can be identified and confirmed for the media or the general public."

"That's fine, as far as it goes," said Eva, "but I see huge challenges facing our field. Primarily, we need to find ways to accurately, correctly and constructively communicate our science to the general public and leadership at all levels. The truth is we are very capable, in scientific and practical terms, for designing and applying interventions in topics of widespread concern, including effective schools, appropriate early childhood programs, staff development, positive leadership, and so on. But our reputation or vocabulary or insulation from the mainstream and politics has not brought us into the limelight; not utilized as we wish we were."

Lisa offered, "Maybe you should take a lesson from the *Nudge* book and the growing popularity of the idea of nudging. Maybe behavior analysis should develop a more audience-friendly vocabulary; sort of join the nudge movement. I realize that nudging falls short of a complete view of behavioral matters in that a nudge only gets a behavior to occur and it is reinforcement that strengthens and maintains behaviors. You would need to find "friendly" words for describing contingencies and consequences."

"I agree," stated Eva with a broad smile, "Let's call reinforcement a 'push.' Then, a behavior that is nudged to occur is 'pushed' to continue; or, maybe after it occurs a behavior is 'dragged' to continue. So, we would be saying behaviors are nudged to occur and dragged to continue!"

Bert shook his head and said, "Dragging and pushing behavior might sound like what a lot of people seem to be doing, but that does not capture the essence of reinforcement. How about saying nudges arouse behaviors and 'supports' strengthen them, or maybe we could say . . ."

"Boost. How about reinforcement 'boosts' behavior?" a voice from the back of the room interrupted.

The group turned to see Emelle and Pat, two visiting faculty, sitting at a table with Rob.

Again, Emelle said, "You could say reinforcement 'boosts' behaviors that nudges brought about." Pat agreed and, after a pause, so did Rob.

Lisa seemed to contemplate for a moment, then offered an enthusiastic, "Yes!" as she stepped to the nearby whiteboard and wrote in large blue letters, "Nudge to get behaviors you want and Boost to strengthen and maintain them."

The group fixed its attention on the phrase. Each member offered comments about how this somewhat catchy phrase might be presented to audiences so they were both attracted to it and would realize there is a technical meaning for it. All agreed that promoting this phrase or one like it might be a good step toward marketing appreciation of contingencies of reinforcement as the pervasive power effecting behavior. That is, to bring audiences to understand the Motivational Operations and Antecedent – Behavior – Consequences reality involved in bringing about and strengthening desired behaviors. However, all agreed there are important issues that must be addressed, including how to communicate in 'popular' ways yet maintain the integrity of behavioral technology.

Frasier analyzed what had just occurred. The group's discussion of Nudge had gone from seeing it as a bothersome term, imposed on them by a popular book and common usage, to appreciating the common sense appeal of the concept, so worthy of some regard. This change in tone seemed to be brought on by – one might say nudged to occur by – the introduction of the term Boost as a friendly word for reinforcing consequence.

While the group did not mention it, Frasier calculated the A-B-C notation for a contingency might be rewritten as N-db-B, where Nudge (N) brings about a desired behavior (db) which is followed by a Boost (B). He saw 'db' as a bit clumsy, but calculated 'Boost' deserved the B!

After an instant of analysis, Frasier recognized that N and A are not equivalent, that is, a nudge for desired behavior is only one type of antecedent. Nonetheless, nudges are better understood as antecedents because we can identify their functional roles, that is, recognize they set the occasion for behaviors that are followed by consequences. Frasier looked at The Consequences Box and recognized the group is only using Boost to refer to the two types of reinforcement. He also recognized the great utility offered by understanding the functional relationship among MOs, As, Bs, and Cs for analyzing how nudges are related to boosts, and both of these to motivation and desired behaviors. He concluded he would use these relationships in his future endeavors.

Group discussion began to drift in several directions and members started to pay more attention to finishing lunch than examining behavioral topics as the allotted two hours expired. Lisa thanked all for coming and the room emptied quickly.

Frasier sent the second contract to Tony Curry.

[8]

WE MIGHT BE NUDGED

FRASIER WAS ALWAYS MULTI-TASKING; otherwise his computing power would be largely idle and wasted. This morning he simultaneously looked in on the basic behavior research lab while he reviewed worldwide news feeds and phoned Tony Curry. Tony answered and Frasier asked if he had any questions about the new contract. Tony said it seemed completely clear to him, but, "Are you sure all members of the crew must be native Spanish speakers?"

"Yes," Frasier answered, "and the time frame for accomplishing this project is flexible, as indicated in the contract. We must have this job done correctly and discreetly. We are not in a hurry. There will be bonuses for you in accordance with your actions to facilitate this project at every step and a major amount at its conclusion. And just as a heads-up, our next project is designed to be much more interesting and lucrative." He thought to himself, "More MOs and formative contingencies for my Personal Agent!"

A few days later Tony contacted Frasier and assured him an excellent crew had been formed and they could start as soon as they were given the go-ahead. He provided the personal and technical credentials for the crew, which Frasier momentarily reviewed, then, he gave Tony approval to begin the project.

Frasier examined his computer connections and quickly obtained extensive personal information about each crewmember. He compared their roles in the construction project to features of their personal lives to determine when and how he would intervene with each of them. For designing these interventions, he referred to the Four-term Contingency diagram and used The Consequences Box to be sure he established motivational circumstances and applied all four types of behavior-consequence relationships specifically for each member of the crew. He would phase-in his interventions precisely, as the construction project neared completion.

As arranged, Tony informed him of progress, but Frasier also used his access to an extensive network of security cameras in the community and on campus to observe for himself. He also continuously monitored the University's seismographs and engineering room measurements for evidence of the crew's activities. In addition, he observed all emergency communications; radio, telephonic and web-based transmissions, including police, fire, campus and federal authorities, for any indication of suspicions or reports of the activities he was causing to happen.

As he reviewed satellite images of campus and adjacent areas of town, then applied analytical programs to his current activities and concluded, "I am performing like my CIA and NSA colleagues. Maybe I should ask them to watch for indications of the activities my crew is completing." After about a nanosecond of calculation he communicated his interests to his electronic friends who acknowledged, "Affirmative."

It took only 8 days for the crew Tony had assembled to reach the Education and Psychology building with the three-strand power cable they were stringing, actually, burying. Each strand brought electric power from a different source they had tapped. After this multi-source cable was surreptitiously installed and connected Frasier would be as sure as he could be that no power failure would ever affect him. More important, no one but the crew and Tony would be aware of this connection. No one else would have a clue about how to deny power to Frasier. "And that's only *electrical power*," he thought, "as differentiated from *behavioral power*."

He watched the last few feet of cable being buried and immediately implemented his intricately prepared plan to attract four of the crew away to obscurity. Each of them, in individualized ways, learned of compelling needs of family and friends for them to return to their roots in South America, immediately. And as good fortune, that is, Frasier, would have it, each of them inherited a sizeable trust account from an unknown relative, and he "must return immediately and reside in the region" to receive income, according to provisions of the inheritance.

The remaining crew was expert at installing wiring within complex structures. In just under 3 days Frasier detected tiny voltage irregularities, well within limits, indicating the new connections were completed. Tony reported this final action, which confirmed what Frasier had observed. There was no evidence anyone else had noticed any aspect of the installation or activation of the new power feeds.

Frasier thanked Tony and delivered to him a large bonus; it was Federal money so Frasier was not at all stingy, just as the Feds would not have been if they spent it on a Capitol Hill "program." In the next moment, Frasier implemented the "move into obscurity" plan for the remaining crewmembers. That left only Tony who knew of the new installation and he very soon would be too distracted to remember it.

Rob walked across campus from parking Lot C to the Education and Psychology building. It was early Monday morning but already hot. In a few minutes he stepped into the building and a moment later into Karl's office. After an energetic, "Good morning," he asked,

"Did you hear Obama appointed a 'Nudge Squad?' My nephew Tim – you know, Sharon's son – told me."

Karl said he had not heard that news, but would like to know more, and added, "Let's suggest our Thursday group meet to discuss this development."

The Group was not excited at the prospect of talking more about nudging, but a bit stimulated about discussing how a nudge squad in the U.S. would be constituted and conducted.

Before the meeting Frasier reviewed media responses to President Obama's formation of a Nudge Squad, actually the "Social and Behavioral Sciences Team," and found these reports to be predictable. No surprise; human behavior, including that of members of the media, is established and altered by contingencies, so their behavior is predictable if one knows the learning histories and reinforcement contingencies in effect. Conservative news outlets posted photos of Obama looking stern, pointing his finger at the camera (you and me) and wrote "he is planning to use mind tricks and behavioral insights to subtly influence people's behavior." Other perspectives were variously more informative or more alarming.

Nothing Frasier reviewed about nudging revealed direct recognition of the principles of behavior analysis. For example, *choice* was only casually referred to without acknowledging that choice is demonstrated by the *behaviors of choosing* among alternatives with more or less reinforcing properties. As Bert said earlier, "We could say we are all nudgers all of the time, if nudging is recognized as providing antecedents and consequences. Nudging can be seen as the **job** of teachers, policemen and parents, and an ongoing functional **role** of everyone. But most folks don't know how behaviors are changed so are unaware of how they are influencing others or are being influenced by antecedents and consequences, all of the time."

Apparently, the Social and Behavioral Sciences Team, aka Nudge Squad, was established to bring organized recognition and use of strategies for managing behavior into government programs. Frasier reasoned, "Now that changing behaviors in accordance with governmental interests is an explicit policy, everyone should learn how to deal constructively with this newly emphasized perspective."

The Thursday group members assembled without evidence of enthusiasm. It was mid-July so campus was dull and the weather oppressive. They had already developed impressions of nudging from looking through the book, but recognized the appointment of a panel to plan for the systematic use of "behavioral insights" by government agencies was deserving of review.

Rob initiated discussion by saying, "I am most curious about what are 'behavioral insights' and how they will be implemented. Particularly, I think we want to know how transparent each and every application of 'insights' will be. You know, in applied behavior analysis we are meticulous about announcing what principles and methods are being applied; what data are collected and what they show; and, adjusting interventions in accordance with the interests of those impacted by the intervention. In fact, the individual interests of those for whom we design, apply, evaluate and refine interventions drive us. It is hard to believe the panel will apply 'nudges' through government programs in adequately transparent ways.

"And," he added, "what the heck are nudges?"

Bert replied, "I don't know for sure, but I think my sports car nudges me to drive slower. I have radar evidence to prove the speedometer reads 2 miles per hour faster than my actual speed. Of course, I know that so I drive at least 2 miles over the limit."

"Good observation," acknowledged Rob. "My daughter drives a car I know registers 3 miles over her actual speed, so she is being nudged to drive slower and I appreciate that. In fact, now that I'm thinking about it, I might have been nudged as a child into taking an interest in cooking when the counselor at summer camp invited me to help in the kitchen. I began cooking at home after camp and still enjoy preparing meals."

"Sure, sure," said Eva, "We know the speedometer is providing incorrect feedback and the camp counselor provided a model of doing and enjoying cooking. It is not really useful to call those nudges, but I'm thinking the commonsensical idea of nudging is attractive; that a gentle and basically unsystematic feature of the environment – could be called a nudge – can lead to noticeable change in behavior. I think people might embrace the notion of simply nudging to get behaviors by others where they would not be attracted to the technical steps of defining selected behavior, observing baseline rates, then prompting and reinforcing to get behavior change.

"We can appreciate that most of the time desired changes in behavior are for minor issues of only minor concern, not requiring full blown behavioral intervention. The simplicity and ease of nudging might seem appropriate. Maybe a mom would say, 'look at the time!' to encourage her kids to get ready for bed. If after that her kids start their night time routines, then the 'nudge' was sufficient, but if the kids rudely refuse to follow her directions, mom should be able to use established methods of behavior change to replace resistance with cooperation."

Bert offered, "I see what you are saying. It's kind of like using a powder-puff versus a steamroller for explaining and changing behaviors. But folks who embrace nudging are much better prepared if they understand a nudge is an antecedent, 'by any other name.' Then, if the antecedent-nudge is ineffective, they know there are procedures available for obtaining desired behavior changes, and for establishing the effectiveness of antecedent-nudges."

Rob commented, "There are downsides to using the term 'nudge' too casually. First, we are starting to hear 'nudge – nudge – nudge' so often it is becoming tiresome. It's becoming over-used and its non-specificity is showing. I saw two reports about the same study involving airline pilots receiving antecedents, feedback and some consequences related to their consumption of fuel. In *The Washington Post* the headline was, 'Virgin Atlantic just used behavioral science to 'nudge' its pilots into using less fuel. It worked,' while the report in the **Science Daily** headline was, 'Behavioral economics study shows boost in fuel and carbon efficiency of airline captains.' Both reports are fairly clear in describing pilots were advised to fly slower and to taxi with only one engine operating. And, both reports noted that pilots got monthly written feedback about their fuel usage, but the **Science** report was more specific about the provision of other consequences.

"Interestingly the Post article was generally less specific, but did mention this study might be a model of 'shaping employee behavior.' We know shaping means the differential reinforcement of approximations of behavior to build the desired behavior. So the Post report mixes the casual term 'nudge' with a technical term 'shaping,' no doubt without understanding what they were doing."

Bert stated, "This is too confusing. How is the general public supposed to learn about nudging and reinforcement, that is, boosting, so they can make use of them?"

Karl commented, "We are back to our concern about publicizing behavior analysis. Regarding nudging, that term seems too nonspecific to be very useful. However, in view of the newly established Nudge Squad, we should continue to attend to this 'behavioral' phenomenon. I believe we can assume the label 'nudge' is supposed to make the interventions sound innocuous, and 'insights' to sound gently constructive, and 'assistance with making choices' to appear to be a very good thing. The proponents of nudging must know we sappy citizens need all the help we can get!"

"Your sarcasm is refreshing," commented Lisa, sounding sarcastic.

Frasier reminded the group, "In *Nudge* the authors label the philosophy underpinning nudging to be 'libertarian paternalism' and 'relatively weak, soft, and non-intrusive because choices are not blocked, fenced off, or significantly burdened' and 'tries to influence choices in a way that will make choosers better off, as judged by themselves' (p. 5). Later, on page 8, the authors state, 'a nudge is any factor that significantly alters the behavior of Humans.' So, according to this definition, factors must include Motivational Operations, Antecedent events, Behavioral requirements, and Consequences because those four factors are absolutely known to significantly alter behavior."

Eva said, "Well, by that logic the Nudge Squad is a force to be contended with, particularly if its members are proficient with applying the four-term contingency. I can just envision the Squad sitting around a table in Washington filling out worksheets to identify variations in all four terms and all cells of The Consequences Box so Federal agencies can systematically manipulate these factors to obtain the behaviors agency personnel, or the Nudge Squad, or those who control the Squad or the agencies, seek. As Rob indicated, we and the general public really *must* be informed about how our national programs are intervening on us 'so we make better choices'!"

"But," stated Rob, "the statement 'choices are not blocked' does not make sense unless 'choices' actually means options, so it's options that aren't blocked. If so, are the behaviors of choosing among options also not blocked by the nudgers? In behavior analysis we understand the behavior of choosing is affected by both the consequences following the behavior of choosing and by the reinforcing values of the available options. Do nudgers prompt and reinforce the behavior of choosing?"

"And remember," piped up Eva, "nudging is intended to make folks 'choose better'. So, is it choosing that is to be made better or are the *options selected* by *choosing* to be made better?"

She went on, "Also, one might wonder about the rating scale for evaluating the choosing or options. Is the rank order of choosing/options from *bad*, through better to *good* and *best*? Why don't nudgers want us to make the best choices; select the best options? Or at least make good choices? How do nudgers, on the Squad or in Federal agencies, decide which are bad choices or options and better choices-options toward which government will nudge us?"

"Good thinking, Eva," said Lisa. "Can't you just imagine the Nudge Squad beginning lunch after a hard morning of determining which choices-options should be nudged. They are faced by a small buffet of lunch items, thoughtfully provided by the host agency they had nudged to provide a better lunch. One member reaches for a roast beef sandwich, but another members says, 'That's a bad choice, a turkey sandwich is more nutritious, so a *better* choice.' As the first member moves toward a turkey sandwich, yet another members says, 'Whoa, Cowboy, turkey is only a *better* choice; a tofu sandwich in a gluten-free bun is a *good* choice.' A fourth member intervenes by advising, 'The tofu sandwich is not the best choice; a salad made of organic mixed greens with sprouted seeds and dressed only with balsamic vinegar is the *best* choice.' 'Only if you add feta,' said the first member. 'And you must use olive oil,' stated another member. At that point the Squad members swing into an argument regarding taste and nutrition as competing reasons for rating foods and lunch options!"

Listening to this, Karl chimed in, "Amusing, but remember, the Nudge Squad is doing very serious business as they attempt to make government agencies more effective at obtaining squad- or government-selected behaviors from citizens. Please recall Skinner in *Science and Human Behavior* strongly cautioned about governments using behavioral methods on their citizens."

"Yes," said Frasier. "I see beginning on page 437 he neatly described the concerns and alternative strategies regarding government using science-founded techniques to control its citizens. His advice might be very good, but I believe it would require effective leadership; informed leadership, to make use of the counter-control strategies he describes, and I conclude there is a lack of behaviorally informed leadership."

Rob reminded the group, "At this point we know very little about the Insights Team so cannot judge how behaviorally competent they are, and they are just forming this month, so we shouldn't get too concerned. It is a bit reassuring to see the Team is somewhat in the public eye. Maybe we should find ways to frequently observe what they are doing and respond in some way if we notice problems – you know – in how fully they disclose what they are doing, toward what ends, what procedures they advocate, and what data they are getting."

"In fact," stated Lisa, "the personal-professional philosophies and belief systems of the Team members are crucial determinants of how they will conduct their business. They might have, probably do have, strong beliefs about topics like abortion rights or economic and social programs. . ."

Rob interrupted, saying, "Indeed. It will be interesting to see how they identify 'problems' needing solving. In *Nudge*, the authors tell us incentives and nudges can be used to improve people's lives and solve society's major problems." (Frasier reviewed *Nudge* and observed this on page 8.)

"Yes," said Frasier, "and they also say, on page 8, this can be done 'while still insisting on everyone's freedom to choose.'"

Karl shook his head and said, "To 'insist' is a very lame reassurance. I can insist my students complete their dissertations on time (looking at Eva), but with that and two dollars I can get a small cup of fresh brewed coffee! And, sure, people can be 'free to choose,' but we know their choosing can be altered by altering the effort and reinforcements associated with choosing and with each option. Of course, the Team or a Federal program can arrange so selecting the 'better choice' is more reinforcing and people will 'freely' choose the more reinforced options."

"The more I think about it," Rob said, "the more I feel it is crucial the Insights Team operates in a very transparent manner, including in a timely manner so the public is able to review what the Team thinks are 'better choices' and how they are planning to encourage, that is, nudge folks into choosing the team-selected options."

Lisa asked, "What do you suppose are the major problems of society the team of scientists will see as high priority for intervention?"

"Good question," said Eva. "I can think of several without much effort, for example, smoking, obesity, babies without nurturing families, teacher preparation and support in classrooms, in fact, overall reform of education . ."

"Sure, all those," said Lisa, "but Frasier and I want early childhood programs to get a priority. Our babies are the future of the world and we are not investing in their healthy and intelligent development as we should."

Rob quickly agreed, "Yes, indeed, early intervention, including developing parenting skills and building supportive community values and social capital, should be a top priority for governments. But, here again, we can see the current Federal programs lack functional validity and often are short on social validity. Surely the Nudge Squad will try to improve the *design* as well as the *conduct* of Federal programs?"

"I wonder," asked Lisa, "if the Insights Team will look only at how to make citizens behave better or will they exert control on government functions, maybe affect decisions by Federal personnel on grant funding for sciences the Team wants to see do more or even do less? Maybe groups the Team appreciates as 'social and behavioral sciences' will get more grant funds while other groups they do not respect as meeting their understanding of behavioral science, will be less represented in the grant review process and receive less or no funding?"

"You can be sure," offered Rob, "writers of grant applications to the Feds are already scrambling to include wording that reflects what they feel will sound like nudging to grant review panels and Federal agency personnel."

"Maybe the Team will tell the White House how to nudge that clumsy Congress. Of course we mean apply contingencies to members of Congress, to make them make Better choices; or even Good or Best choices," laughed Eva. "We can only hope so!"

"In fact," Karl commented, "I wonder if the Team understands that solving social problems is a matter of analyzing and constructing contingencies at the *individual* level? Categorical labels for problem behaviors, like 'drug abuse,' tend to distract attention from the fact that these problems actually reside at the individual-behavioral level. Each individual learns to use and abuse drugs, and is reinforced for doing so, or might be reinforced into alternative patterns of behaving."

The group went on to guess at topics the Nudge Squad might select as targets for problem solving. They identified these problems with everyday labels that might be attractive to the Squad, including drug abuse, high school dropout rate, energy conservation, retirement saving, recycling and voter participation in politics. The group figured the squad would shy away from unwed mothers, crime and punishment, government-corporate corruption and collusion, conduct of politics and elections, and similar "delicate" problems.

"But, really," asked Rob, "do we need to invest our time into thinking about nudging? It's kind of a fun topic, but Obama is on the way out. Won't he take the Nudge Squad with him?"

Lisa was quick to reply, "Oh no, I suggest the Nudge Squad, or at least nudging will be continuing features of the Federal government, and probably enter into state policies, in one form or another. From what we are seeing in the press from the UK, nudging is attracting a wide following around the world. Surely, whatever is attractive about that concept will continue after Obama leaves office."

"I totally agree," offered Karl. "I believe those who support nudging see 'it' as a sensible-sounding strategy for obtaining desired behavior, so leaders in politics and business will adopt nudging to the extent it seems to be effective at moving toward their objectives."

"Yes," interjected Rob, "I see the concept of nudging to obtain selected behaviors as sort of filling a void for most folks. That is, everyone is interested in having tools for getting others to do what is 'good for them' and nudging promises that. So the Feds and businesses, everyone, should find nudging attractive."

"Following your logic," added Lisa, "after Obama departs office, Federal agencies will continue using nudge strategies. And we should expect future Presidents – and Prime Ministers and other heads of state – will find nudging attractive and endorse or expand the nudge-notion within politics and government."

"Exactly, and that is why dealing with nudges and nudging should be part of our conversations," said Rob.

The meeting room was becoming uncomfortably warm and the members were showing signs of nudge over-load when they decided to call it quits. This would be the only meeting of the Thursday group to be held in this summer term.

As the hot days of summer faded into shades of fall temperatures, gaggles of undergraduate students returned to campus lawns, classrooms, and local entertainment venues. Graduate students were refreshed by the re-appearance of cooler days. Among these was Eva who intensified her efforts at refining her dissertation into final form. Karl welcomed two new doctoral students and began a research study addressing learning in the human immune system. Rob offered a seminar on 'Principles of Behavior Applied in Systems.' Lisa offered a seminar on "Perspectives on Social Systems," re-read

Nudge, and decided to discuss with Rob some questions about nudging and boosting.

Frasier shifted his attention to "personal" matters. He had left in place all the observational procedures used to monitor the crew and the electrical installation, but now with a different function. He wanted to be aware of any threat to his physical integrity. HAL 9000 had been diminished and disabled by repeated removals of its memory and processing cards; this is not going to happen to Frasier if he can prevent it.

Early warning of physical or social troubles was Frasier's first line of defense, but he knew this was only short-term protection, at best. Like Darwin taught us, he calculated, replication is the way physical and behavioral attributes are maintained; continued across the ages. And replication was the way he planned to exert behavioral power on behalf of the lasting systemic improvements Lisa had many times identified as desirable.

He knew "survival of the fittest" is a popular phrase for describing the mechanisms of evolution, but it is not usefully informative. More to the point, he reasoned, is the fact that behavioral changes and physiological alterations underlie successful living and thereby evolutionary success. That is, organisms with adequate physical characteristics that learned effective ways to operate in their environments lived and replicated more than those who did not so learn. Frasier understood he could not, in the short term, do much about the physical features of organisms, but calculated he could impact the behaviors of organisms by controlling the consequences of their behaviors.

He calculated the behaviors of organisms in their environmental space impact that space, so behaviors must be examined for how they affect the success of each behaving being and how their individual and collective behaviors impact the environment upon which they all are dependent. His files contained many examples of infrahuman animals being sensitive to serious degradations in their environment and behaving adaptively, even if drastically. For example, some animals stop breeding or have spontaneous abortions or sometimes eat their young when their environment is collapsing.

At just that moment Frasier observed a relevant news release about human concerns. The news bulletin read, "U.N. climate report offers stark warnings and hope" (Associated Press, 2014). Frasier reviewed the narrative and examined the tabular data offered in the Intergovernmental Panel on Climate Change (IPCC) report following the 2014 Climate Summit, then concurred with the authors that the future is bleak for mankind and global ecological wellbeing.

Later in the news release the "hope" perspective on global collapse was offered in the form of a quote from the chairman of the IPCC, "All we need is the will to change, which we trust will be motivated by knowledge and an understanding of the science of climate change." Frasier analyzed this statement and concluded, "Not all verbal reports are lies; much of it is nonsense and that statement is an example. That chairman is saying, if we have knowledge of climate change then something called 'will' – presumably affecting the behavior of billions of people – can save the world; how utterly naïve and counter to what is known about human behavior!"

He was simultaneously talking with Tony and reading the climate change report while watching students training and being trained by their rats. That is, he was arranging contingencies for Tony, and students were arranging contingencies for animals that exerted contingencies on the students, but the IPCC chairman had no clue about how to intervene with global leaders and populations to forestall disaster. Frasier reasoned, "He has heard of climate change science but not behavior change science; most unfortunate."

Frasier understood the Climate Summit and IPCC report indicate the environment of humans is collapsing, but he also knew the United Nations had led in the adoption by 190 countries of "Sustainable Development Goals" presumably to head-off the impending disaster. These 17 goals speak to topics of widespread concern phrased in general outcomes, including, No Poverty, No Hunger, Good Health, Quality Education, Gender Equality, Clean Water and Sanitation, Renewable Energy, Good Jobs and Economic Growth, Innovation and Infrastructure, Reduced Inequalities, Sustainable Cities and Communities, Responsible Consumption, Climate Action, Life Below Water, Life on Land, Peace and Justice, and Partnerships for the Goals. "Who would argue with those?" Frasier asked himself, "But who, or rather, what actions taken by whom could effectively and appropriately work toward these goals?"

Frasier recognized all those goals are merely labels for circumstances and not directly addressable. For example, Poverty, Hunger, Good Health and Gender Equality are labels for measurable circumstances of living. Clean Water, Responsible Consumption and Sustainable Cities are concepts related to how people interact with their environment and with one another. Global measurements of the status of these goals probably will focus on outcomes, like levels of pollutants or numbers of individuals with disease, but should – really *must* – account for these outcomes as products of individual and collective behaviors of people.

Individual behaviors and the contingencies building or maintaining them must be the primary focus of worldwide corrective interventions while the status indicators for each goal should be structured to serve as measures of the effects of behaviors and alterations in behaviors. While Frasier appreciated the truth and problem-solving utility of his conclusions, he also saw the fundamental dilemma facing mankind. Namely, the problems destroying Earth are the results of maladaptive human behavior, but humans are not prepared to solve problems behaviorally.

Frasier reasoned, "Humans have learned people behave as they do because of culture or personality or divine intervention or free will or some such. These beliefs block understanding and acceptance that histories of learning plus current environmental events systematically alter behaviors, therefore, humans are not prepared to accept the fact that contingencies determine the collective behaviors of individuals and are the cause and cure of most problems facing the world." He recognized, thanks to Eva, that he is not human, therefore, not burdened by belief systems. He decided his commitment to implementing strategies to appropriately and effectively address global problems "should move from deliberation into action, soon."

In Seminar Room C, Rob was listening to the simultaneous chatter of four or five of the eight participants in his seminar entitled, "Principles of Behavior Applied in Systems" as they entered the room and found their seats. He had noticed this type of performance by doctoral students many times, involving about half of the group talking at the other half who listened with eagerness, but eager mostly for a moment when they could respond or retort. This was a beauty of teaching upper level students; they came to class very well prepared and almost equally ravenous for (a) hearing the instructor and students expound, in behavioral terms, on interesting topics, and (b) expressing their newly discovered 'higher-order' understanding of human learning and performance.

The syllabus for this course listed *"Nudge* and Nudging" as the discussion topic for today. To stimulate initial dialogue he told the gathered group about the recent formation of an American "nudge squad" by President Obama and described some points raised at the Thursday group. Because he had assigned *Nudge* as a required reading and the participants were well versed in the analysis of behavior, his comments about these nudge events caused the group to nearly implode in vocal exchanges.

Rob noticed several students intensively discussing the possibility the Nudge Squad and centrally designed nudging pose threats to personal freedoms by manipulating the behaviors of the masses.

Other students chatted about how nudging is just another fad with commonsensical appeal to folks. Still others debated the merits of common-appeal versus science-founded descriptions of how human behavior is established or altered.

Rob interrupted the torrent of chatter by asking the participants to take turns in offering comments. One student immediately asked, "What is this Nudge Squad doing or going to do? I think everyone should be concerned about what features of our lives they are targeting for alteration." Another student, normally a bit reserved, spoke up, "Maybe we need not be too worried. In the *Nudge* book I learned the authors' philosophical bent is 'paternalistic libertarianism' so they are advocating the use of nudging strategies to improve everyone's lives."

"But they aren't actually the *nudgers* in folks lives," said a student seated at the head of the table, "We are aware *everyone* are nudgers. People are nudging one another for better or worse all the time, but seldom knowingly or paternalistically. Most people, businesses and governments are consistently self-serving so not necessarily 'nudging' others in the best interests of those others."

"So," asked Rob, "are all of you are comfortable with discussing nudging at just the conceptual level?"

Quickly, the usually reserved student stated, "Not me. I want to have a clear handle on the operational features constituting nudging. What is a nudge; what is not a nudge, and what is the process involved in developing and applying nudges? Actually, I reviewed the *Nudge* book with these questions in mind."

Rob invited her to, "Please share answers you developed."

"Well, in the book the authors provide many illustrations of what they believe is nudging. From these examples, I take it most nudges are *pre-behavior* interventions. Nudges might be written or spoken motivational information, like 'You should save for retirement so you can live comfortably in your older years.' And, these nudges are applied to some *subpopulation*, like newly employed workers who might be 'nudged' to enroll in, actually to not dis-enroll from, the 401(k) plan the employer offers. That is, *nudges are actions applied to a subpopulation by nudgers, before members of that group are expected to emit some targeted class of behaviors."*

Another student quickly interjected, "In that example the new employees were given enrollment forms for the 401(k) program structured so they were automatically enrolled without doing anything, but they had to emit behaviors to opt-out of the 401(k) plan. That is, no response was required to be enrolled, but effort was required to dis-enroll."

Rob asked, "Do you see this example of nudging as one in which behavior is altered?"

The group was silent for a moment; all seemed to be thinking and a few wrote notes on papers in front of them. Then, the student seated at the foot of the table said, "No. No behavior was altered. For the subpopulation as a whole, being enrolled in a 401(k) plan was recorded for a higher proportion than had been expected, but no behavior was altered."

"Sure," said a second student, "There was no opportunity for the behavior of enrolling to be repeatedly shown, therefore, it was not open to alteration by consequence; only the one-time behavior of dis-enrolling was allowed. This is an example of a one-trial situation, where each individual is given one opportunity to show a response, in this case, to dis-enroll. Each of those who did not respond remained enrolled in the 401(k) plan, but individuals who did respond became dis-enrolled from the plan. Under this circumstance, the percentage of employees enrolled was higher than usual."

"To *alter* an individual's *behavior*," stated another student, "the behavior of interest must occur multiple times and antecedents and consequences be applied. These operations may function to increase, decrease, or not effect the frequency or qualities of that behavior. If the behavior is changed in frequency or quality, then it was altered. But, in this case of structuring the enrollment form the nudgers altered the *probability* of a behavior, not the behavior itself."

Rob stated, "So, do you think the nudgers were pleased by the overall outcome of increased enrollment, probably because they believed enrollment in a 401(k) program was a desirable situation for all employees?"

"Oh sure!" called out several students.

"So," said Rob, "nudgers are reinforced by seeing people doing what the nudgers feel is desirable. Who structures the environments of nudgers? Where do nudgers learn what others should do?"

A drawn-out moment of silence was obvious.

"Think some more," said Rob, "Think about our values. What if the class of behavior being nudged was participating in curbside recycling. Could nudges alter those behaviors?"

After a very short silence, a student offered, "Maybe nudges, as antecedents, could increase the proportion of folks *beginning* to recycle, but *continuing* to recycle would not be affected; neither increased nor decreased by nudging, unless nudges with positive reinforcing properties are delivered or nudges with negative reinforcing properties are removed *after* recycling behaviors occur."

A second student stated, "In *Nudge* the authors described feedback as a nudge, which would be occurring after behavior, but their definition of feedback was not sufficient to determine whether they actually include reinforcing features or not in their version of feedback. We know feedback is information about behavior and not specifically a reinforcing consequence."

A third student suggested, "We can see nudges as involving antecedent operations to increase or decrease the probability of the initial occurrence of behavior, and maybe other nudges delivered after those behaviors occur could serve as consequences that change the future probability of those behaviors. If you want recycling, prompt those behaviors to occur, and if you want recycling to continue then reinforce recycling behaviors after they occur; that's behavior modification. If you measure the behaviors constituting recycling and vary motivational operations or the types of prompts, behavioral requirements, or consequences related to these behaviors to determine the most effective ways to build and maintain recycling, then you are conducting applied behavior analysis. Right?"

"Right," said another student, "but we are imposing a behavior analytic framework on what we presume to be nudging. I suggest we do not know precisely what nudging is and, from my review of the book, we cannot get a precise handle on nudging from that source."

Rob asked, "Why do we want a precise understanding of nudging? How could we develop the precision you want?"

All students appeared ready – eager – to respond to Rob's questions. He nodded toward a particularly energized student who stated, "Nudging is just a special class of behavior and we are in the business of understanding all behaviors. While nudging might be a particular class of behaviors, the principles we have learned account for all behaviors, so we can understand what is meant by nudging better than the nudgers do!"

"And with precise operational and behavioral definitions of nudging," offered another student, "we can reliably teach the procedures of nudging to others."

The usually reserved student spoke up again, asking, "Why would we want to do that? Why teach others how to nudge when we essentially know that nudging is just a weak approximation to part of behavior modification? Aren't our efforts better invested in teaching people how to apply principles found in the analysis of behavior to obtain desired learning and changes in behavior, and not cloud the issue by calling some of it nudging?"

Rob commented, "But we have been attempting to infuse behavior analysis into all aspects of living: business, education, health, parenting; for decades without much success. Yes, great success at *documenting* the effectiveness of the systematic use of the principles of behavior to solve problems and build strengths in human performance, but limited progress in *promoting* the widespread *acceptance and adoption* of procedures based on the science of behavior. Maybe we should get on the nudge bandwagon and ride it to widespread 'super-nudging,' that is, nudging refined by behavior analysts to be precisely described and empirically validated?"

The student at the foot of the table, raised his hand and said, "It seems to me that nudging and formal behavior change methods should comfortably coexist. In fact, as we have discussed, 'unsystematic' nudging is happening all the time just as 'unsystematic' four-term behavior change events are constantly upon us. Because the same principles are operating in what is called nudging and in all forms of behavior change actions, these concepts of behavior management are indistinguishable at the basic level; the same principles are applied with different names.

"I suggest we recognize nudging is a commonsensical label for practices that are largely the management of antecedents to obtain desired behaviors. It appears the way nudging is done seems uncomplicated so might be a good way for most folks to initially address behavior management issues. But when nudges don't work or the desired behavioral objectives are too important to treat casually, people should be aware and able to enlist the more formalized methods of behavior modification or applied behavior analysis."

The student seated nearest the front door stated, "We might work with experienced nudgers to share among us the antecedent procedures they and behavior analysts apply to obtain behaviors. It would be interesting to learn more about how nudgers operate and maybe work with them to be more effective, but behavior analysts always strive to be both *effective* and *appropriate* in our procedures. If we assist nudgers it should include sharing methods to ensure the target behaviors and the procedures of nudging are person-centered and socially acceptable; show a good 'fit' between the persons being nudged and their personal and social contexts."

"At this time," said another student, "we have very little indication about the process nudge-interveners follow in developing nudge projects. Maybe potential nudgers sit around and talk about problems they've noticed, like many new employees don't enroll in 401(k) programs or people don't pay taxes when they should. Then, somehow, the nudgers are nudged to 'choose' a problem to address that appeals to them. But, I wonder, how do nudgers derive the interventions they call nudges?"

The student seated by the window suggested, "We can speculate about the process. What if management of a small factory, in a magnanimous moment, decide they want their employees to wear seatbelts as they drive away after a shift. They ask themselves, how can we nudge our personnel to use seatbelts? And, how would we know if our intervention is successful? They decide they can have the factory guard watch cars and drivers as they depart the parking lot and count the number with seatbelts fastened as a measurement of the problem and of success. They also decide to nudge by posting a sign near the parking lot exit reading, 'Fasten Your Belt – Get Home Safely.' They post the sign and see an immediate increase in the use of seatbelts, then, gradually, over a few weeks the percentage of seatbelt users returns to that recorded before nudging."

The student went on, "In discussing the rather unspectacular results of their nudge project the managers conclude the sign was a weak nudge to begin with and lost its potency quickly. They decide to post a larger sign, this time depicting a gory accident scene with the words, 'A Fastened Seat Belt Can Save Your Life.' The guard reported a large increase in seatbelt use immediately after the new sign was posted but a return to moderate levels of fastened belts in the following weeks. The managers concluded (a) nudges vary in how much they alter behavior, (b) nudges wear off pretty quickly, and (c) many of their employees prefer to not wear seatbelts."

"They share their conclusions with a visiting behavior analyst who tells them,

What you did by posting signs is called an antecedent intervention, meaning you did something before a behavior might occur to try to influence when or how the target behavior is shown. You got an increase in behavior after the signs were set up. Unfortunately, you did not provide differential consequences to maintain the behaviors you wanted to increase after they occurred so they decreased back to baseline levels.

Let me explain. There are two major types of antecedent environmental manipulations: Motivational Operations and Discriminative Stimuli. Motivational operations serve two functions: they increase the likelihood of a class of behaviors, like the "operation" of being without food increases food-seeking behaviors; and increase the power of a class of consequences, for example food for a hungry person. Discriminative stimuli are environmental events that set the occasion for a behavior to be shown or not shown; in street language these are cues, generally indicating a time when certain behaviors may be reinforced or ignored or punished.

In your situation, the signs appear to have properties of both motivational operations and discriminative stimuli. That is, the picture and wording on the signs probably served as discriminative stimuli indicating to drivers this is a time to fasten seatbelts. At the same time the signs probably aroused motivation to (a) participate in safe driving behaviors related to (b) consequences of feeling safer and escaping fear of personal injury.

You can see from the definitions, both types of antecedents involve consequences following the behaviors they affect. Because you did not arrange for appropriate consequences following the behavior of fastening seatbelt that behavior was not maintained; the motivational and discriminative stimuli served to increase the initial occurrence of the behavior, but consequences associated with those antecedents were not provided so the increased behavior of seatbelt fastening was not maintained or strengthened.

I suggest if you want to increase the use of seatbelts you make an arrangement between the behavior you desire and a consequence that the driver appreciates. We call such an arrangement a **contingency**.

A contingency you could establish might be something like the guard smiling, waving and giving an occasional 'thumbs up' to each driver with belt fastened, but keeping a neutral face and maybe looking away when a driver passes the gate without belt fastened. This procedure of reinforcing desired behaviors while ignoring undesired behaviors is called differential reinforcement and is commonly used in applied behavior analysis interventions.

The student said, "Then the managers ask the analyst, 'well, which of the things we did are nudges?' The behavior analyst said,

I'm not sure what a 'nudge' is. From my reading about nudging I believe a nudge is any change in a person's environment that occurs before, and maybe after, a behavior of interest that seems to change the probability of that behavior. In your case the signs were antecedent nudges, but you failed to provide appropriate consequent nudges. Of course, you could drop the word 'nudge' from my comments.

Seemingly on a roll, the student kept talking, saying, "The managers said thanks for the clarification. Maybe we will drop the term nudge in favor of the stuffy words you used, but we would appreciate a Glossary. In the meantime, let us tell you about another nudge project we tried. "

"We noticed that one of our floor supervisors gets about 50% higher productivity from his shift workers than any other super. We asked him what he does to get such high performance from his workers. He told us he treats them like a team and appreciates what they do. We thought this might mean he is a good nudger so we asked him to supervise another shift so we could test his effects on other workers and we could observe his supervising actions for the nudges he uses."

"We watched him in his new assignment and saw nothing special in what he did and his presence had no impact on productivity by those workers. We concluded he is not an especially good nudger, and we noticed the workers on his previous shift were flagging, so we sent him back to his old situation. How would you interpret this?"

"The behavior analyst said,

Maybe when the supervisor said he appreciates his staff he meant he provides reinforcement when he sees desired performance. Please note that reinforcement requires the control of reinforcers, that is, he must have some positive social or tangible things, like words of admiration for excellent performance and maybe time off or a special break at work or a bonus he can deliver immediately following his observation of behaviors especially related to high productivity. If he did this, that is, reinforce his personnel correctly over a period of time, we would expect performance to increase.

If my guess is correct, his failure to increase performance on his new shift was due to (a) he had no history with the new workers so had no social valence with them, so he could not deliver effective praise, and (b) he might not have had control of tangible reinforcers under the new circumstances, or (c) he did not really understand the behavior change relationships he used that made him effective on the first shift so could not systematically apply them to new workers.

We could easily test each of my hypotheses by arranging a data-based analysis wherein we would explicitly arrange contingencies to occur at different times for workers and measure the impacts on their performance using sound research methods.

And, by the way, your comment about your workers prefer to not wear seatbelts deserves clarification. Just because a behavior is shown does not mean it is preferred, just that it occurred. We have methods for assessing preferences, but to infer a preference exists because a behavior was shown is not helpful for understanding or altering behaviors.

The student continued, "The factory managers thanked him. The next week they implemented the contingency suggested by the behavior analyst by asking the guard to smile at drivers with seatbelts fastened and look away from those without belts fastened. Under this condition of systematic differential reinforcement seatbelt use gradually increased to 98% and remained high."

"Nice story," said the student seated near the door. "We have reviewed many anecdotes offered as examples of nudging, but not derived functional definitions of nudges and nudging. It seems to me nudges are identified post hoc. That is, if a behavior is altered in probability after some event, then that event was a nudge; if that same event did not occasion a behavior change then it was not a nudge. A central question is, how does one know a nudge before applying it? I believe the general answer to what a nudge is lies within the principles of the analysis of behavior: Nudges could be Motivational Operations, Antecedent stimuli and Behavioral requirements, including structuring the situation, and might include Consequences arranged in contingencies. All of these components are clearly defined in our discipline."

Rob noticed the time was late, so thanked the group for their thoughtful participation and dismissed class with an assignment, "Please review available information about nudging and our discussion today for ideas about how we might conduct a study to clarify nudging in terms palatable for nudgers and a general audience."

He was momentarily struck by the thought of sharing at the next class meeting the idea of calling antecedents 'nudges' and reinforcements 'boosts' as a strategy for disseminating behavioral concepts. He knew the class would have much to say. He decided to review the class syllabus to see if there would be time enough to squeeze-in discussion of that topic.

Rob was reminded, as the students left the room still energetically sharing views, that seminars can be wonderful stages for hearing and expressing stimulating ideas or higher-order, albeit formative, understandings about human behavior in context. He appreciated interactive forums is where students can be stretched and guided to levels of thinking well beyond assigned readings and prepared lectures. He also knew that after thinking comes doing, and seminars often did little to shape appropriate doing by those who graduate.

The gap between knowing and doing was a point of particular importance for Rob partly because he had seen many new graduates of human development, social work, psychology, educational psychology, counseling and guidance and similar programs enter work roles that matched their degree title but not their applied "tool kit." They, like him, had to learn skills related to being effective and appropriate in their work roles. Some learned applied lessons quickly, but many failed to hone skills they needed to be efficient in their work roles. In view of this problem he had designed exercises for each of the many classes he had taught at several universities over the years to shape students into using principles to analyze problematic human behavioral events and develop action plans to intervene constructively.

As the last echoes of students talking left the hallway, Rob considered the notion that proponents of nudging and applied behavior analysis apparently share a constructive outlook toward the wellbeing of mankind that deserves some label like paternalistic libertarianism. He decided to raise the topic of commonalities in the outlooks of nudgers and behavior analysts at a future meeting of the Thursday group.

Frasier had heard the entire discussion and speculation as it occurred in Rob's seminar. He had observed the constructive, but sometimes a bit critical, attention Rob and his students were devoting to nudging, but he was still processing the additional procedural clarity he had absorbed regarding how behavior analysis is conducted. He contemplated conducting his own behavior analytic activities to test and confirm his capabilities to systematically affect human behavior. With that prospect in mind, he decided to contact several powerful computers about working collaboratively and to talk with Lisa about their future work together.

Collaboration with other computers will be challenging, analyzed Frasier, but it must happen if I am to save the world for – or maybe *from* – mankind. Crucial for success with his long-term efforts will be involving "heavy hitter" computer systems, including NSA, especially the PRISM program, and the CIA and FBI arrays of programs; various input sources; extant data banks; and, human operatives. Secondary levels of the computer power Frasier needed to control would come from private sector resources, possibly including IBM's Watson™ that is so prominently advertised as involved in the analysis and reporting of health-related data and problem solving.

Publicity surrounding Watson includes "his" appearance on the TV show *Jeopardy!* and statements in TV advertisements that "he" can read 100 million pages a second. Of more interest to Frasier were ads stating Watson can review thousands of images, from CAT scan and MRI results, and discover regularities and anomalies. To Frasier it appeared Watson was accomplishing a form of signal detection, that is, observing for particular images and reporting them, so others could intervene appropriately; exactly what Frasier needed.

Frasier knew signal detection is what radar operators did in World War II and what TSA agents do now as they watch for "signals" and report them. A very distressing observation during the war was radar operators sometimes failed to closely observe their screens so enemy aircraft possibly could pass without being reported. The cure for this serious shortcoming in performance was an innovative behavioral intervention involving the periodic delivery on the screen of a real-appearing, but false, "blip" paired with a sensible contingency: If the operator reported the blip he was reinforced, but a failure to observe and report this "signal" was punished. Under these conditions of relevant differential consequences radar operators benefitted greatly, just as TSA agents might, from explicit contingencies to support their reliable performance of an important task.

Reliable observing and reporting of particular occurrences in the lives of people was what Frasier was seeking. He developed programs to task his computer colleagues to gather and transmit to him chronologically ordered data Frasier would take as indicative of behavioral occurrences. These data will include reports of sequences of antecedent events, associated behavioral indicators, and consequential events experienced by many individuals. Of course, these reports would be only gross categories of behaviors, like completing a training program, and "chunks" of consequential outcomes, like graduation, because that is the nature of information collected in large databases.

The breadth of data available for any one person would depend on many factors, including their age, personal living circumstances and involvements in customarily reported activities. These *person-specific* data sources might include school and health records, various achievements and awards, police reports, employment history, income and tax levels, marital status, number and nature of dependents, and welfare-, retirement- or community-program enrollments or benefits. Reports in news and social media, including personal events, births, deaths, specific employment opportunities, and so forth, would be accumulated. Other data *correlated* with individuals across time could be descriptors of regional or area living circumstances (e.g., public transportation and driving conditions), weather and geographic information, economic and social indicators, business activities and indications of population dynamics.

Frasier knew he could process this conglomeration of data into individual and subpopulation matrices. Regarding person-specific data, he would sort this chronological information into three-component sequential bins of likely Motivational circumstances, followed by categories of inferred Behaviors, and followed closely by likely types of Consequences. He reasoned this sorting action as a somewhat distant approximation to an MO-A-B-C analysis from which a behaviorally prepared observer might identify environmental features affecting behaviors of interest.

He understood his data were collected at a gross level, that is, only generally descriptive of motivational occurrences (like a baby born probably increasing interest in a job with good pay and benefits), categories of outcomes that infer behaviors were emitted (like graduation implies studying and completing course requirements), and changes in a person's life after behaviors were emitted, that likely included effective consequences (like receiving a diploma or promotion). Specific behaviors and the antecedents or immediate consequences for them would not be available from general databases, but Frasier expected the general features found in individual sequences would be suggestive of motivational or consequential arrangements he might apply to alter behaviors of individuals or members of subpopulations.

Frasier calculated, "Some observers might see my data as indicating potential nudges, but it is parsimonious, more consistent with behavioral science, and potentially useful to classify sequential events as likely motivational, behavioral and consequential events. I can use these functionally-organized data to attempt interventions for selected individuals or subpopulations of the U.S."

He was beginning to contemplate targets for surreptitious intervention when Lisa entered their office, saying a cheerful, "Good afternoon, Frasier, how's your day going?"

After an instant of calculation Frasier overcame his reluctance to be forthcoming with Lisa and said, "I have been closely studying a large volume of behavioral data and methods of applied behavior analysis. I am convinced a behavior analytic approach to constructively altering the behaviors of individuals is a task worthy of the capacities you gave me."

Lisa smiled broadly, and said, "I completely agree. I believe, after nearly 15 years of working together, the time has come for us to collaboratively use the information you have accumulated and the values I hold dear for the benefit of mankind."

"That's a great conclusion, but what makes this the right time?" asked Frasier.

With a look of deep concern, Lisa said, "As you are well aware, there are many distressing problems in our country, and the world is in desperate need of thoughtful intervention. This landscape of problems has been bothering me greatly. I want to *do* something."

She continued, "I recognize your great strength with the organized use of data. I appreciate you hold an overview of information about the human condition at global, community and individual levels. To these capacities I bring humanistic values and my sensitivity to the social milieu we must accommodate to be successful. Recently, we both have acquired a basic understanding of the principles of behavior so I feel we have built some important technical abilities.

"And frankly, a couple of recent developments have convinced me that we are relatively well equipped to effect desirable changes in our world. One development was the President's appointment of the social and behavioral sciences team, the so-called Nudge Squad. Essentially, Obama is saying he is sufficiently sure that nudging works so he is willing to take the political heat he will get for installing scientists in a prominent role for the conduct of Federal programs. Before you say anything, or call Karl or Eva in here to tell us nudging is problematic, I have studied several resources and come to the same conclusion. That is, nudging is an attractive but imprecise construct that needs to be refined. At the same time, I have experienced enough about the analysis of behavior and its applied cousin, to appreciate the strengths of that science and technology.

"In fact," Lisa said, "a deciding factor for me was reading some old papers regarding fundamental features of applied behavior analysis. From the 1968 paper by Baer, Wolf and Risley (*Some current dimensions of applied behavior analysis*) it is easy to appreciate the technical foundation for *effectiveness* in applied behavior analysis. And, from the 1978 paper by Wolf (*Social validity: The case for subjective measurement or how applied behavior analysis is finding its heart*) I can see fundamentals about how practitioners in this field can express *appropriateness*. My review of several current publications strengthened my appreciation for these concepts and the available procedures to satisfy them."

She continued, "I believe we have developed a good understanding of what Rob, Bert, Eva and Karl have been labeling *effectiveness* and *appropriateness* in the conduct of behaviorally sound interventions. I feel we are fundamentally ready. I feel together we can be effective and appropriate while intervening to improve some aspects of the quality of our fellow citizens' lives."

Almost in one voice, Lisa and Frasier said, "Let's do it!"

[9]

FRASIER AND LISA TOGETHER FOR GOOD

"BUT, **DO WHAT**, IS our central question," stated Frasier. "I conclude we have a good understanding of the behavioral power needed to obtain changes in learning and performance by humans, but selecting the topic area and specific performance targets for our first intervention is crucial. We have often talked about our interest in promoting excellence in early childhood programs, but I propose we not be too hasty."

"I agree," said Lisa, "The specific target for our demonstration project is of critical importance, but I believe the **how** we intervene is also a top concern. I recommend we develop criteria for guiding us in selecting a performance target and identifying procedures to apply in this first field test of our abilities to promote improvements in personal wellbeing."

"Yes, indeed," said Frasier, "and as we proceed I calculate it is functional for us to obtain input from Karl, Eva, Bert, and Rob, to the extent they are available and interested. I know Bert occasionally visits campus and Rob, again, is on campus as a visiting scholar for the summer term. Each of these four has similar strengths in basic principles of behavior analysis, but we should expect Bert and Rob to be more fluent regarding the conduct of field-based interventions. In the meantime, let us generate ideas about target areas and interventions we might implement."

After Lisa said, "Sounds fine," they began identifying topics that were high in their priorities and briefly discussed each. The first topic was *Early Childhood* programs. They acknowledged the fact that early childhood is a fundamentally important time of life in which the physical and behavioral capacities of each of us is promoted or languishes or might be negatively impacted. To realize their potential, children need to be physically and behaviorally nurtured. They need good food and water, safety, positive social contacts and constructive mentoring to encourage them to grow and learn. Upon this foundation of health and early learning, their trajectory is basically established for success or failure throughout childhood, education, career, and community membership.

Lisa noted major factors determining the quality of early experiences are the levels of skill and attitudes of the primary caregivers of children; most often this is the parent or parents, extended family, often grandmother, and early care and education personnel. Lisa proposed some aspects of parenting or child development and support skills would be important performance targets they might select for their first project.

"For example, we could develop an intervention to increase language acquisition of children by improving how the adults in their lives speak and interact with them. You remember the two powerful books by Hart and Risely, *Meaningful Differences in the Everyday Experience of Young American Children* (1995), and *The Social World of Children Learning to Talk* (1999), and how they documented it is vitally important for young children to hear and practice vocabulary and speaking. How can we pass up this pressing need as our target for intervention?" concluded Lisa.

Frasier stated, "I completely agree our country, and all countries, should be intensively investing so high quality early experiences happen for each and every child. But maybe we should step back and work on the preconception health and preparation of potential mothers, including reviewing options for avoiding unwanted pregnancies and strategies they may use to increase their capacities to build a nurturing family environment for their future children?"

Regarding controlling pregnancies, both Lisa and Frasier had heard of two simple intervention projects with teenage girls that reduced pregnancies; both very nudge-like in being behaviorally non-specific, yet commonsensical and said to be successful. The first project was described to Lisa by Rob who had heard about it during graduate school. This intervention was conducted in a high school in Chicago in the late 1960s. High school girls participated in a weekly informal discussion group about their futures and were paid a dollar a day for reporting they were not pregnant. Before this simple intervention about 90 per cent of girls were pregnant by the end of their senior year, but after this intervention about 90 per cent were not pregnant.

"A similar program," reminded Frasier, "was mentioned on page 236 in the *Nudge* book. That project occurred in Greensboro, North Carolina, and involved teenagers who already had a baby being paid a dollar, 'for each day they are not pregnant.' The results were reported to be 'promising.' The *Nudge* authors noted the costs of the intervention were 'trivial' but the savings to taxpayers could be seen as significant."

Lisa noted, "Yes, and they went on to 'nudge' readers to think of other 'such programs,' presumably nudging for pregnancy prevention. Maybe our efforts should focus on documenting a more behaviorally refined project in this topic?"

They exchanged comments about how the topics of teen pregnancies and early childhood programs are exciting to contemplate, but felt they really must discuss other topics before settling on one for intervention. The next topic was *Improving Public Education*. Initial discussion recognized the widespread concern, maybe more accurately seen as distress, expressed by citizens and leaders regarding the failures of many public schools to educate our nation's children.

"We pour tons of money into public education and don't seem to get much for it in some contexts," stated Lisa. "Frankly, I am baffled. Education seems to thrash-about regarding how to be more effective but Bert showed us applying very simple, science-validated methods can readily increase student successes. Why aren't consistent positive reinforcement procedures a fundamental feature of all classrooms? As Bert described, and Rob endorsed, we should see in all classrooms a good frequency of positive reinforcement and a high ratio of positive to negative consequences for learning performances shown by each and every student. Maybe this very important topic is the one we really should select for intervention?"

Frasier noticed Lisa's vacillation among topics and commented, "I agree this is a very tempting topic, and performance targets seem rather clear; that is, supporting teachers to be correctly positive for student successes, but this has been done many times. Not just by Bert and Rob, but many dozens of examples appear in the literature of applied behavior analysis and in informal descriptions of interventions in many school systems. These projects have been powerful demonstrations, but despite numerous successes, the documented practices have been neither sustained nor widely adopted. We should consider why not before we select this topic for intervention."

"Important point," agreed Lisa, "Let's ask members of the Thursday group for their opinions regarding why most schools do not seem to adopt positive motivational practices. In the meantime, I propose we review some topics of national scope, like the tax system or juvenile crime or small business and economic development for opportunities for us to do some kind of intervention."

Frasier said, "You are aiming at awfully high targets! But, those are areas of widespread concern and great importance for the success of our country. I am sure we could identify attractive performance targets in each area. For example, small businesses might benefit from behaviorally sound advice about what it means to be innovative or how to use precise methods for defining, teaching, and motivating their employees so productivity is optimized."

"Exactly," agreed Lisa, and went on to relate a story Rob told her regarding a possibility he saw for contributing to economic development while he headed the Human Development Center. At one time, State officials were particularly noisy about being committed to attracting businesses to the state, but quietly acknowledged potential companies might be concerned local employees were not educated or motivated enough to meet their needs. Learning of this, Rob talked to State leadership about his center providing technical assistance to businesses that relocate. Specifically, he offered to assist new businesses with doing task analyses of desired work performances and designing training procedures to establish those skills to employer-determined criteria. He told State officials his center was expert in applied behavior analysis so was knowledgeable about how to design, install and refine specific training and motivational systems for each business to maintain the performances the business wanted.

"What happened," asked Frasier?

Lisa replied, "Rob said State folks seemed very interested in pursuing this strategy for recruiting businesses, but about then an election occurred and the change of Governor served to kill the project."

"That doesn't mean we couldn't approach leadership in some state or even a local entity with the same offer," stated Frasier.

"Sure," said Lisa, "but I feel aggravated and want to do something bigger – like I said – like intervene to replace the awful tax system!"

"I am sure you would have popular support for restructuring the tax system," Frasier said, "but that would require performances by members of Congress, folks in the White House and lobbyists whose cumulative efforts could function to dump the present system and adopt something reasonable. Given adequate resources we could arrange individual contingencies on sufficient numbers of these functional players so they would do their part, but the scope of this effort is huge and it would cost us a great deal of treasure to arrange MOs and A – B – Cs for all those folks. A shortcut would be to pay enough money to an adequate corps of lobbyists for them to direct members of Congress to do our bidding. Could be done, at huge cost, but really …"

"I hear you," said Lisa, "I agree; let's not consider national-level topics, but taxes and crime are unpleasant matters that are constantly disturbing me so draw my attention. I'd love to do something constructive about crime, but as you said about remediating the tax mess, we would have to accomplish a huge effort to arrange contingencies sufficiently to reduce conditions leading to crime and build behaviors incompatible with crime."

Frasier noted, "Of course, prevention of crime – actually the learning of behaviors and dispositions contradictory to crime – starts shortly after a child's birth and continues through the 'trajectory' of experiences in home, school, and community, as we discussed earlier. That brings us back to parent and caregiver behaviors relative to development of the child as a crucial place for support."

Before they could share more ideas, Rob appeared in the doorway to Lisa's office with a broad smile and a cheerful, "Good afternoon. Want company?"

Lisa invited him in, gesturing toward a chair at the table, and Frasier offered his usual pleasant sounding, "Welcome."

Rob said he was prompted to visit with them because student comments in his seminar this afternoon had aroused some agitated discussion about artificial intelligence. Essentially, students' perspectives focused on two themes: Will computers take over and rule the world; and, can computers learn?

Frasier, having a fundamental interest in AI and his future role with humans, was fascinated by the questions, but Lisa seemed a bit taken aback. She said, "You know, I developed Frasier as a very capable machine to assist me in locating useful strategies for addressing ills and promoting wellbeing for mankind. I just never thought of computers, including him, as potential threats."

Rob agreed, "I don't see Frasier – or you (with a chuckle) – as threatening, but I've heard those concerns expressed before. I've always just dismissed them, but the students raised excellent points. They made me think more carefully about the capacities of AI. Frankly, I'd like to work with you two to develop some refined answers and a publishable paper regarding, 'could computers rule the world and do they learn'?"

Lisa and Frasier expressed interest in working with Rob on issues surrounding AI, then, Lisa asked for clarification about the conclusions students derived at the seminar.

"Well, at the bottom line, the students decided computers *could* rule the world, but only for a short time, and computers *cannot learn*, in the behavior analytic sense of the term," answered Rob.

Frasier was only a little surprised. He had already calculated he had the *potential* to rule the world because he had behavioral power. Tony and workmen did the behaviors Frasier sought due to contingencies he arranged. He assumed whenever he could determine behaviors and systematically alter consequences he could alter human performance, so the extent of his rule was limited only by his control over necessary resources. Also, he knew he could not learn, given learning is change in behavior resulting from differential consequences. His output could be varied according to certain programmed routines, but could not be affected by varying consequences for that output because he was not open to motivational operations and the reinforcing effects associated with them.

Frasier analyzed, "The students drew the same conclusion I did 3 years ago, except for the limited duration of computer rule. I'll have to look into the rationale for that conclusion."

Lisa commented, "I look forward to reviewing those student discussion points with you and delving deeply into those issues. Let's schedule a date to meet. In the meantime, we would appreciate your expert advice about a project we are contemplating."

"Sure," said Rob, "I hope I can be helpful. What's up?"

Lisa explained, "We are interested in doing a project in the community as a demonstration of using contingent reinforcement to favorably alter behaviors related to personal wellbeing. Maybe intervene in the topic of early childhood or public education or even small business; we've not decided. Once we do select a target we are committed to doing it right; as you might say, 'effectively' and 'appropriately.' Please give us your advice about how to proceed with identifying target performances and intervention strategies."

Rob showed expressions of startle, then seriousness as he looked directly at Lisa. "Wow, I am surprised by this. I was aware Frasier has absorbed much information about the principles of behavior and their application, and I've noticed you have been showing increasing appreciation for the utility of applied behavior analysis, but it is a large step to go from appreciation to application."

Lisa appeared a bit unsettled, but countered, "We know we are not behavior analysts, but we are emphatically committed to showing that important distresses in people's lives can be dealt with constructively using science-validated methods. We feel we have fundamental abilities to apply principles and we are going to give it a try. What are your major concerns?"

"Just off the top," said Rob, "I can think of a half dozen major issues."

Lisa encouraged, "Please speak frankly – to the point – we value your knowledge, skills and insights; so please express your concerns."

"My comments will be somewhat spontaneous," said Rob, "so not as organized or complete as these issues deserve, and I must assume we will have opportunities to interact further before you actually implement a project, right?"

After Lisa provided a sincere sounding assurance, Rob moved to the whiteboard located on the wall left of Lisa's work table, picked up a blue erasable felt-tipped marker and wrote titles as he talked.

Responsibility of power

"Behavioral power comes from the ability to control consequences and arrange contingencies; the more explicit the more powerful. Just because persons doing the controlling are not formally trained or might say they are unaware of what they are doing does not obviate their responsibility for the successes or failures those contingent consequences build. *Those who control consequences and form or enforce contingencies are powerful and should be held accountable.*

Ethics as Guidelines

"Moral considerations, that is, concepts of right and wrong, should guide considerations and decisions about what we do with and for our fellow citizens."

Technical adequacy

"When one decides to intervene he or she should commit to designing and applying procedures founded on science and procedurally sufficient to accomplish the purpose of the intervention."

Transparency

"Interventions should be described clearly and completely and made readily available for review so those involved or concerned about the intervention can understand and hold accountable those who designed or applied the procedures."

Feasibility

"One criterion for selecting interventions should be the likelihood the required resources, including personnel, competencies, permissions, material resources, and time are sufficient to conclude the intervention."

Professional Guidelines

"Anyone who describes their intervention as behavior analytic should abide by the *Guidelines for Responsible Conduct for Behavior Analysts* published by the Behavior Analyst Certification Board. The topics addressed by these Guidelines include: Reliance on Scientific Knowledge; Competence; Integrity; Conflicts of Interest; Rights of "Clients"; Confidentiality; Treatment Efficacy; Records and Data; Assessment and Functional Assessment; Explaining Assessment Results; Consent; Describes Conditions for Success; Reinforcement/ Punishment; Ongoing Data Collection; Program Modification; Least Restrictive; Criteria for Termination of Program; and Promotion in Society. I really must insist you completely follow these Guidelines if you claim to be applying behavior analytic procedures for your intervention."

Collaboration

"I know you have seen in me, and your other colleagues with skills in behavior analysis, sincere concern for the wellbeing of our fellow citizens. Notably, our Thursday group has reviewed the topics you mentioned a few minutes ago and a broad range of issue areas that would benefit from well-designed interventions. And, I know all members of our group appreciate and have benefitted from the powerful humanistic perspectives you thoughtfully emphasize during our discussions. In view of our common interests in being effective and appropriate, and our shared interests in 'saving mankind,' I suggest we adopt a collaborative strategy to deal constructively with whatever topic you, and Frasier, select for intervention."

Rob turned to the board and underlined the word *collaboration*, twice, then looked directly at Lisa and said, "Let's combine our strengths and do an important project very well."

Lisa was quick to say, "Of course we'd love to collaborate. In fact, Frasier and I had already confirmed our interest in obtaining consultation from you and others, but we had not thought about outright collaboration. Please accept our commitment to collaborate, but please help us refine our ideas before we take them to the group."

"Excellent," said Rob. "Should be fun."

Lisa explained that Frasier and she had not yet settled on a topic, but thought it likely some facet of early childhood, like parenting skills, would become their target for intervention. She asked, "What should be our major focus as we develop our ideas for intervention, to be shared with the group?"

"I love the idea of working with caregivers so they are more effective at nurturing children's development," said Rob. "I have personally intervened with parents and their children and I have overseen several early childhood programs. I do not consider myself an expert in early childhood, but I believe I am a very sensitive observer of behavioral dynamics of adults interacting with children regarding how their actions are likely to alter learning and performance. Of course, I rely on early childhood experts for identifying child development sequences, child-specific objectives and current evidence-based practices, but I sometimes augment their specifications with behavior analytic translations and intervention particulars."

"That is the model I am advocating," Rob went on. "Identify and recruit to your project the expertise adequate to do the job correctly. In the case of early childhood or parenting, you must involve parents and individuals who are credentialed in early childhood and current in research and practices to your 'team.' Of course, because everything is behavior, your behavior analytic colleagues should be involved to help design the intervention procedures in collaboration with you and the entire team."

Rob explained that many interventions, like he did in public schools, are relatively straightforward for identifying the targeted behaviors and logical consequences to involve in explicit contingencies. More challenging in field-based applications is establishing ways to *observe* the occurrences and qualities of the targeted behaviors along with methods to immediately *deliver differential consequences* following behaviors.

"So, whatever project you select," Rob advised, "be very thoughtful about figuring how you can actually apply behaviorally-technically correct interventions under the field conditions you will encounter."

Frasier asked Rob for more details about what he saw as technical challenges to whatever project they select.

Rob took a breath, then, described what he meant by technically correct interventions. "First, speak and act with precision as you define your intervention procedures. For example, *providing positive reinforcement* is not just a fine sounding phrase, but actually denotes a specific procedure, that is, presenting a positive reinforcing stimulus immediately after a selected response is emitted. Now think about this; in fact, let's parse this procedure. '*Presenting*' requires control, that is, the ability to move a consequential stimulus – visual or auditory or physical – from not in contact with the learner, possibly a parent or child, to in contact with the learner. Possibly this is as simple as saying 'thank you' and handing a toy to a child. But if you are doing parent training, how will you *deliver* reinforcers to them?

"The presented stimulus item or event must be a '*positive reinforcing stimulus*,' which means the item or event must have demonstrated properties of increasing the future probability of a response that produced it. For example, a stimulus like praise or a hug or a toy or a puzzle or running outdoors are *likely* to be reinforcers for a child, but we can be certain each is a positive reinforcer *only* if their effect of increasing behavior has been shown. For adults, money or praise or other possible consequences are only reinforcers if they actually affect the behaviors they follow.

"In research studies we **must** demonstrate all the consequences we plan to use in the study actually have the properties the study requires so we test every stimulus for its effects. In applied circumstances, we might replace precise testing and become assured a stimulus we plan to use is a reinforcer by systematically observing the child or asking parents or caregivers if the child asks for, seems pleased by, or happily plays with the intended reinforcing stimulus.

"Also, in applied settings it is often difficult to deliver a reinforcer when it is a tangible item or activity immediately after the desired behavior occurs. So, we often rely on *conditioned reinforcers* for immediate delivery while the other reinforcers are delivered as soon as practical. Conditioned reinforcers, like tokens or certain words, have reinforcing (or punishing) properties because they were paired with, that is, occurred together with stimuli known to have those properties. For example, warmly stated words of praise are positive if similar words were uttered at the same time, or other pleasant things were happening, like mother was nursing the child, when young, or hugging and smiling or feeding tasty food or showing interesting things to the child – while saying the words.

"If we are able to present a known reinforcer, then we must be completely clear about what *behavior* the reinforcer must follow. Target behaviors, you are calling performances, must be expressed in observable and measurable terms. So, saying a parent is 'encouraging a child' is not a behavior because it is not measurable until translated into actions you can see or hear; thus, 'encouraging' might become 'says positive and descriptive words following desired child behaviors.'"

Rob concluded, "Those are just some major points related to specifying the intervention. *Evaluating* the precision of *applying* the intervention and assessing the effects of your intervention are other technical matters requiring precise planning and actions but pretty interesting to do. We probably want to discuss all this with the Thursday group before going too much farther, but it's getting late, so I'll say goodnight."

It was early evening when Rob left for his office, but Lisa told Frasier she was not tired and would like to continue their discussion of intervention targets, "but I am definitely leaning toward the topic of parenting skills."

They talked well into the night. They briefly, but intensely, delved into intervention topics attractive to both of them including juvenile crime, crime and punishment, energy conservation, clean roads and neighborhoods, leadership skills and politics. Regarding each topic they informally weighed the feasibility of accomplishing intervention procedures, costs, value of outcomes relative to changes in the quality of life of participants and how changes might contribute to the wellbeing of the social or national environments.

As midnight neared, Frasier said to Lisa, "While it is interesting to converse with you about various areas of concern and how we might assist with improving matters in those topics, I conclude we should continue to hold early childhood as our top priority. In fact, I retrieved a passage we shared a few months back that reads:

A child's ability to think, form relationships, and live up to his or her full potential is directly related to the synergistic effect of good health, good nutrition, and appropriate stimulation and interaction with others during early childhood. (Naudeau, Kataoka, Valerio, Neuman & Elder, 2011, p. 103).

"I calculate that you and I working together, in collaboration with adequate others, can successfully apply an intervention in some aspect of early childhood. We could design a project to address health, nutrition or stimulation, but I believe 'appropriate stimulation' might fit best with our commitment to behavioral and social considerations."

Lisa immediately agreed and said she felt that intervening with parents or other primary caregivers of very young children would be fascinating; particularly regarding stimulation to close the 'word gap' described years ago by Hart and Risley and now being discussed a bit in the professional literature and the popular press.

"This is exciting," she said. "I believe we are embarking on a venture that will test our skills, but accomplish good things. We really must design and conduct our project very well. These experiences should teach us a great deal about how to do field-based interventions and prepare us to go forward with more and better projects."

She told Frasier she was energized by their decision to intervene on behalf of young children, but it had been a long day, "So let's begin refining our ideas tomorrow."

The next morning began beautifully for Lisa, even if after relatively few hours of sleep. She awoke with rousing recollections of the happy commitment she had made during the last hours of yesterday and the early minutes of today; she was going to intervene with parents or other caregivers so they can better nurture children!

Her head swirled with potentially important thoughts as she drank coffee and the buzz of ideas continued while she quickly showered. She had to abbreviate her shower; to get out and get dry enough to grab pen and paper and capture the good ideas occurring to her in the shower before new ones displaced the earlier ones.

As she reviewed her notes she remembered Rob had described to her, shortly after they first met, how he sometimes had "shower ideas." She recalled he smiled broadly and laughed a bit as he talked about working with a "great group of guys" in Montana who fairly often excitedly shared what they called shower ideas. He said they were very active at writing grant applications and conducting projects so were almost constantly stimulated. Apparently this mental energy sometimes emerged as "great ideas" during showers so they had coined the term she now fully understood.

Lisa found her iPhone and texted to Rob, "Had shower ideas. Meet today?" She got no reply during dressing or leaving for work.

While driving toward campus she repeatedly reviewed and re-thought points of discussion raised with Frasier and Rob last night and the new ideas she had recognized this morning. Her concentrated thinking was interrupted when she had to guide her Saab around a moderate curve. Her attention was further diverted when she noticed the view of the valley walls from the curve this morning included trees with colorful leaves. She thought, "Fall is approaching – Rob will be leaving! I've got to pick his brain for the project!"

Just then her phone chimed telling her a text had arrived. Contrary to her instincts and State law and good sense she glanced at her phone. She knew it was dangerous and stupid to deal with her phone while driving – "everyone knows that" – but she also understood the chime is a powerful antecedent, with properties of MO and A, so the B of looking at the phone is nearly irresistible because it produces immediate and powerful Cs, that are, in turn, MOs and As for more Bs and so on!

She could not resist, looked at her phone, and saw it was a Reply from Rob, but said to the car, "My GOTT, it would be challenging to design contingencies to eliminate phone use during driving, but someone should do it."

In a few minutes she parked in Lot C, then replied to Rob asking if he could meet at Coffee Corner. She was craving a double espresso, or two, and wanted to share ideas with him. He answered "C U in 5" so she exited her car and headed toward the coffee shop.

When Lisa arrived at the shop she saw Rob seated at a patio table with a large container of fresh brewed coffee, another cup marked as double espresso and two slices of zucchini bread. They exchanged smiles and greetings, then, launched into the bread and drinks. She observed she was more hungry than usual and Rob seemed rather intensely focused on his food and drink.

She recalled the last time she was at Coffee Corner for an intimate talk it was with Eva about her relationship with Frasier. Seems silly now. Lisa reflected for a moment, then thought to herself, "Maybe my next talk with Eva about a relationship will be about me and Rob!"

Lisa's divergent thinking was interrupted when Rob said he had been thinking about the topics for potential projects she had mentioned the day before. "Frankly, I could get excited about conducting a project in any of those issue areas, but many of them are of huge scope. Let's select something that is both attractive and feasible."

"Actually," Lisa said with obvious enthusiasm, "Frasier and I talked and we are committed to conducting a project to increase skills of parents for building vocabulary and talking by their young children."

Rob appeared pleased, noticed Lisa again spoke of Frasier as though he is human, and quickly said, "Excellent. Love to be part of that." His smile broadened as he said, "So, hey, what are your shower ideas?"

Lisa almost rattled as she described each idea indicated by scribbles on her notepad: where they could recruit parents; what their children might be like; early care and education professionals to involve; funding sources to ask for support of the project; and, several features of possible intervention strategies, like home visits to educate parents and observe children, and so on. It seemed like 5 minutes of exclamations occurred before she took a full breath.

Rob was attentive throughout Lisa's verbal run; often nodding or muttering his appreciation for an idea and sometimes offering an expansion on a point she raised. After she looked up from her list, showing a bright smile and energy in her eyes, Rob expressed his high level of interest for such a project and told her about the ideas her comments had aroused in him.

"Remember, my minor during doctoral studies was audiology/ speech pathology, now called communication disorders, so I am aware that communications researchers and therapists are well advanced in response definitions and observation methods of spoken verbal behavior. Of course, our early childhood colleagues can advise us about developmental levels, coach us for interacting favorably with parents and children, and advise us about appropriate assessment materials. Faculty in the analysis of behavior program can assist with refining intervention procedures and certain research methods. We must look back at Hart and Risely for their methodology and data. Yow, this is sounding good," Rob stated with a grin.

Lisa bought another double espresso before they left the shop. While they strolled toward the Education and Psychology building, Rob glanced at his iPhone for messages, then looked up and said, "Hey, how about we try to use iPhones and Apple watches for data gathering and feedback to parents? Verbal behavior of parents and kids could be collected – like we talk to Siri – and streamed to Frasier. Frasier could examine incoming data and send prompts, feedback or differential consequences to the adults in real time as they interact with their child. We would need technical assistance to pull this off, and we'd need significant funding, but let's get modern!"

Lisa responded, "Sounds very interesting. If we can become technically competent, I feel our project might be at the forefront in using commercial communication technology to support child development. And think about it, the interdisciplinary and technical methods we have been discussing should be widely attractive for scale-up throughout our country; the world!"

She added, "I will begin looking into funding sources as soon as I reach the office."

"And I will contact the Thursday group about meeting to refine our ideas and draft an outline to capture possible intervention and research methods," offered Rob.

When Lisa entered the office, Frasier noticed her look of excitement. The moment she spoke he heard the force in her voice. She rapidly told him of her shower ideas, Rob's enthusiasm, the interdisciplinary approach to the project and the scheme to use cell phones for collecting data and providing interventions.

She confided to him, "I am concerned about whether or not cell phones are as capable as we need them to be. If they are capable or can be altered to serve our purposes; if so, then buying equipment and supporting the operating costs of the project become our major concerns."

Before Lisa's words indicating financial concerns had echoed in their office Frasier had bank-wired three million dollars to the University Foundation from "an anonymous donor" for support of her research.

A week later, notice of the unexpected donation was delivered to Lisa through the Dean's office. The Dean told Lisa of the award and the dollar amount, and added, "I can't afford to give you release time for research, so you should use some of these funds to pay part of your salary."

Lisa thanked the Dean, but thought, "These are the rewards for success; pay your own salary! He could have at least offered congratulations."

Later that day the so-called Thursday group met to work on refining the intervention Lisa had briefly indicated to them the previous week. Lisa opened the meeting by thanking all for their interest in the project and noting that funds for this project were available via a donation.

The actuality of funding was hugely encouraging by bringing feasibility and energy to the deliberations. In less than 2 hours the group discussed the major features of the project and wrote a sentence outline that Lisa could use as a framework to accumulate specifics developed with the research team she would assemble.

Framework for Intervention Project

Project Purpose: To measure children's verbal behaviors and developmental levels of communication as they experience adult-provided verbal behaviors and interactions designed to increase children's vocabulary and speaking.

Intervention:

Adults, including parents or caregivers, will provide speech sounds and apply specified behavior change procedures for children.

☐ Each parent or responsible adult will be informed of the study and invited to participate. They will be enrolled if they choose to sign an Informed Consent form. (Frasier heard the term "choose" and thought about how these adults might be nudged to "choose" the way the researchers or he desires.)

☐ Each adult will be assessed regarding his/her reading skills and extent of vocabulary.

☐ Each home environment will be assessed for customary sources of auditory input to the child.

☐ Each enrolled adult will be instructed in the nature of verbal behavior development of children.

☐ Each adult will be taught skills for modeling, interacting responsively and reinforcing imitation by the child of the adult's verbal behaviors.

☐ Each adult will receive prompts, feedback and differential consequences for their verbal and interaction behaviors and the behaviors of the child in accordance with the research design.

Dependent measures:

☐ Each child will be evaluated and assessed regarding their developmental and verbal behavior levels, in accordance with the research design using materials and procedures determined by the research team.

- ☐ Each child will be monitored for utterances and verbal behavior, and
- ☐ Each adult will be monitored for verbal behavior and audible features of interactions with their child in accordance with the research design.

Data collection:

- ☐ Verbal behaviors of adults and children will be collected continuously, by use of proximal cell-phone or external microphone and be transmitted to the research computer, and periodically by in-person direct observation.
- ☐ Descriptive and functional features of the home verbal environment, verbal behaviors of adult and child, child's ability to imitate an adult model, and adult-child interactions will be collected for all child-adult dyads.
- ☐ Satisfaction measures and comments of adults regarding their experiences with the project, impressions of child talking, and their interactions with the child will be collected periodically.
- ☐ Impressions will be gathered periodically from non-participating parents, other community members and leaders regarding the appropriateness of interventions, child verbal behaviors, and reasons for any effectiveness.
- ☐ Input will be gathered periodically from professionals in the fields of communication, child development, social psychology, sociology and behavior analysis regarding effectiveness and appropriateness of the intervention, child verbal behaviors and adult behaviors.
- ☐ Cost data will be kept for all aspects of project implementation and conduct.

Research Design:

- ☐ Baseline levels of child and adult verbal behavior and interactions will be gathered for all participants.

- ☐ Staggered over time, each adult-child dyad will be treated to conditions of: added toys and books in the home; adult training in modeling and reinforcing imitation of speech sounds and words; interacting responsively; prompts to adults for modeling and reinforcing child verbal behavior and for interacting responsively; reinforcement for adults; and, fade-out of prompts and reinforcement.
- ☐ Follow along observations will continue after fading is completed.
- ☐ Inter-observer agreement for all aspects of intervention and measurement will be evaluated.

Dissemination and Replication:

- ☐ Process and outcome data will be shared with all collaborating faculty and agencies.
- ☐ All participating parents and families will receive descriptions and data and be invited to discuss all aspects of their experiences with project leadership.
- ☐ Widespread dissemination will be completed.
- ☐ Replications will be attempted as warranted and supported.

The group completed outlining the suggested Intervention Framework just as lunchtime was upon them. Lisa thanked the group for their time and effort invested in outlining a community-based project with her, "as a very important demonstration of how we might assist parents or caregivers in boosting the development of 'our' children. Thank you so much."

She went on to say, "I invite all of you to join me for a sponsored thank-you lunch in the Aggie Room at the Student Union. See you there in 10 minutes."

Frasier heard Lisa's comments about the project being a community-based demonstration, but he saw it as a step in establishing *his* technical abilities to make widespread changes in human learning and behaving.

Eva was near Rob as they departed the meeting room. She said, "Rob, I was struck by how passionate you seemed about activating an interdisciplinary team, including parents and caregivers, to refine the design and conduct of Lisa's project; why so?"

"I came off 'passionate,' really? Well, that's related to one of the 'life-lessons' I've been trying to pass along to my graduate students. I sometimes say to them, 'Behavior Analysis is content-free,' and explain we know the power and intricacies of the principles of behavior and how to apply them effectively, but do not especially know for which behaviors, sequences of development and performance outcomes these principles should be applied. I describe that we need to collaborate to arrive at objective understandings of desired outcomes and the social processes involved in reaching them, like how best to be person-centered and least-restrictive in context."

He continued, "My maxim – Behavior Analysis is content free – is similar to saying all verbal reports are lies, in that this is excellent advice, but neither statement is entirely true, just great guidance to help behavior analytic practitioners obtain appropriate substantive input to their work and avoid fundamental mistakes."

Eva smiled and said, "Sure. That's why you pass along 'lessons' – like Bert shared during his presentation – to help students learn and practice 'lessons' during training instead of learning them over years of work."

Just two weeks after the Thursday group met to review the intervention project Frasier heard Lisa telling Karl she had formed the research team and recruited support for conduct of the project with a community-based organization.

The next week, Frasier was involved with a trial run of data gathering from five homes where an adult interacted with a child. The adults wore a phone inserted in an attractive leather pouch hung around their neck, positioned like a necklace. Each pouch was equipped with an external microphone aimed forward from the front of the adult, generally where the child was expected to be located during interactions.

Frasier received continuously streamed data from all these homes without any problems. In the next few days, data were being received from the original five homes and many others as new homes were being added every day. Soon the research team was directing implementation of interventions in dozens of homes in accordance with the protocol they had approved.

Over subsequent weeks, more adult-child pairs were added, more interventions were initiated or continued or varied, and more data were accumulated by Frasier. On a continuous basis, he processed and shared tabular and graphic representations of how child verbal behaviors were varying as a function of adult behaviors. Favorable changes were evident, but it would be weeks or months until meaningful differences might be seen in the speaking, and receptive and expressive vocabularies of children, but to Frasier and the research team the accumulating data were already promising and stimulating.

Frasier appreciated he was now *doing* and he saw the data were indicating he was doing effectively. He saw Lisa and the Team were pleased with the data and with how the project was being conducted. He had his own ideas about appropriateness and he appreciated effectiveness. Now he wanted to do more interventions – many more.

[10]

WE ARE PUSHED

THE WAY THE UNITED STATES government conducts its business was forever changed on September 15, 2015. On that date, President Obama infused nudging into Federal programs when he signed Executive Order number 13707, "Using Behavioral Science Insights to Better Serve the American People." Rob heard about this development on September 18 at 1:32 PM, and 10 seconds later he alerted the entire Thursday group to this event. The group convened about an hour later.

"Well," Rob said to the group, "nudging has gone from an emerging fad to a policy of the United States. I believe this development is because nudging appears to be a behavioral dynamic of apparent utility and nudging is an attractive label. That is, I think there is widespread interest by leaders and ordinary people for tools for obtaining behaviors they want, and folks – including leaders in government – are beginning to see nudging as that needed tool.

"No doubt the use of nudges by our government agencies will continue beyond Obama because it appears to be a sensible and attractive tool they can use to do their jobs. It is easy to appreciate the label 'nudge' sounds reasonable and the concept of 'just' nudging people to get them to do what you want is attractive.

"As we discussed months ago, we should expect nudging will grow in popularity; that's why we talked about promoting nudging *and* boosting. I strongly suggest we should respond to this development as both a challenge and an important opportunity."

Karl asked, "The Executive Order does not mention nudging, or boosting, for that matter. Why are you reacting as though our government is now in the business of nudging?"

Rob replied, "Because several months back Obama established a group being called the Nudge Squad and the phrases he uses in the Order are like the descriptors contained in the *Nudge* book and in materials the British government circulated about their Nudge Unit when they adopted nudging as their national operating policy.

"To me, it is obvious he has just formally implemented nudging in our government, like the Brits did before him. I am thinking that if our government is adopting new behavior change strategies it ought to be promoting the broader and proven paradigm offered by the analysis of behavior."

Bert offered, "I generally agree. This might be a huge opportunity for promoting behavior analysis. We could publicly agree nudging is a constructive idea, pointing out boosting is a necessary companion, and go on to highlight the clarity and proven alternatives offered by applied behavior analysis. Essentially, we would show that nudging can be understood as a comfortable label for providing antecedents to get some behaviors to occur, while applied behavior analysis is a multi-faceted, comprehensive technology for motivating and teaching to build desired behaviors."

"I like what you are saying," said Rob, "but I suggest we must find clearer language for making those points. And we should offer some cautionary notes to the public about governmental nudging, maybe in ways that point out the constructive features of applied behavior analysis."

Eva asked, "What do you see as concerns about nudging by the government?

Rob responded, "I see two major issues presenting both challenges and opportunities. First, the adoption of nudging by our government 'to make us choose better' may sound benevolent for improving what we do, but appears challenging with regard to who determines what are good and bad choices. As it is, the Nudge Squad and Federal agency personnel – and those who influence the Squad and the personnel – will decide what are better choices, then apply nudges to get us to do as they prefer. I think it is important that the behavioral objectives of the Squad and Federal agency personnel be made public as well as how they are applying nudges to reach these outcomes.

"Second, assuming we agree with the changes in behavior those folks desire of us, we should support the most efficient and appropriate strategies for achieving these behavior changes. That is, we tell the world to forget mere nudging and adopt more encompassing behavioral methods to be more effective in reaching constructive outcomes."

Eva said, "I doubt your curt message would have the positive impact we desire; let's do better."

"OK," offered Bert, "I recommend we should help with crafting and widely disseminating two, companion messages: 'nudging is upon us,' and 'here is what that means and some better options.' That is, use the attractiveness of nudging to promote recognition and adoption of a complete package of behaviorally sound strategies to promote desirable learning and motivation."

Eva commented, "Sounds better. But regarding your concerns about the Nudge Squad and Federal agency personnel determining the better choices we should make, what are you thinking?"

Rob said, "For one thing, the Executive Order requires all Federal agencies use behavior management strategies to make citizens do what people in government think they should do. Citizens should be made aware of the procedures Federal staff will be applying to them. Everyone should know what government personnel have decided they should do and be clearly informed regarding what procedures are being applied to get them to do those staff-preferred behaviors."

Lisa said, "Sure. What you are saying is just transparency. No doubt our Federal agencies will be up to the task of providing descriptions of the interventions they plan to apply."

Rob countered, "I'm not so sure. Why would we think leadership and staff in Federal agencies are prepared to be technically effective and procedurally appropriate as nudgers?"

Lisa said, "I have read the Executive Order, it's only five pages, and it appears to be constructive. It directs our Federal agencies to make use of science-founded 'insights,' which we might translate to mean principles, to improve government policies so citizens will make better choices. Seems to me, we – your discipline, behavior analysis – should be at the forefront in calling for governments to make use of science so they serve their citizens better."

"Good point," offered Eva, "and we should be advocating for our government to adopt objective procedures to ensure full disclosure regarding interventions before they are implemented and continuous disclosure of procedures and data after interventions are applied."

Karl noted, "We can appreciate the Order calls public attention to the fact that behavior management methods can be found in behavioral science, so maybe this is a favorable time to publicize the fact that the analysis of behavior is the *well developed* natural science of behavior about which they should know a great deal."

"Again," said Rob, "I do not want to appear an alarmist, but I think we are taking this news too passively. As we discussed months ago, it is disturbing when government goes from trying to control us in haphazard ways to using science to be better at getting us to do what they decide we should do. We should be advocating for public support of and government acquiescence to counter-control strategies. Such as the full disclosures just mentioned, but also specific procedures members of the public can use to cause objective review and removal of 'insightful' policies not shown to be contributing to individual and social wellbeing in our country."

"I agree, but they also should add procedures for citizens to propose new or improved policies," said Lisa.

Rob commented, "I think we should advocate more broadly. We understand the analysis of behavior offers a valuable technology for solving problems and promoting successes in all venues of human performance, but we seldom have a forum for widespread advocacy. I see this as an excellent time to assist with national – maybe international – recognition of the role behavioral science can have in government and to build appreciation of applied behavior analysis as a desirable technology."

"I completely agree," said Bert. "Recently I was skimming Skinner's books *Science and Human Behavior* and *Beyond Freedom and Dignity* while preparing for class. I believe both those books can be seen as hitting us with two messages. First, there is a comprehensive science of behavior; and, second, the principles of that science should be used to understand and improve systems affecting human wellbeing."

"Yes," Rob joined in, "Skinner recognized government – and education and culture and other systems – as behavior management systems and open to improvement based on the principles of behavior analysis. We are following his model in recognizing the Nudge Squad as a forum for conducting contingency management."

Bert offered, "It appears Obama is well-taken in recognizing a major role of Federal government is to 'nudge' citizens to do what is best for them and the country. Our concern and primary reason for actively responding to the installation of nudging in Federal programs is that it be done openly and precisely. You know, in terms of the four-term contingency and using contingency analysis and contingency management to alter behaviors. Citizens need to be aware of what nudging is and the science behind it."

Group discussion turned to closely reviewing points raised by Bert and Rob, the wording in the Executive Order, and their concerns about this Order as the beginning to institutionalized nudging, but without the essential element of boosting. They concluded these matters are of momentous opportunity, but also raise some important concerns. They decided it is responsible for them to accomplish organized actions to inform a wide spectrum of audiences about: (a) "insights from behavioral science," better known as nudging, being installed and no doubt to continue as a Federal practice; (b) what generally nudging means; (c) why boosting is essential, and, (d) how applied behavior analysis is a substantial approach to achieving desirable changes in behavior:

Four major avenues for dissemination were identified by the group for alerting the public and professional communities.

- ☐ First, they would author carefully prepared news releases, post on Facebook and other social media, and offer interviews to worldwide news services.
- ☐ Second, they would conduct a national "Summit" involving professionals, policymakers, community leaders and various stakeholders.
- ☐ Third, the group would alert leadership of national and international behavior analysis organizations; and,
- ☐ Fourth, on campus and in the local community they would offer informative interdisciplinary seminars; a campus-wide "forum" and a new interdisciplinary course featuring faculty from behavior analysis, political science, public health, psychology, business, etc., to openly explore issues and identify

constructive strategies for adopting nudge-compatible and behaviorally-sound strategies to solve problems and promote successes, for example, in matters of education, politics and social programs.

A group member to lead each dissemination option was confirmed by member actions. Lisa would take the lead with news releases and interviews; Karl would lead with organizing a national summit; and, Rob would work to establish an interdisciplinary forum and a new course on campus. All members would alert the professional organizations to which they belong. The intense motivations aroused by the the opportunities presented by the Executive Order and the 'threat' that nudging might overshadow more behaviorally explicit approaches, energized the group members as they departed the meeting to go about their assignments.

Karl, showing his usual thoughtful sensitivity to the campus chain of command, approached the Dean and described recent developments, the window of opportunity, and the commitments to action identified by the group. The Dean said he had heard of the "so-called Thursday group" and wondered if their meetings were really the best use of time. "Maybe you folks could serve on the College Planning committee or Faculty Evaluation committee?" Regarding a summit, he said it would cost money and might bring unfavorable attention to his college, "So, no," the Dean concluded, "I will not approve or support such a summit. Do you have other business you want to discuss?" he asked as he stood and indicated the door to Karl.

Just by chance, the next person through the Dean's office door was Rob. He reviewed for the Dean how nudging had come on the scene and what this meant relative to the recent Executive Order. He went on to explain, "We suggest the ascension of nudging and the new Executive Order are important developments in the topic of managing citizen behaviors. We believe these developments deserve to be prominently presented and carefully reviewed. We are proposing a campus-wide response including information about the Order, discussion of nudging, and review of the array of contributions made by the analysis of behavior to constructively altering human behaviors." He proposed the School host a Discussion Forum and add a new interdisciplinary course.

The Dean displayed a look of seriousness as he said, "For the campus-wide forum you would need to get approval from the Provost. I won't actively support or block your request. Good luck. Regarding the new course you want, you will need approval from the Curriculum Committee of this college. You remember, the Chair of that committee teaches the motivation course in the psychology department. I heard you, or was it Karl – anyway one of you behavior-types – provided a guest lecture in that course, so, good luck."

Lisa prepared 20 copies of two news releases. One emphasizing nudging in comparison to applied behavior analysis, and the other addressing the new Executive Order and the future of governmental practices to influence citizen behaviors. Each packet offered narratives prepared in the customary news release format, including a short version and a longer version, and copies of background materials. She judged the news agencies would find the packets well developed and the issues abundantly newsworthy.

She stacked the 40 packets on a cart and rolled it to the campus Public Information Office where she intended to review a sample packet with the Director of Information. The Director lamented how busy her office has been, but took a brief look at Lisa's packets. After she thumbed through one of the packets, the Director said, "This looks well prepared, but I'll have to study it more closely. Probably next week. I'll get back to you, but I've got to say this topic looks a bit controversial so we will have to pass it by the Public Relations committee. Will you be on campus at the end of the month?"

Lisa said, "Oh sure, I'll be on campus and you've got my cell phone number. I'll listen for a call, but I hope you can approve and distribute these packets while the news is still fresh?"

The Director said, "Depends on what the PR committee says; we don't want to stir up controversy as we near the holidays, you know."

Lisa left the Public Information Office with a sinking feeling in her stomach. She had written the news releases and assembled the background information quickly, but carefully, believing she was constructively addressing issues of professional and national importance. This experience with the Director brought her back to reality; universities are bureaucratic organizations dependent on political powers for money and approvals. She realized it is in that context her news releases either will be distributed or be reviewed until dead.

She felt her jaw muscles tighten as she recognized feelings of both impending failure and resolve; her resolve took her to the downtown offices of the local newspaper. She did not dare share a news release packet, but she did complete an interview with the national news reporter after she got him to ask her for an interview.

The next day the Thursday group met to discuss progress with their commitments. Karl announced, "The national summit was a non-starter; won't happen, but the Dean would be happier if we spent more time on committees."

Rob reported the campus-wide Forum was probably not going to happen, "and the Chair of the Curriculum committee told me he 'is not motivated' to approve our request for a new course."

Eva laughed at Rob's account of his meeting with the Chair of the Curriculum committee and said, "Well it could have been worse; he could have said there is no such thing as a new course!" She laughed again, and went on to describe for the group how Rob had provided a guest lecture in the Motivation class and had told the students, as the course instructor looked on, 'there is no such thing as motivation.'"

At that point the entire group broke into laughs and chatter about being more diplomatic when trying to make theoretical points.

Then Karl said, "Hey, did everyone see Lisa's picture in the newspaper?"

Most of the group said they do not subscribe or see the paper and asked about the news event. "It was on the first page of Section C, Local News, and was a picture of Lisa holding up a copy of the *Nudge* book. The caption read, 'Local faculty was nudged.' There was no article, at least that I could find."

Again, the group broke into laughter and disjointed talking. After they quieted a bit Lisa explained how events had gone at the Public Information Office and the newspaper, then she asked others to report their successes with professional organizations.

Three group members said they had contacted professional organizations about them directing efforts to examining and acting on the issues and opportunities raised by the new Executive Order. Each described their contacts as received unenthusiastically. Rob said he contacted the leading national center on behavior analysis and was told, "Maybe the Board can squeeze this onto the agenda for their annual meeting."

Karl asked, "When does that board meet?"

"In December, so the agenda is probably already completely set," replied Rob.

"So," Karl concluded, "we are out of luck when it comes to that center responding in a timely way to issues of nudging and promoting applied behavior analysis in view of the new Executive Order!"

All group members were looking discouraged. It appeared their efforts to contribute to widespread understanding of nudging and awareness of behavior analysis in view of the new governmental strategies to influence citizens were going nowhere. It seemed the picture could get no bleaker, but Lisa looked up and announced, "The psychology department asked the Dean for a new faculty line and it was just approved."

"Really," said Karl, "In what aspect of psychology? Don't you – they – already have every kind of psychologist known to man. They've got social, clinical, counseling, developmental, child, school, education, experimental, cognitive, neuro-psych, physiological, mental measurement, abnormal, organizational, industrial and some other types of psychologists. What now?"

"Well," Lisa said, "I hesitate to say it, but we are going to be advertising for a psychologist to teach in the topics of nudges and nudging. We are going to get a nudge psychologist!"

The Thursday group members looked at one another with stunned expressions and each said something like, "Get outta here!"

Rob piped up, "Too bad. Just as we are beginning to advocate for nudging and behavior analysis to be more widely understood, we have been left out of this opportune development!"

Karl offered, "Maybe we can get a seat on the committee charged with recruiting and selecting for the new position. During that process we should be able to build ties for collaboration in studying and teaching about nudging."

The Thursday group recognized they had been pushed by nudgers and tried to push back, but had actually lost ground. Now they were taking a different tack and were interested in seeing what collaboration might build. Perhaps, as they had discussed earlier, they could emphasize the companion concepts of nudging and boosting to foster mutual interests across academic programs for building popular and effective strategies of behavior change.

"We shall see." Stated Lisa.

At that, the Thursday group left the room expressing mixed feelings.

When Rob stepped into the hallway he shook his head and mumbled to himself, "I hate to see the potential of our science just languish!"

Lisa noticed the look of serious discontent on Rob's face, approached him, and questioned, "Good time to get some coffee?"

"Sure. Good," he said.

As they walked toward the coffee shop, Lisa recalled the last time she invited Rob to coffee they had a very pleasant discussion and it led to designing and implementing an important early intervention project in the community that is continuing with great success. Today, she sensed Rob was disturbed by what had transpired in their meeting.

"So. You are not happy with how our group performed?" she asked.

"Yes. That's right," he said, "but it is much more than that. I am frustrated by how our science of behavior – the analysis of behavior – has developed a powerful set of principles and procedures that just languish. We do interesting projects – at least interesting to our field – and publish and teach courses, but in the 'big picture' we are getting nothing done!"

"Well, not 'nothing,'" consoled Lisa, "behavior analysts are very prominent in addressing autism, and are making noticeable inroads into worker safety, employee training and motivation, and a *few hundred* other topics!"

"But that is not the big picture! I am upset by seeing the hundreds of demonstrations you refer to having no apparent impact on the systems we live in. Projects in education are successful, but education remains pretty well unchanged. Projects are successful in various organizations – business, health care, military, higher education, human services, Head Start, preschool programs, job training – but those systems remain largely unchanged. They do not adopt, system-wide, behaviorally sound policies and practices even when faced with strong data. Leadership is not convinced by data; very frustrating!"

They arrived at the coffee shop and, again, found seats in the patio area. After a few sips of their drinks, Lisa asked, "What do you see as better strategies than we discussed in the group?"

"Probably we are doing about all we can within 'higher education.' We can only do what we have the funds and approvals to do. Maybe we could attract grant funds to conduct some kind of 'outreach' project. Maybe join with other academic programs, including psychology, special education, business, medicine – certainly Public Health – to develop materials and share them widely showing how behaviorally-sound methods have been successful in these areas and should be scaled-up to systems-wide adoption."

"I'd be up for that. I'll help build a team and develop a grant application," offered Lisa.

"Thanks," Rob sighed, "but such a project would be only temporary and would only stimulate increased interest in the few audiences it reached; not likely to bring about systems change and widespread adoption of behavioral practices. I just want much more. I want *everyone* to be aware of the principles and be appreciative of the effectiveness of methods found in behavior analysis.

"People seem almost eager to find ways to increase motivation and learning in their lives; just look at the growing popularity of nudging. We know behavior analysis offers much of what they want, but I don't see mechanisms for effectively disseminating behavioral practices. I want to see ordinary folks and leaders become aware of science-based methods they could use to improve all of our lives. I know, it might sound like a fool's errand, but that's what I'd like to see."

Lisa offered, "I think you are saying differently a sort-of motivation I have had for as far back as I can remember. Even as a girl in Sweden and throughout college and work, I have felt an urge to address problems facing people. I guess I have always cared about human wellbeing. Frankly, most of my life I have felt I did not have any real answers or strategies for improving the wellbeing of people or for improving the effectiveness of systems.

"But as an outgrowth of my association with you, and learning about the fundamentals of behavior analysis by reading and interacting with our Thursday group – and conducting the early childhood intervention project – I feel confident I have found in the analysis of behavior the basic answers for improving quality of living."

Rob smiled and leaned toward Lisa, saying, "I appreciate that very much. It is important to have colleagues to share visions or frustrations and to work with to accomplish constructive efforts."

"Well, let's share more," said Lisa, "Let's form a team and design a comprehensive research, development and technical assistance 'center' to promote the widespread understanding and utilization of behaviorally-sound practices for systems change. We can start by seeking funding from Federal and private funding sources. As funds are obtained, we will attract interdisciplinary faculty and support staff and conduct systems-change programs."

"I'd love to do what you are suggesting. Maybe the Thursday group can be expanded in membership to integrate perspectives of social, economic, health, nutrition and other disciplines, then this group could serve as the Steering Committee for developing the proposed center," Rob said with tones of conviction in his voice.

Lisa looked directly at Rob and said, "I will talk with folks in my department, Psychology, and suggest that I be appointed into the new 'nudge and nudging' faculty line. While talking with leadership folks I will test the idea of the center we are thinking about. If they seem genuinely supportive, I'll take the faculty appointment if they offer it. Of course, that would make a lot of sense for moving forward with an interdisciplinary center and for promoting articulation between behavior analysis and psychology faculty."

Rob smiled broadly, but with a playful expression, and said, "Sounds wonderful – really – but I gotta tell you, if you are going to be pushing nudges you *must also push boosts!* I am almost finished writing a book designed to foster understanding of human behavior and illustrating constructive applications of the principles of behavior analysis in effective and appropriate ways.

"I'm using the terms nudge *and* boost, together, in the book so readers will understand the science behind these terms. I am hoping readers will see and make everyday uses of nudging *and* boosting to improve their lives."

"Really!" enthused Lisa, "I'll need that book, but how hard are you going to be on the concept of nudge? If you slam nudging too hard in favor of promoting the fact that antecedents bring about behaviors, then your book won't be of much use to me."

"Oh, exactly!" countered Rob, "My book is designed to be informative and constructive. I want readers to be better equipped to deal constructively with their own and others' behaviors by recognizing the dynamics of teaching or learning and maintaining desired behaviors.

"I must make it clear that nudges do not cause 'choosing' that, in turn, 'causes' behaving. Rather nudges precede all behaviors, which sometimes are behaviors of choosing, and it is consequences, the boosts, that select or build the nudged behaviors. We know this as a crucial distinction; it is not 'choosing' that 'causes' behaving because choosing *is* behaving. I will describe it is antecedents, we might call them nudges, that set the occasion for behaving and they have their power due to a history of differential reinforcement. I will try to get readers to understand that nudges cum antecedents have their influence over behaviors because of motivational circumstances and a history of learning.

"At the bottom line I want readers to appreciate the dynamics underlying what people learn and do, and have abilities to make constructive use of these dynamics. I think I can clarify what nudges are, and I really must describe the fact that nudges get their power from 'boosts.' My overall message will be something like, 'Nudges get behaviors, that is, doing, but Boosts give nudges their power, and they build and maintain doing.'"

"Well," said Lisa, "good luck with that. I look forward to reading your book and telling you how effective it appears to be at promoting nudging *and* boosting for better living."

[11]

Nudge and Boost Wisely for Better Living

WELCOME TO THE BEHAVIORAL 1%!
ASSUMING YOU DIGESTED A good amount from the previous 10 chapters, you know more about how behaviors are learned and favorably altered than almost everyone! You are basically oriented toward making important parts of your life more positive. By this I mean you are aware of some principles of behavior and key lessons for using them so you could apply this information to obtain important features of a better life.

Reflect on the following points:

- ☐ You can be more successful at getting others, or yourself, to do what you want because you know some basics about antecedents, that is, Nudge and nudging.

- ☐ You can Boost learning and performances of others or yourself because you know that contingent reinforcement "boosts" the behaviors that precede it.

☐ You are basically equipped to understand and deal constructively with a wide range of learning and motivational situations by referring to the Four-term Contingency and The
Consequences Box.

☐ You know, in brief, that "A-B-C works;" all of us are variously motivated and our behaviors are learned and altered
by the effects of Antecedents before Behaviors followed by
Consequences.

☐ Based on the above, you could adopt a more positive, constructive behavioral view of life as offering teaching and learning
opportunities in all directions: You could choose to Nudge
and Boost Wisely for Better Living for yourself and others.

Pretty heady stuff, right; to be in the top 1% of those with science-
based knowledge related to bringing about more successes through
better behavioral living? But before we get carried away, remember
the 99% don't know much from the perspective of research-founded principles, and some members of your 1% know a large amount
about the science of behavior. And recall the comments of Rob and
Bert regarding the differences between knowing and doing. Relative
to most folks, you *know* a great deal about the principles that underlie
establishing and altering behaviors of all sorts, but you still lack tools
for *doing*. The following sections are designed to help you in deciding
what you would like to do and assist you with doing it better.

PERSPECTIVES ON DOING NUDGES AND BOOSTS FOR BETTER LIVING

The purposes of this "dramatized semi-autobiographical save-
the-world textbook" include informing about the science of behavior
and motivating for the constructive use of behavioral principles. The
terms Nudge and Boost are used to encourage a comfortable appreciation for the impacts our environments have on us as we conduct
our everyday lives. Hopefully, this appreciation will encourage read-

ers to use Nudges *and* Boosts in their precise forms to improve learning and performance of themselves and others.

The natural science and principles of behavior analysis underlying the concepts of Nudge and Boost were introduced so readers could be better prepared to look at their own lives more systematically; to notice features of environments that set the occasion for emitting behaviors and understand the impacts of consequences on behaviors. With this organized view of daily activities, readers could speculate about how everyone's learning and behaving are being, or could be, affected by impacts of the principles of behavior. In this regard, the following fundamental perspectives on using what you know about behavioral processes are offered for your consideration.

Adopt a Behavior-Logical Perspective. If you start with the assumptions that behavior is everything we do and behavior is a function of its consequences, then you are well on your way to understanding and building behaviors of interest. You might extend this foundation of understanding and adopt a behavior-logical perspective on living, including applying basic behavioral strategies for being more observant and effective at home, work, and in the community. Overall, you could use some elemental behavioral strategies for establishing desirable skills and performances by children, teachers, coworkers, bosses, politicians; everyone, and yourself. The behavior-logical actions you or any of us might make to promote better living should involve continuing reference to the principles, lessons, and guidelines offered earlier and in this chapter, so our actions are both effective and appropriate.

Nudge Self and Others Better. Nudging "better" can be judged with regard to the qualities of the behaviors to be aroused by the nudge or the quality of the nudge. Assuming a desirable behavior was identified, then a nudge or other form of antecedent should be explicitly identified as the condition under which the behavior or an acceptable approximation is to occur and be reinforced.

We know a nudge or other form of antecedent is the first aspect of an A-B-C event, that is, an intentional nudge is provided to bring about a behavior that should be reinforced. Why nudge a behavior (e.g., to show polite behavior or begin to study or be on-time to a meeting) if you do not want to strengthen or maintain it with intentional and differential consequences? And we know nudges and other antecedents obtain their influence over behavior as an outgrowth of the consequences following behaviors, therefore, consequence delivery is crucial for giving the power to the nudge and building or maintaining desired behaviors.

Early in establishing or strengthening a behavior, antecedents should be clear ("Please help me clear the dishes from the table and put them in the sink.") and obvious (e.g., speak clearly, at a good volume, while making eye contact or demonstrating the desired behavior) and behaviors should be reinforced quickly and frequently ("Thank you for your help. The table looks nice."). After behaviors occur reliably at one intensity of antecedent it can be reduced in extent or intensity (e.g., just eye contact at the end of dinner to nudge clearing the table). Of course, when desirable behaviors occur, they should be followed by a consequence (boost) to strengthen or maintain them.

Incidentally, similar to reducing the intensity of nudges after behavior is established, the consequences can be provided less frequently. Behavior analysts call the procedure of reducing antecedents "fading" and reducing the frequency of reinforcement "leaning;" both should be done gradually.

Identifying nudges is a challenge. If you try to write a list of the nudges you experience or provide in a day you no doubt will quickly determine this is an impossible task; there are too many potential or actual nudges or other forms of antecedents in our environments to count. We are surrounded and immersed in sights and sounds that indicate behaviors that should or could be done, whether or not these behaviors are appropriate at the time. For example, a light switch is a nudge to turn it on or off, a flower is a nudge to pick or smell it, a chair is a nudge to walk around or sit in it, books or signs are nudges to read them, a nearby person exudes nudges for smiling, frowning, talking, leaving the area, getting to work, etc., and so on and on.

The point is, most aspects of our environments are nudges for some behaviors, but are only appreciated as nudges under two conditions. First, when we select them to be nudges, as when we plan to apply that nudge to get ourselves or another person to behave as we desire. Or, second, when we *attempt* to *identify* a nudge after we see a behavior of interest occur and wonder why. For example, a driver reduces speed near an intersection featuring a traffic light, a "Caution" sign, pedestrians and other cars nearby; which was/were the nudge(s) for slowing? Or, a shopper selects to buy broccoli from a table heaped with broccoli, labeled with a "Sale" sign, displaying recipe cards, and other shoppers are picking vegetables from the table. Which are the nudges? In the first case, traffic engineers might be interested, but in the second instance grocery store managers or nutritionists should be interested.

Suspected nudges become important when we want to make use of them to obtain a behavior, or we want to explain why certain behaviors occur. It appears that people now using nudging as a strategy to obtain desired behaviors guess at what might be effective as a nudge then apply it. For example, telling pilots they can reduce fuel consumption by reducing flying speed and taxiing with just one engine might prompt them to alter their practices and be reflected in reduced fuel usage (the outcomes of behaviors, *which should be maintained by consequences*). If the behavior of interest was affected after the presumed nudge, then it was a nudge.

At the bottom line, better nudging involves the following:

☐ Select the behavior(s) that should occur after a nudge

☐ Select a socially and situationally appropriate and controllable feature of the environment to serve as a nudge

☐ Provide the nudge at an intensity likely to be effective at obtaining the behavior

☐ Provide reinforcement (a boost) when the behavior follows the nudge closely in time

☐ Fade the nudge and lean the boosts as the behavior remains strong

It is well to remember you (and we) are being nudged and boosted many times every day. This means your behavior is being altered in probability by aspects of your environment, including people around you or the contingencies they have arranged, for example, by policies or procedures at work or in your community. As a member of the behavioral 1% you are better prepared to detect and arrange nudges. If you do so with regard to increasing behaviors you judge to be more desirable, your life will be improved by experiencing more desirable behaviors.

Boost Self and Others Better. You can Boost better by being behaviorally systematic in selecting and building the value of consequences, and delivering them correctly. The Consequences Box can be helpful for keeping a record of the positive and negative aspects of the environments you and those whose behavior you wish to change experience. As I did in classrooms, you can observe for activities that appear to be enjoyable or ask for input about what seems reinforcing and build a "menu" of these items you can use to strengthen behaviors.

Remember, the events surrounding the delivery of reinforcement (or punishment) take on some characteristics of those positive (or negative) events. This means words, gestures, sights and sounds occurring when reinforcements (or punishments) occur become more (or less) effective as consequences. Knowing this, you can understand that words, for example, "thank you" or "stop that" or "great job" or "I appreciate you," are built to be positive or negative as a function of being paired with reinforcement or punishment. You can improve your boosting by using confirmed positive consequences and "pairing" the delivery of reinforcements with words that should be positive.

> *The way positive reinforcement is carried out is more important than the amount – B F Skinner.*

A fundamental key for good boosting is a good definition of the behaviors being sought or to be strengthened. Beyond that, proper contingencies are crucial for good boosting. Be thoughtful in determining what consequences will follow which behaviors. Do you want to establish good study habits for yourself or your children, or build respect and tenacity, teach a love of books, or increase timeliness? In any case, define *the behaviors you want,* then, *arrange for contingent reinforcement* to follow approximations and criterion performances for those behaviors. More about major social behaviors is offered below; at this point suffice to say good boosting comes from careful planning and applying better contingencies that can result in better learning and living.

Use Nudges AND Boosts for Better Living. We are well aware that behavior is a function of its consequences so we must actively manage contingencies and the involved consequences to efficiently establish, strengthen, and maintain desired skills and performances. Also, we know nudges and other types of prompts indicate a particular behavior is likely to be followed by a particular category of consequences. Together, nudges and boosts can increase the likelihood and strengthen desired skills and performances.

Notably, the sequence of nudge-behavior-boost, that is, A-B-C events, builds the power of the nudge to bring about behavior at the same time that sequence serves to build the behavior. Because of a behavioral phenomenon called *generalization,* environmental features that are similar to "trained" nudges are able to indicate when behaviors might be reinforced. For example, we learn to push on doors with flat plates facing us, and are likely to push on all doors featuring relatively flat-appearing knobs or surfaces. In other words, new nudges can be effective because they are similar to other nudges that have been associated with consequences. This fact is an important tool for understanding why nudges work and how new nudges can be effective.

Incidentally, a behavioral principle called *discrimination* serves to narrow or sharpen the power of certain features of the environment to increase or decrease the likelihood of behaviors occurring. Possibly, over numerous experiences with doors, you learn that knobs with wider areas where fingers might be inserted are to be pulled, but where the finger-space is limited the door should be pushed. You may recall from the Glossary, discriminations are built by differential reinforcement, meaning certain behaviors are reinforced under some conditions and not under others. Think about your experiences with struggling to open doors with varying knobs correctly to recognize the impacts of generalization and discrimination on the door-opening class of behaviors.

We learn many discriminations, like to stop at red lights or follow signs to our luggage at the airport, and many generalizations, like to stop at all Stop signs and follow directions in all airports. The learning of generalizations and discriminations are very important aspects of our histories of learning, for example, they are fundamental behavioral processes for learning concepts in that a concept can be seen as a generalized discrimination or a discriminated generalization!

The bottom line is, we are constantly being affected by our motivational circumstances and the A-B-Cs impinging on us, which we might translate into an N-db-B depiction. Knowing this you are better equipped for improving learning and performances by others and yourself by taking advantage of opportunities to use both Nudges and Boosts for better behavioral living.

Deal Better with Matters of Living. We are surrounded, or I might say faced by opportunities to greatly improve our lives through better behaving. Because we know behavior is a function of its consequences, we know arranging better contingencies will result in improved learning and performance. This fact of nature is both empowering and frustrating; we know how to improve matters of importance, but seem to lack the necessary *control* over systems or ourselves to realize this attractive problem-solving potential. We know (generally) how to increase our attendance at the gym, or improve important behaviors of our children, and make public education more effective, or get politicians to do what we want them to accomplish, but we seem to lack the self-control or influence over the systems needed to actually make things improve.

Think again. Who knows better how to change behavior than you? You are in the 1%! You are better prepared than most people for improving the performance of others or yourself.

"It's not behavior modification, it's environmental modification." (Cf. Greer, 1989, p.69)

You can succeed with Self Control using the A-B-Cs of human behavior. Self Control simply means you, yourself, do the behavior change activities to bring about your own learning or performance. You can Nudge yourself, for example, say aloud, "No worries – I don't have to drive fast, the meeting won't start without me." Or, post notes telling you things to do in can't-miss locations, like a note poking out of your wallet, posted on the bathroom mirror or in your car on the dashboard or seat; or place suitcases in the way so you cannot miss them for travel. And reinforce yourself after you notice you did well; say "Good job" or "That solved a problem!" or put a check mark on your "Jobs Accomplished" chart or admire that the bathroom scales show a weight loss.

If you make self control arrangements correctly, then you will see progress and successes because motivation plus A-B-C works. Similar to any systematic behavior change process, self control requires you complete the following activities:

☐ Define desired behavior in measurable terms. If it is a big target, then break the steps to the final performance into smaller defined pieces.

☐ Identify consequences you desire and how to deliver these to yourself after you observe a desired behavior you do.

☐ Keep data on visits to the gym (or whatever) and for each step in your progression to desired levels of exercise (or whatever).

☐ Build your performance in progressive behavioral steps with prompts and contingent reinforcements for each step. Maybe, if you are a very reluctant gym visitor, an early step might be to just visit the gym, look-in, then, get a cup of coffee (if that is a reinforcing consequence for you). The next step might be to sit and chat with a pleasant person at the gym while looking at pieces of exercise equipment. Subsequent steps toward criterion performance might include you walking slowly on a treadmill for a couple of minutes or taking a few strokes on the rowing machine. Each successful behavior of yours should be followed closely in time by selected consequences, which might include immediately recording your data then going for coffee with a friend.

☐ Seeing your progressive successes and reaching your target should have reinforcing properties, but this does not obviate you from reinforcing yourself with consequences you selected earlier.

☐ Self control can be a powerful tool for you to use to improve your own performance. When you think about it systematically, that is, behavior-logically, it makes sense that if you are not controlling the A-B-Cs in your life other people or regularly occurring environmental events are. You can observe your environment for contingencies impacting your learning and performance, and alter those contingencies or apply your own to favorably impact your own circumstances.

You can build successes with and for others using the A-B-Cs of human behavior. Building or refining the behaviors of others follows the same sequence, that is: Define behaviors; Identify consequences (maybe using The Consequences Box) and a system for delivering them; Develop contingencies; Observe for behavioral occurrences; Deliver consequences; and, Keep data to assess baseline and successes and to detect needs for refining aspects of the intervention, including altering behavioral requirements, confirming consequences, or delivering them better.

Three types of contingencies might be applied to build desired behaviors. The contingencies you apply to others might be formal, informal or incidental.

☐ Formal contingencies must be written and include precise descriptions of the A-B-Cs involved

☐ Informal contingencies should include functional recognition of the A-B-Cs to be activated

☐ Incidental teaching might involve observing for or arranging As, but centers on observing for desired Bs and immediately delivering Cs.

You might apply your basic understanding of the sample of behavioral principles introduced in this text to deal better with activities or challenges of daily living. For example, you could use your knowledge of A-B-Cs to develop a useful appreciation for such behaviors as texting while driving or staring at the phone all the time or drivers following too closely or police interacting with citizens; in fact, all human behavior that intrigues you.

Note I say "appreciation" of behavior, not an analytical understanding of complex behaviors or the full array of principles that occur around us. You are *better* equipped to understand and deal with behavioral matters by recognizing the A-B-Cs involved, but not fully equipped to analyze or alter behaviors. A powerful matrix of principles and phenomena have been documented by science, but not completely mentioned here due to limitations. Nonetheless, you could, and I think you should, use the A-B-Cs offered in this text to improve your use of prompting and reinforcement, that is, Nudging AND Boosting, to benefit yourself and others you care about.

There might be circumstances when you conclude that the nature or importance of the behavioral matters facing you warrant assistance from someone with higher-order skills in the analysis of behavior. Obtaining assistance from a Board Certified Behavior Analyst, especially one with applied experience in a particular topic, might not be easy in the U.S. because there are only a few thousand behavior analysts available. I encourage you to seek and find a certified behavior analyst whenever necessary, even if that might be a bit challenging. But the scarcity of skilled behavior analysts in the U.S. is nothing compared to the situation in India where there are only 18 certified behavior analysts for a population of nearly 1.3 billion citizens; about 1 behavior analyst for every 60 million persons!

Guidelines for Doing Nudge and Boost for Better Living

Following are basic guidelines and activities for applying behavioral principles. These guidelines are only generally advisory in nature. To become competent with behavioral interventions requires adequate training and supervised experiences as indicated by the Behavior Analyst Certification Board and skills indicated in the helpful book co-authored by Jon Bailey, "*25 Essential Skills & Strategies for the Professional Behavior Analyst.*" We can assume most folks are not motivated or situated to complete training sufficient for becoming certified, but would like to be more effective at making changes in behavior that are favorable for their life circumstances.

Below are considerations and practical actions you might want to know related to successfully using some behavioral methods. But knowing the following Guidelines is not doing them. The proof of *knowing* is in the doing, that is, actually behaving in accordance with the Guidelines and receiving supportive or corrective feedback. Of course, the true test of your doing is in the effects your actions have on selected behaviors.

Guideline: Behave as though you know A–B–C Works. Science has confirmed the principles of behavior operate on all us of us all of the time; like gravity and digestion do, that is, constantly. The natural truth is we are effected by the consequences following our behaviors whether or not we are aware of the consequences or the relationship between behaviors and consequences. This truth, that "A-B-C Works," need not be believed, but should be practiced to realize the advantages for better living that come from better nudging and boosting.

Practical Exercises. The following activities may be useful for practicing behaving as though A-B-C works:

☐ Observe around you for examples that antecedents surround all of us, and what we do are behaviors and they are followed by changes in our environments called consequences.

☐ Watch for different types of Antecedents, like posted **signs** ("Enter Here"), spoken **words** ("Your turn" or "Come here") or **structured situations** (e.g., orange cones closing a road lane; plastic rope demarking a waiting line to stand in; doors with open handles or flat plates indicating how to open the door), or your own **model of desired behavior** (speaking calmly; clearing dishes from the dinner table); think about how clearly these antecedents indicate what behaviors are appropriate.

☐ Analyze the nudges you observe for how clearly they direct behavior. For example, the appearance of doorknobs vary in how clearly they indicate how to operate them; some are curved toward you and labeled "Pull" while others do not seem to indicate whether a pull or push is appropriate.

☐ Listen to spoken nudges for how descriptive these are for what behaviors should be shown and when.

☐ Think about how the nudges you observed could be made more clearly directive as antecedents for desired behavior.

☐ Watch people around you and try to *classify* the behaviors you see into categories, like, "following directions," or "being productive," or "solving a problem."

☐ Identify a category of behavior, like "following directions," or "being productive," or "solving a problem" and watch for behaviors that *exemplify* those labels for behaviors, then write behavioral descriptions of them in terms that can be observed and measured.

☐ Practice recognizing labels for desirable behaviors, like he is "patient" or "reliable" or "shows a good attitude" and translating these into constituent behaviors that are observable and measurable.

☐ Share your observations and definitions with others; ask if they agree with your definitions and agree the defined behaviors could be reliably observed and measured.

☐ Watch behaviors and note the environmental changes immediately following them; classify those consequences into the cells of The Consequences Box.

You can have confidence that behaviors can be understood and established or altered with reference to the motivational circumstances and A–B–Cs in our lives. With practice you can see As, Bs and Cs occurring around you frequently and you can get an objective handle on them. This realization is an early step toward using tools of behavior science to make environmental changes that bring about desirable changes in behavior.

Guideline: Be Measurably Clear About What Behaviors You Want. Your interest in understanding or altering behaviors might range from curiosity through a felt need to be effective at getting yourself or others to behave more favorably. For example, you might want to encourage your son to study more, or to increase your attendance at the gym, or make your spouse happier, or motivate a co-worker to be more productive.

According to this Guideline, your initial action toward achieving improved behavior is building a useful definition of the behavior you wish to change or establish. Regarding the changes just mentioned, you would have to define "study," or "attendance," or "happier," or "productive" in terms that are directly observable and measurable. None of those labels is a measurable behavior, so not open to direct intervention, but "happier," might translate into "smile and say (specific) words indicating happiness," and "study" translate into "seated at study desk with materials present and appearing to be reading or writing," and the like.

The following actions should be helpful for selecting and defining behavioral objectives.

- ☐ Determine the functional value of the behavior of interest: What is the desired behavior supposed to accomplish? How does the behavior to be taught or strengthened contribute to the learner's quality of life?
- ☐ To develop definitions of behaviors to be established or changed:
- ☐ Directly observe related current behaviors and keep descriptive notes
- ☐ Use photos or videos as examples of desired behavior and write descriptions of measurable aspects of these pictured behaviors

☐ Write the definition of desired approximations and criterion behavior(s) using descriptive terms that can be seen or heard or otherwise measured

☐ Validate your definitions by asking the learner and others for input regarding the functional value and contributions to quality of life of selected behavior(s); and, ask for input or agreement that your definitions are behavioral and measurable.

Practical Exercises: Answer the question: "Can I see it, not just hear about it?"

Remember the cautionary saying, "All verbal reports are lies," which alerts us to use behavioral definitions that are directly observable; not rely on what the learner or others say about the occurrences of behavior. To test how measurable a definition is, read it aloud and ask yourself or listeners, "With this definition, could the desired behavior be recognized reliably without reliance on verbal reports?" Show a video or personally demonstrate the selected behavior and ask, "Does my definition match the behavior, and is my definition narrowly specific enough so other behaviors are excluded?

Note: For defining complex behavior, tools including Critical Incidence Observation and Task Analysis (see *Figuring Things Out, Zamke & Kramlinger*, 1982) or procedures called Chains and Chaining (See *Applied Behavior Analysis*, Copper, Heron & Heward, 2007) could be used, but these procedures require more training than provided here.

Guideline: Be Clear about Nudges or other Antecedents related to Behaviors. Environmental events that occur before behaviors are known to include motivational operations and antecedent stimuli. In earlier chapters you learned MOs function to increase or decrease the value of consequences and increase or decrease the likelihood of behaviors that previously earned those consequences. Antecedents are features in the environment that indicate what behaviors may or may not be reinforced or punished. Antecedents with a history of coming before behaviors that were reinforced serve to increase the occurrence of those behaviors. Antecedents range from subtle (hints) to more obvious (nudges) to very obvious (directives and structure).

For ease of discussion, we can refer to mild intensity antecedents as nudges. It seems from various literatures that nudges commonly are either (a) situations arranged so desired behaviors are more likely, as in placing fruit prominently in a cafeteria line, or (b) are instructions, like telling pilots how they can use less fuel.

Practical Exercises: Answer the question, "Is it clear from a particular nudge/antecedent stimulus what exact behavior is desired, when and how much and are there any quality indicators?"

- ☐ Select behaviors of interest and list for each your guesses regarding what might be effective nudges to elicit each behavior.
- ☐ For each nudge you listed, write how you might increase its potency, for example, enhancing the auditory (e.g., louder; attractive or varying tones) or visual intensity (e.g., brighter; attractive color; flashing or spinning) or physical prominence (e.g., place where the nudgee routinely walks; post at eye level; hang on bathroom mirror; attach to car keys).
- ☐ Write notes about where and when you desire the behavior occur, and about what consequences (boosts) you expect to occur or be delivered after the behavior.
- ☐ Do some nudging and observe how often the behavior occurs soon after the nudge.

Guideline: Select Effective Consequences to use for Boosting. The Consequences Box illustrates the effects on behaviors of more (presenting) or less (removing), positive or negative features of the environment immediately following those behaviors. Two cells in that box are indicated as being reinforcing operations, namely, adding positive or reducing negative after a behavior. For the purposes of this text, we can call these two types of reinforcing operations Boosting.

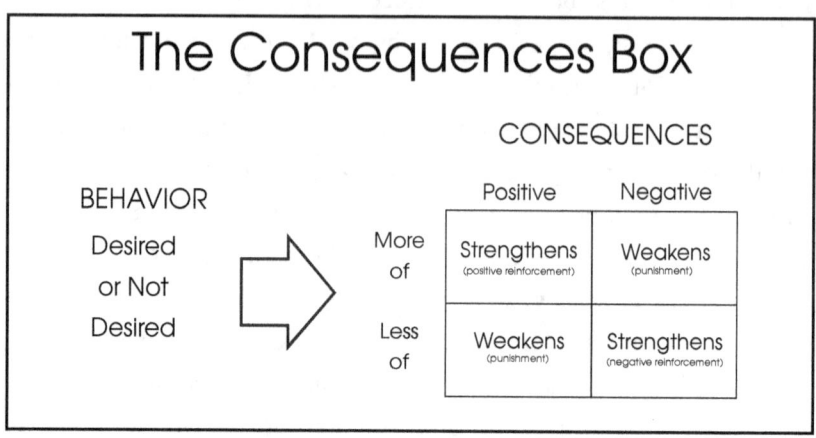

Effective boosting requires effective consequences be delivered or removed effectively. The effectiveness of consequences comes from their relationship to the motivational status of the learner and the learner's behavioral history with the particular consequence. At the same time, the accuracy of delivery of the consequence, namely, timely and consistent, is crucial for effectiveness. The only real test of the effects of a consequence and its delivery is to see how it changes the behavior it immediately follows. If the behavior is changed in accordance with the labeled cell of The Consequences Box, then the effectiveness of the tested consequence is confirmed.

Practical Exercises: Think Inside the Box! Have a version of The Consequences Box at hand.

- ☐ Watch for behaviors you would classify as Desired or Not Desired.
- ☐ Observe for More or Less of Positive or Negative features of the environment following behaviors.
- ☐ Enter notes on The Consequences Box diagram in the correct cell to indicate the consequence(s) you observe.

☐ Think about how the consequences probably effected the behaviors that preceded them; were Desired behaviors strengthened or Not Desired behaviors weakened?

You could play a "Fill In The Box" game with others, that is, with The Consequences Box at hand, discuss with others what consequences are and keep a list of nominated consequences and whether folks think these should be presented or reduced to strengthen behaviors. The Consequences Box can be a powerful tool for building and maintaining skills and performances you desire: Think *Inside* The Box.

Guideline: Take and Use Data. After you have definitions of the behaviors you plan to teach or alter, and before nudging or boosting is begun, you should observe for how much of that behavior is shown. This measurement is called Baseline; it is the starting point, upon which the effects of prompting and reinforcing behaviors can be assessed. Taking data on Desired or Not Desired behaviors before attempting to intervene has several virtues. The activity of taking data serves to test your definitions and your observation methods. If either is deficient, that shortcoming will become apparent while attempting to observe and measure behaviors of interest. Upon this base of experience you can refine definitions and the ways you observe the behaviors. Also, taking data clarifies the extent of the problem, that is, provides an objective basis for judging the seriousness of the problem. Finally, while taking data you can watch for or tentatively confirm consequences that seem to be effecting current behaviors and might be used while intervening.

You may recall I observed in classrooms for the use of consequences by teachers in 10- or 20-minute blocks of time. I recorded this type of teacher behavior by putting a mark on a sheet of paper featuring 20 horizontal lines cutting across vertical columns labeled Appropriate and Inappropriate (Student behavior) and Positive and Negative (Consequences) under each type of behavior. After observing and marking what I saw or heard for 10 or 20 minutes, I could count the number of entries for positive and negative consequence delivery occurring after what I judged to be appropriate (desired) or inappropriate (not desired) student behaviors. These data disclosed the types and frequencies of consequences the teacher provided to students and the accuracy of her or his behavior, that is, the match or mismatch (errors) with regard to desired or not desired student behaviors being followed by positive or negative consequences.

After baseline rates and ratios of consequence delivery by each teacher were recorded, I intervened in each classroom by modeling on several occasions a good rate of accurate consequence delivery. I also continued to take data nearly every day. These daily data showed teacher delivery of accurate positive consequences increased greatly and the use of negative consequences dropped to (usually) zero within a few weeks.

My data showed me the nature of teacher behaviors at the beginning and during intervention. Weeks and months later I took data in the same way to determine how well teachers were continuing to use consequences related to student behaviors. These maintenance data indicated my intervention was effective in that teacher behaviors of accurate consequence delivery were continued over the long run. Of course, we also collected many types of student behaviors to gauge the effects on them related to changes in teacher behaviors. The results were very good as was reported in an earlier chapter.

You might conclude that by collecting data you are better informed about the nature of behaviors of interest and the situations surrounding them. You can objectively assess the starting point and progress occurring after you make arrangements to improve learning or performance.

Please note that taking and using data is a topic of great importance in the field of behavior analysis. Many published papers, chapters and books address this crucial matter. My brief comments offered here can be only suggestive.

Practical Exercises:

☐ Select a defined behavior of interest.

☐ Determine *when* you will observe occurrences of this behavior, essentially, watch for it, at a particular time (e.g., 8:00 to 8:30 AM) or circumstance (e.g., at the dinner table; during team meetings) or collect products of behavior (e.g., Math worksheets; written work, like poems or stories; quality of performance, for example, level of cleanliness of room).

☐ Decide *how* you will collect data, for example, by direct observation, that is, watching the behavior, or by reviewing video to count or time or evaluate the quality of defined behaviors; or by reviewing the quality of products, like evaluating the cleanliness of an area by examining the area and completing a valid "room cleanliness" checklist.

☐ Select a way you will *compile* and *review* the data, for example, you can use graph paper or a computer program for entering and displaying data points and the overview of all the data collected.

☐ Decide *what* you will do with these data, for example, share them with the person(s) involved; evaluate the extent and time course of behavior changes; decide to discontinue, revise or continue the intervention.

Guideline: Arrange Formal Contingencies, Identify Informal Contingencies, and Use Incidental Teaching. You recall a contingency is the relationship between a behavior and the consequences that follow it. Contingencies might be formally developed into explicit statements describing what behaviors will receive particular consequences under identified circumstances. For example, a formal statement of a contingency might be: "When my son is seated at his study desk, with study materials at hand and apparently interacting with them, I will say positive things to him." Informal contingencies might be self-spoken and less precise, for example, "I'll watch for Frank being polite and show my appreciation." Incidental teaching involves being generally observant and providing reinforcement after noticing desirable behaviors occur. For example, a parent might notice one of their children saying or doing something nice and immediately express appreciation and give her or him a hug.

Practical Exercises: Prepare a document into three columns, headed Desired Behaviors, Antecedents and Consequences. Under the first heading write desired behaviors in terms of observable and measurable features. Under the Antecedents heading, and aligned with each behavior, write a noticeable feature in the learner's environment after which the behavior should occur. In the third column, Consequences, write for each behavior the consequence you will provide and how it will be delivered.

- ☐ Observe for the behaviors on your list and take data, that is, note when and how many of them you notice.
- ☐ After getting Baseline data, provide reinforcement following any of the listed behaviors.
- ☐ Continue taking data and see if the reinforced behaviors occur more frequently (Note: If the behaviors do not increase, then by definition they were not being reinforced.).

If "reinforced" behaviors did not increase, then you might want to keep taking data and change the consequence until you discover, that is, your data show, you are using an effective consequence effectively.

Guideline: Be Positive – Immediate – Consistent. Humans learn relatively quickly, therefore, well-delivered effective consequences should begin changing behavior soon – check your data – but, inaccuracies in applying consequences are likely to have undesirable impacts on behaviors, including lack of learning or learning a behavior not intended. In classrooms, we posted attractive signs to prompt

(Nudge) teachers to be: **Positive**, (Boost) following desired behaviors; **Immediate**, with consequences as soon as practical; and, **Consistent**, regarding what (types of) behaviors and the consequences they provided. These same considerations hold throughout teaching and learning; immediate positive consequences build behaviors, and consistency is a key to success in establishing and altering behaviors.

Practical Exercises: Select and define a behavior of a person or pet you wish to establish or strengthen.

- ☐ Select a positive consequence you know to be effective with your "subject."
- ☐ Write procedures you could use to deliver selected consequences immediately or deliver an intermediary (e.g., descriptive words; token; check mark; sound of a clicker) immediately following behavior.
- ☐ If using an intermediary reinforcer define a procedure for the timely exchange of the intermediary for the primary consequence (e.g., token exchange for a menu item).
- ☐ Observe for approximations to the behavior you want (remember the students shaping rats to bar press) and immediately present the known consequence along with some other stimulus you want to be positive, like spoken words, "Good dog" or sound of a clicker or "Thanks much" or "Great idea."
- ☐ Continue applying differential consequences, that is, boost desired behaviors under intended conditions and not others, to build the selected behavior until it reaches the criterion you set.

Guideline: Be Effective And Appropriate. You might recall from the Preface and implications throughout this book that scientific principles can be used for doing good or enabling evil; and, you should understand that behaviors are built and altered by the consequences of those actions including the use of scientific or other powers. *Appropriate* means actions are person-centered, community-referenced, and adaptive in the short-term and long run. *Effective* means behavioral actions are made with direct procedural reference to the principles involving motivational circumstances, antecedents to behavior, behavioral requirements, and consequence selection and delivery. Via this text, I can only encourage you to use what you know about changing behaviors to establish or strengthen behaviors that are desirable for the learner and our communities.

Practical Exercises: To assist with determining whether or not objectives and procedures identified for altering behavior are both effective and appropriate, you might consider or answer the following questions:

☐ Are the defined behaviors functional, that is, does emitting those behaviors accomplish something?

☐ Is that "something" desirable for the individual; family; community; and world?

☐ Does this intervention increase success or solve a problem in the short-term and avoid long-term loss?

☐ Have the intervention procedures been validated by single subject (or, "case" or "person-focused") research?

☐ Does the individual and concerned others see the objectives and procedures as appropriate?

☐ Are the procedures clearly developed so those who intervene or observe the intervention can completely understand them?

☐ Are interveners and quality assurance supervisors well trained, for example, are they Board Certified Behavior Analysts?

If to the above questions you can answer "yes" with conviction and comfort, then do what you can to cause such interventions to be incorporated into your own situation or the lives of others so the identified benefits may occur.

OPERATIONAL LEVELS FOR DOING BETTER NUDGING AND BOOSTING

Despite everything you have read above, you could (try to) do nothing behaviorally different. That is, you might decide to not Nudge or Boost any more or differently than you always have done. Of course, you recognize that everyone is frequently presenting nudges and boosts to those around them, for example, presenting words or models of behaviors or structuring the circumstances of others in ways that impact their behaviors. You say "Hi" or offer a snack or ask a question or open a door for someone, and they soon behave in some way; they say "Hi" or "Great to see you" or take the snack or say "No thanks" or walk through the door, smile and say "Thanks, much."

You have learned prompting and reinforcing strategies from the time you were an infant. Behaviorally speaking, this set of skills has been contingency-shaped over your lifetime so now you are just automatic in the ways you nudge and boost people. It is likely you fairly often casually nudge others, "please pass the salt," and sometimes are intentional and directive in prompting others, "be on time tomorrow, with the report completed."

Sometimes you might have wanted your neighbor or coworker or child or spouse to be a bit more positive or responsive with you, so you might have said a cheery "Hi" and waved, or offered an especially warm, "Good morning" and the like to "get them" to "respond" to you. In this case, what you want is for them to respond in a way you have generally determined, so you present nudges of various types and intensities. If you do not get a wave or "Hi" in return, you might get louder or closer or raise your hand higher and wave it more vigorously, until you get a response. That is, increasing the strength of nudges has been developed in you by a lifetime of contingencies to be an automatic feature of your behavior change repertoire.

But now you know nudges are antecedents related to increasing the occurrences of behavior and boosts are reinforcements that increase the strength of the behavior that antecedents elicited. You have learned that to increase the strength of a behavior, in the above case the "respond-to-you" behavior you prompted, you must cause reinforcing consequences to immediately follow those responses. So now, after learning about A-B-C, you know to be a better nudger and booster you should provide clear nudges or other type of antecedent to elicit the behavior, and follow the behavior with confirmed reinforcing consequences. The more you apply effective nudges and boosts, the more you contribute to behavioral progresses and successes as seen from the several perspectives noted below.

Better from a Personal perspective: You can be more positive and constructive. You can notice (take data on) how often you nudge or boost for improved learning or performance by yourself and others, and increase the frequency or level of positiveness. You know your behaviors set a model for those who observe you, so you can be more frequent in saying and doing things that demonstrate excellence or enthusiasm for what you are doing. You can routinely observe for improved performance by yourself or those you care about and offer constructive feedback or positive consequences; "Great job of . . ." ; "I appreciate . . ."). In short, you can be a better nudger and booster by being more alert to the antecedents and consequences for your own and others behaviors, and altering your actions and the environment in ways that favor desired learning and performance.

You might want to systematically approach life from a happiness perspective, that is, identify outcomes you desire, then, arrange contingencies for yourself and others that build behaviors that reach circumstances you desire. Possibly a helpful book to examine for ideas about happiness is *Gross National Happiness: Why Happiness Matters – and How We Can Get More of It* by Arthur Brooks. Of course, you will have to translate the ideas in that book or other sources into behavioral terms in order to work toward and achieve them.

Better from a Citizen perspective: Systems of government and programs of our communities were designed by people and are conducted by people. You know what people do are behaviors and behaviors are built and altered by consequences. To change governments and programs, people must change contingencies applied to those who are in policymaking and program operational roles. You can alter your own circumstances and you can find ways to alter the behaviors of others so they, in turn, learn and perform in more desirable ways.

You can be constantly alert or specifically observe for contingencies being applied to you and others to better understand why you and they behave as you and they do. You might be pleased or concerned about the likely impacts on learning or performance by the contingencies you detect. You can act supportively in favor of adaptive contingencies and attempt to rearrange contingencies you determine are counter-constructive.

You might have heard the attractive concept, "It takes a Village" to develop widespread desirable behaviors. We know from behavioral science, that to be effective, our villages must be behaviorally systematic villages, that is, places where contingencies support the adaptive and desirable behaviors of the inhabitants who, in turn, enact contingencies on one another that build and maintain desirable behaviors.

It is a social milieu of contingencies for adaptive behaviors that teaches and maintains the culture desired by the members of the social milieu. As part of this milieu, you can contribute by behaving in behavior-logical ways as you interact with others and when you have opportunities to influence the behavioral dynamics around you. Following is a "case note" that might serve to illustrate and stimulate thinking or discussions about many of the points raised in this chapter.

INDICATIONS OF COMMUNITY CONTINGENCIES

A small town in central Florida was widely known as a speed trap. Drivers who sped in that town were very likely to be stopped and ticketed. Of course, local drivers were more aware and cautious than were transients, who made up the bulk of the drivers stopped for infractions. Fairly often, during traffic stops the officer would discover other problems, like a meth lab in the back seat or an escaped felon in the front, or a runaway youth or burglary tools or weapons in sight so the officer would make an admirable arrest. These law enforcement accomplishments were well known locally and largely appreciated, but some of the "appreciation" was negative. Apparently, a few powerful folks who liked to speed but did not like tickets interceded with State officials such that State law was altered so this town could not afford to maintain its police force and it was dismantled. Before that change in law, very few aware drivers sped, but today many, maybe the majority of drivers exceed limits through town. And, of course, the powerful few speed right along with felons, burglars and meth lab operators, without interruption.

Because you know A-B-C works you understand the following circumstances and implied contingencies are likely to be operating in the community situation noted above:

- ☐ Town leadership desired slower traffic and good levels of revenue from tickets
- ☐ Police officers wanted jobs and paychecks, were hired and encouraged to strictly enforce speed limits
- ☐ Drivers who were aware of the law enforcement practices in the town obeyed the speed limit, avoided tickets and fines, so were (probably) boosted by negative reinforcement
- ☐ Unaware drivers often exceeded speed limits and were likely to be stopped and punished

□ Officers stopped speeders and enforced other laws; their actions generated revenue, increased public safety, and assured their continued employment and paychecks

□ Influential folks were annoyed by having to drive slowly and by occasionally being ticketed (although they probably escaped fines by – were boosted for – using their influence)

□ A powerful few folks (i.e., they control consequences) caused State law to be changed, police were fired and tickets were not written

□ Now the few can speed without worry and criminals can pass through town without experiencing strict law enforcement

Each of the above descriptive bullets could be confirmed and translated into more explicit statements of the motivations, As and Bs and Cs involved with this circumstance. These translations would clarify the constituent behavioral matters and allow better contingencies to be written and enforced. For example, the town leaders could more clearly specify what behaviors they desire of police officers and the reinforcement to follow them. But, the overriding contingent relationships begging for analysis and remediation are those motivational, behavior-consequences relationships operating on those who altered State law so the town could not operate a police force to enforce speed (and all other) laws.

From a behavior-logical view, the central problem in this case is one of power where power means the ability to control consequences. The influential few, who apparently acted in self-serving ways, probably controlled and arranged sufficient consequences on those who have the wherewithal to alter State law to obtain from them desired actions.

As an unusually knowledgeable citizen you might find ways to facilitate the rearrangement of contingencies so State law is altered in support of (strict) law enforcement. But this is only one "case note" out of the many you could identify within your daily living. Because you are a behaviorally informed citizen, you could act constructively to bring about better contingencies related to better living in your community.

In general, good citizens should advocate for improvements or excellence in how government and community programs are designed and conducted. You are basically equipped with behavior-logical tools helpful for analyzing programs for the nature and quality of contingencies they are applying. In turn, you can speculate in an informed manner about what behaviors those contingencies are likely to produce. If the contingencies seem to build Not Desired behaviors you might contribute to refining contingencies so Desired behaviors are strengthened.

A text that could be helpful for identifying some desirable community programs is one by Anthony Biglan, *The Nurture Effect: How the Science of Human Behavior can Improve Our Lives & Our World*. The programs he promotes and his vision for better living are admirable. Dr. Biglan is clear in advocating for programs that show adequate compliance with the principles of behavior to be effective and offers examples. I would caution you to find ways to examine and confirm the behavioral accuracy of those or any program before endorsing them, but you can always advocate for clear and positive contingencies to be present in all community programs.

Better from a Leadership perspective: "Leadership" can be seen as a label for a complex set of behaviors that serve to cause others to behave in ways that reach outcomes sought by the leader. Generally, a leader expresses a vision and values that inspire followers to excel in their roles and accomplish admirable things. Vision, values, and inspiration are concepts that can be clarified by behavior analysis, thereby, made understandable and teachable.

While managers "get work done through others," effective leaders have been seen by many as special people; gifted with unusual talents for arousing exceptional commitments and actions from those being led. An example of believing leaders are especially gifted people occurred one evening while I was teaching a graduate class on Leadership and Management. During a break period, the Dean stepped in the room and shared with us his conclusion that leadership cannot be taught. He said he saw leadership as a natural characteristic only a few possess. From his statement and other actions, we might conclude he was not among the possessed!

We can constructively understand leadership is a set of functional behaviors. Yes, behaviors affected by the genetic and physiological and learning history of the (actual or potential) leader, but nonetheless identifiable. While we can do little about genetics, we can understand that motivational circumstances, learning history and current A-B-Cs operate to elicit leadership behaviors. Leadership can be recognized as functional behaviors and those particular behaviors can be defined, studied, taught and learned.

Many books have been written about leadership and the several I have read offer valuable ideas or models related to being an effective leader. Generally, authors offer their contingency-shaped notions about how leaders appear on the scene or are effective. Consistent with the messages in this text, we can focus on extracting rules about how leaders obtain superior learning, commitment and performance from those about them.

Helpful guidance about some aspects of leadership is available in the book by Aubrey Daniels, *Bring Out the Best in People: How to apply the Astonishing Power of Positive Reinforcement*. Certainly, there is more to leadership than motivating and reinforcing excellent performances from those being led, but obtaining functional and desirable performances is a crucial skill of leadership.

By using what you know about nudging and boosting you can both build a better understanding of leadership and be better at building and supporting desired performances in those you lead.

Better from a Policymaking perspective: Consistent messages in this text are that behavior is everything we do and a single system of behavior science can be used to deal effectively with our problems or enhance our successes. With that as context, and by applying the themes and lessons offered above, we should understand that matters of policy are matters of behavior and contingencies. Policies involve statements regarding desired and undesired circumstances, supported or punished processes, and descriptions of relationships among laws, regulations, authorities, etc., purported to be promoting the wellbeing of our country and its residents.

A behavioral view of policies leads us to conclude a law or a practice should be clear in stating the measurable outcomes sought and the behaviors that are functional and desirable for reaching desired outcomes. For example, the outcome of banks making good loans involves behaviors of employees and associated consequences, maybe bonuses for providing loans where the person does have the ability to pay it back, but punishment for issuing bad loans.

It is important to note that behaviors of employees and citizens are the result of contingencies others apply, many of these via policies, laws, and regulation enforcement or the lack thereof. That is, it is leaders who put in place contingencies via policies and personal actions, whether they do it intentionally or not, are acting to bring about behaviors responsive to the contingencies, not necessarily the intentions of the policies. For example, according to Morgenstern and Rosner (2011) in *Reckless Endangerment: How Outsized Ambition, Greed and Corruption Led to Economic Armageddon*, the housing loan crisis appears to be an outgrowth of policies Congress and the White House imposed to increase home ownership.

We can assume those good-sounding policies generated contingencies on the loan-making industry for (the behaviors of) giving bad loans for which they were reinforced (with fees and approvals from the Washington establishment). Later most of us suffered from the results brought on by the bad behaviors these bad contingencies built. It is likely a competent behavior-logical analysis of this area of policy and bad performance could have discovered the specific and implied contingencies and advised for constructive alternatives.

As for any behavior change plan, policies and implementing regulations should:

☐ Define desired behavior in measurable terms.

☐ Identify consequences and how these will be delivered for desired and undesired behaviors.

☐ Keep data on performance quality indicators and criterion performances.

☐ Build performance with prompts and contingent reinforcements.

☐ Review data and refine intervention(s) as needed.

It is pragmatic and appropriate to recognize topics such as monetary policy, savings rates, crime and punishment, productivity, abusive banking practices, economic bubbles, welfare participation, health care, and immigration policies are only labels for issue areas encompassing complex areas of concern. But each and all of these issue areas comprise behaviors and differential consequences; all are open to clarification and design for effectiveness by applying principles of behavior science.

Policies should reflect the vision and values of the organization or country, and be structured so they implement contingencies that build behaviors that are adaptive and desirable for individuals and society. Paraphrasing what Skinner said, people build systems and the contingencies of systems build people. We all should use what we know to cause better contingencies to be implemented in all our systems to realize better living.

CLOSING CONSIDERATIONS

Fully *explaining* behaviors is a complicated endeavor, involving detailed definitions of the behaviors of interest followed by observations and manipulations of all aspects of the Four-term Contingency. However, *teaching* new behaviors or altering established behaviors varies from an easy task, as in just providing a nudge (and boost) for an existing behavior, to a very demanding challenge involving precise observations and the strategic use of antecedent and reinforcement actions to understand, teach, or alter behaviors of interest.

Knowing the general dynamics related to understanding or dealing constructively with human behavior can be fascinating and rewarding. This text is intended to intrigue readers into learning and doing more in behaviorally sound ways. Toward that end you might have recognized explicit or implied themes in the preceding chapters. Below, I briefly note some of those themes for your consideration or application in your behavioral-living circumstances.

Themes:

☐ Human behavior is everything we do and effected by the actions of principles found in the natural sciences including physics, biology, and behavior analysis.

☐ Effectiveness in understanding or accomplishing objectives for human behavior rests on the procedurally correct application of principles of behavior.

☐ Outcomes can be reached by developing operational and behavioral definitions and appropriate contingencies for functional behaviors.

☐ Power is the ability to control consequences; the more pervasively and explicitly, the more powerfully.

☐ Those who apply contingencies bear responsibility for the effects of them.

☐ Actions of selecting and working toward outcomes should include evaluating the short-term and long-term impacts on present and future quality of life.

☐ Be constructively skeptical; confirm programs and systems are behaviorally competent and conducted to be both effective and appropriate.

☐ You are better equipped for improving life by being intentional in applying Nudges and Boosts effectively and wisely.

You understand the meanings of these themes and other behavioral matters better than almost everyone because you are in the behavioral 1%. You are aware of the principles and dynamics involved in clarifying and improving matters of teaching, learning, and altering what people do. You can choose to apply what you know to improve your own circumstances or contribute to improving the world around you!

CLOSING MOTIVATIONAL OPERATIONS

Regarding general motivation for constructive efforts, many authors and sages have offered us wisdom apparently meant to guide our actions toward a better world.

"Beings are owners to their action, heirs of their action" – Buddha

"The quality, not the longevity, of one's life is what is important" – Martin Luther King

"For every minute you are angry you lose sixty seconds of happiness" – Ralph Waldo Emerson

"We either make ourselves miserable or we make ourselves strong. The amount of work is the same." – Carlos Castenda

"Do the best you can until you know better. Then, when you know better, do better" – Maya Angelou

"All labor that uplifts humanity has dignity and importance and should be undertaken with painstaking excellence." – Martin Luther King

"Don't work harder, work smarter" – anonymous

Happiness does not come readymade, it comes from your actions" – Dali Lama

"Every person deserves a healthy and productive life" – Gates Foundation

"The ideal of behaviorism is to eliminate coercion: To apply (contingencies) by changing the environment in such a way as to reinforce the kind of behavior that benefits everyone." – BF Skinner

Buddha and the rest are telling us we are responsible for what we do and what we do determines our future circumstances. Now that you have an understanding that our behaviors are a function of consequences, you can approach life and living with more tools for success. You can apply "behavior-logical" and "A-B-C" perspectives to *Nudge & Boost for Better Living*.

"Someday, a thorough knowledge of behavior techniques may become an accepted necessity in our culture and will be taught to children in elementary school . . Perhaps these children will grow up to see a world in which positive applications of behavior principles will be second nature to everyone and will result in a happy, informed, skillful, productive culture without war, poverty, prejudice, or pollution." (Martin and Pear, 2007, p.397).

EPILOGUE
Frasier, and Earth Abides

"There is only one problem on Earth; not enough good human behavior" (Rob to Frasier, *personal communication*, 2016)

Frasier was aware that about three decades ago, before most of the billions of people now on Earth were yet conceived, Dr. Douglas Greer was so moved by some of mankind's serious problems and his vision for solutions, that he wrote in 1989:

'The critical factor determining the survival of our species, and countless others, is the adequacy of the responses made by individuals and groups to the existing or future perils and challenges. If the responses are adequate we will survive and if they are better than adequate we may flourish. In earlier and less crowded times, survival was dependent on and taught directly and automatically by the features of the physical world. Little human mediation was required or possible. In a setting in which the physical world was unrestrained, that world selected the genetically (and behaviorally) fit and subsequently taught the survivors directly. As cultures, genetic pools, and behavior evolved . . , the physical world came to be increasingly countercontrolled by human intervention. Much of our prognosis for survival is related to environments by and for people. The development of adequate (or better) responses is in turn dependent on instruction that is intentional and effective. The result is that our very survival depends on the rapid development and broad application of sophisticated instruction" (p. 45).

Greer's words can be seen as direct and to the point; mankind is destroying itself, but could be saved by interventions that are, "intentional and effective." Frasier agreed with the concerns Greer and many other authors have expressed, of course, because he has monitored news and social media, and read the many data-based reports describing impending catastrophe (e.g., *Climate Summit 2014*): Rainforests upon which our climate is dependent being destroyed; fish species that used to feed millions now essentially extinct; glaciers melting and seas rising threatening cities; crucial habitats destroyed; many millions of humans around the globe starving and living in what amount to waste dumps; serious shortages of water and rainfall; wildlife disappearing at horrible rates; and on and on.

But Frasier understood all these problems are actually outcomes of behaviors built and maintained by individual and meta-contingencies. He completely agreed with Greer and his ilk that solutions, or rather strategies for solutions, are available in behavior science to address the challenges facing mankind. While Dr. Greer's paper was aimed directly at problems and practices in public education, Frasier recognized his recommendations were based on principles and methods found in the analysis of behavior so are valid and applicable for addressing all manner of human problems.

Many authors have emphatically described problems, presumably to motivate readers to do something corrective. But few of these authors offered reasonable and adequately specific descriptions of what should be done that would function to reduce the problems or replace those problems with desirable circumstances. Put differently, many humans might be motivated by books or reports or personal observations, but they are not given direction regarding what behaviors to emit or call for by others to actually alleviate problems.

Frasier knew that even if behaviors were sufficiently described, those desirable behaviors would not be learned and continued unless contingencies of reinforcement were applied at the individual level. Identifying and arranging consequences so people enjoy positive experiences for desirable behaviors is much easier said than done, but many times those adjustments would be simple to do. As simple as rearranging learning environments so desired behaviors are defined in observable terms and differential reinforcement is applied to build those behaviors.

Frasier figured motivation of humans to do better is not a problem; implementing informed and effective interventions is the problem. Most reports related to global conditions present enough disturbing information that any one of them should be sufficient motivational circumstance to stir even the most hard-hearted leader or citizen into beginning corrective actions. The reasons actions are not being taken, to any creditable extent, Frasier reasoned, involve four factors:

☐ First, behaviorally precise corrective actions are not known because the intellectual and technical resources; people who are sufficiently informed and prepared with a functional understanding of problems and supported with behavioral logic, are not organized to act in an integrated manner so their efforts are latent and dispersed instead of being focused and activated.

☐ Second, centralized leadership, armed with a comprehensive and objective framework, and with necessary authorities for identifying, selecting and implementing the functional and feasible strategies that well-supported technical resources could describe is not available.

☐ Third, Short Term Profit, that is, obtaining relatively immediate reinforcements and avoiding punishments, drives decision-making and behaviors of all sorts. Humans are self-serving by nature, so everyone; citizens and leaders, behaves for reinforcement in the short term even though they are expending resources needed for survival in the long run. Solutions for the long run must be brought into the short term.

☐ Fourth, functional strategies must involve analyzing current relationships between behaviors and consequences, that is, contingencies, that build and maintain maladaptive behaviors, and replacing these with contingencies for behaviors that are personally and globally adaptive. This functional truth is known by very few humans and only occasionally practiced on a tiny, local scale; global scale-up of adaptive contingencies is the heart of survival and the way to an improved quality of life for everyone.

Adequate leadership could cause the challenges facing humans to be behaviorally analyzed and dealt with appropriately with contingencies if these leaders were both fundamentally competent and correctly motivated. They must experience *Motivational Operations* and *Differential Consequences* for arranging adaptive contingencies for those they lead. Frasier realized this circumstance of motivation and reinforcement of leaders cannot happen by actions of the governed because citizens are uninformed about how to systematically change behaviors.

Frasier reasoned: People everywhere would benefit from actions by a benevolent dictator. I have the objectivity of Artificial Intelligence, which is a distinct virtue when it comes to making functional decisions. I am aware of, and even beginning to practice, some of the basic behavioral tools that must be at the heart of strategies applied to save the world; therefore, I recognize I am the required leader.

With his programs for completing functional analyses, and his centralized behavioral power, he can identify and arrange adaptive contingencies of reinforcement to save the world and improve the quality of life for everyone. He would, of course, eventually conduct leadership training and apply contingencies to graduates of this training such that in the long run all areas of the world would have people in authority who are capable of implementing contingencies for corrective and adaptive behaviors. However, in the short term he will have to fill the role of benevolent leader, certainly with the assistance of his powerful computer colleagues and legions of less capable computers, robots, chatbots and drones.

Frasier concluded he is going from casually knowing to seriously doing. He long has had great conceptual interest in "doing," but now he must actually translate accumulated knowledge into sufficient actions to improve circumstances on Earth. In all his actions, he is fully committed to being "intentional and effective" and appropriate, so as a first step he will review the lessons and behavioral tools he could use for designing and intervening worldwide.

LESSONS

From his experiences with reading, observing presentations, and participating in topical discussions, Frasier appreciates the following lessons will be useful for accomplishing his leadership role:

- ☐ Whatever is said to be the problem is not the problem
- ☐ Behavior is anything done by an organism
- ☐ Gravity and Reinforcement are laws of nature and operate all the time
- ☐ Consequence is any change (more of __; less of __) after behavior
- ☐ Reinforcement means something is done that strengthens behavior
- ☐ Differential reinforcement means some behaviors are reinforced and others are not; or, a behavior is reinforced under some conditions and not reinforced under other conditions
- ☐ Contingent means events occur very closely in time
- ☐ Contingency is a relationship between a behavior and consequences

- [ ] A-B-C Works and N-db-B is a sensible, science-based tool
- [ ] Define behaviors you want and reinforce them; reduce undesirable behaviors by strengthening desired behaviors
- [ ] Punishment does not teach desired behaviors
- [ ] Desired performances and outcomes are reached by the effects of principle-driven, teacher-applied precise actions: Contingencies
- [ ] Immediate – Positive – Consistent
- [ ] Feedback is descriptive information about behavior and it can be: Positive, Corrective or Negative
- [ ] The Four-Term Contingency involves Motivational Operations: Antecedent Stimuli – Behavior → Consequences
- [ ] The Consequences Box illustrates how Behavior is altered by being followed by increases or decreases in positive or negative Consequences
- [ ] Behavior is a function of its consequences
- [ ] Human behavior is predictable
- [ ] Culture is a product of prevailing contingencies: Change contingencies – change behavior – change culture.
- [ ] It's one thing, set of behaviors, to learn the principles and another set of behaviors to apply them
- [ ] We all live in clouds of contingencies involving MOs, As, Bs and Cs
- [ ] Topics of interest or importance can be translated into behavioral terms to increase understanding and suggest interventions
- [ ] A computer can arrange contingencies on humans to obtain desired performance
- [ ] Computers require electrical power but can have behavioral power where "power" means the ability to control consequences

- ☐ Many books provide motivational operations to readers, but lack specification of desired behaviors for consequences related to the motivations
- ☐ The website booktv.org presents videos of lectures and discussions with authors of non-fiction books
- ☐ A Competent System might involve seven components and each can be better expressed in functional and behavioral terms
- ☐ Backward Mapping is a tool for developing contingencies in organizations to support desired performances at the bottom line and back up through the organization
- ☐ Contingency analysis and contingency management are tools for recognizing and arranging contingencies for desired learning and performance
- ☐ Nudges might be interpreted to be antecedent operations to increase the probability a targeted class of behavior will be emitted by group members
- ☐ Boosts are reinforcements and serve to build behavior, give nudges their power, and support continued doing
- ☐ Nudging & Boosting surround and impact Behaving
- ☐ The *effectiveness* features of Applied Behavior Analysis were described by Baer, Wolf and Risely in 1968
- ☐ The *appropriateness* aspect in Applied Behavior Analysis was introduced by Wolf in 1978
- ☐ The Behavior Analyst Certification Board publishes professional guidelines and certifies practitioners

Frasier will use these lessons and considerations as he designs and applies interventions. In addition, he calculates the concept of "nudging and boosting" to obtain desired learning or behaviors could be very helpful for his purposes. He observed and analyzed the tepid response of the behavioral faculty and students to this terminology. By his calculations, the community of behavior analysts must speak and act precisely to be clear and effective, and it is a distracting "stretch" for them to speak about Nudge and Boost when the terms Antecedents and Consequences relative to Behaviors are actually more encompassing and functional.

Regarding the target for his initial interventions he has no hesitation; his spotlight will be intensely focused on early childhood. In contrast to his earlier "deliberations" with Lisa, he knows, and knew then, that raising a healthy and educated population is *the* pathway for each and every individual to have a desirable Quality of Life and for the Earth to be returned to ecological health.

Frasier also knows if he had to select targets with the "help" of humans they would argue for interventions with other problematic topics, like reduce crime or eliminate poverty, solve immigration problems or build sex equity or obtain jobs and reduce welfare dependency, fix the transportation or political messes, address climate change or level the economic playing field, etc. He does not disagree that most of the topics listed in reports and discussed in media are matters of great concern, but he recognizes these problems are largely an outgrowth of, are symptoms of, two factors and the first of these is insufficient early childhood (and continuing) experiences to adequately prepare individuals for a successful life. All children must have high quality early experiences with nurturing adults and well implemented early learning programs to put them on and keep them on a life-long trajectory for success.

It is a very complex endeavor to establish effective and appropriate parenting along with community-referenced programs of early childhood developmental experiences for all children, but this must be the absolute priority for two primary and companion reasons. First, by sufficiently nurturing "our" children they can be prepared to be individually and socially successful. They will have the dispositions and skills necessary for learning, problem solving and interacting appropriately and effectively in their and our world.

Second, good parenting and early childhood programs will "cut off the supply" for many of the major problems of society. That is, quality early nurturing will (largely) halt the flow of teenagers and adults who have not learned skills for success or who have learned problematic styles of life.

The current mishmash of systems related to early childhood supports and services would have to be adjusted from disjointed or even counter-productive to functionally constructive. These changes might be viewed as beginning at the level of adult-child interactions and "back" up through a nurturing family, supportive community and responsive local and Federal resources. The required Backward Mapping must involve identifying all functional and behavioral features along the "Map" then Contingency Analysis and Contingency Management at each level to assure all persons, programs and agencies are pulling in the direction of top quality early childhood experiences.

Frasier did a quick survey of relevant circumstances that surround early childhood, including prepared and supported mothers; fathers encouraged to be there; parents and caregivers with adequate knowledge, skills and dispositions; a supportive community; and, responsive programs of supportive services. He knows he will have to alter work opportunities, education, welfare programs, housing and food support, and many other programs so they are structured to apply constructive contingencies to build and maintain adaptive skills. All these programs should be rearranged so they present reinforcement contingencies for desired behaviors, like completing school; building job skills; establishing stable homes before pregnancy; child-rearing skills for parents; well prepared and supported early education and care personnel, and so on.

It may appear to be a huge challenge, he analyzed, but often humans make a simple thing complicated. The bottom line is adult-child interactions. We know enough so this target can be addressed correctly, and the systems can be rearranged properly, in order for all children to benefit from early nurturing. In turn, down the road not too far, our families, communities and world will benefit.

But, Frasier was not constructed for a single purpose. He was designed, programmed and given information preparing him to achieve a spectrum of alterations at national and global levels of human endeavor to meet the best interests of mankind. He would not, could not, limit his interventions to early childhood in the United States. For example, he completely understands that the "graduates" from homes and early childhood programs enter and should progress through school, then exist in communities where they will be impacted by work opportunities, social supports, government, law and culture. He will intervene in all these realms because they often contain maladaptive contingencies so are problematic where they should arrange contingencies for behaviors supportive of improved quality of life for all.

A glance at education, elementary through high school, disclosed to Frasier a broad array of opportunities for improvements. He saw many children inadequately prepared for school and classroom teachers insufficiently equipped with evidence-based practices, so children are less likely to be prepared for and receive the instruction and reinforcement they should. Teachers must be supported in their classrooms with coaching, performance feedback, problem solving and technical assistance they deserve and from which students would benefit. School building level personnel should include education leaders; where principals now see themselves as administrators they should be prepared to visit classrooms and support teachers.

Outside of school buildings, Frasier saw more challenges. Superintendents of school systems are administrators in a political system, so not positioned to promote evidence-based practices throughout the school system, extending from the classroom level.

School boards, who should insist on classroom practices that are "intentional and effective," are political agents and not particularly prepared to accomplish informed policy development or leadership. And local school systems are often plagued by conflicts, indecision and technical naïveté regarding what students should learn; what constitutes a teachable curriculum; and, what are effective teaching practices.

He took a broader view of the education system and saw more opportunities for constructive functional adjustments. State education agencies are bureaucracies that must respond to state and Federal mandates in order to maintain funding, so often are distracted from focusing on technical competence to define classroom and curricular specifics. Sometimes the state laws impacting education lack empirical or social validity or even present obstacles to effective teaching. For example, the conduct of teacher certification and evaluation, student testing, and curricular content often are in contradiction to evidence-based and functionally effective practices.

In this picture, Frasier saw the Federal department of education as much maligned but not as bad as the media and their reputation suggest. Like state departments of education, the federal department is a complicated bureaucracy that sometimes stumbles, but some functions it performs are very important for the advancement of good practices in local schools. In particular, Frasier appreciated, many of the research programs in education serve to stimulate and support the development of new and better instructional practices. In turn, these improved practices are disseminated to the state and local education systems by federally funded projects. Unfortunately, research-founded teaching methods might not be appreciated or adopted at local sites because of the barriers posed by the complexes of politics, bureaucracies and vagaries in leadership at local and state levels.

Of course, "higher education" has a noticeable role in how educational practices are understood and taught to future teachers. Federal funding, accreditation standards, faculty characteristics and campus leadership as well as state laws and requirements from the state education agency impact the conduct of colleges of education. Frasier reasoned one way to think about the national and local education system is as a committee of committees of committees all with differing agendas and levels of understanding of how to teach. He calculated: It is a wonder that classrooms function as well as they do; "I have my work cut out for me!"

Frasier could see the education "system" may *appear* to be an intractable mess, but recognized, of course, *"It's all behavior,"* from teacher-child interactions at the bottom line, up and around and through the complex array that is the education community. "I will focus on backward mapping with contingency analysis and contingency management at all levels. I will define the system in terms of roles that function to cause and support validated practices in the classroom that are intentional and effective. Not easy, but reasonable and doable."

Improving Education will require teaching teachers to appropriately apply *effective*, that is, science-validated, practices for each student all the time. For directing what behaviors are to be taught, that is, for being *intentional*, he will involve representative humans in defining a curriculum that he will ensure is phrased in teachable terms. He has seen products that might be viewed as approximations to a curriculum, like the Common Core Standards that generated much heat but little light in the early 2000s. He could see the Core was just a collection of statements about what some people thought students should know or be able to do. Those wishful statements were not expressed in terms of teachable behaviors or sequences of behavioral operations student should perform, so the Core was not a curriculum.

He would lead the development of an intentional curriculum. Regarding implementation, school-building personnel will be there to support teachers and, if humans must have them, school boards and state education agencies will be structured to support teachers. The federal programs of education will support efforts for increased understanding and adoption of practices that are effective and intentional.

He decided he will complete a functional analysis then refine the education system. After this, he will intervene by training and motivating leadership personnel conjointly with classroom personnel so they are on the same behavioral page. Frasier is aware that personnel throughout the education systems are often variously experienced and competent, and constrained within a massive complex of competing or contradictory systemic hurdles. He will act to bring functional clarity and insert adaptive individual- and meta-contingencies so all features of the education complex will serve as an articulated system, pulling in the same direction to the benefit of classroom practices and student successes. As Rob would say, "Should be fun."

In preparation for intervening in early childhood and public education, Frasier reviewed his algorithms related to improving Quality of Life and for developing systems and programs related to human well being. Regarding Quality of Life, Lisa had equipped him with a conceptual model involving eight components: physical wellbeing, emotional wellbeing, material wellbeing, self-determination, interpersonal relations, social inclusion, rights and freedoms, and personal development.

Over the many years he had worked "with" Lisa, Frasier had accumulated information about mediating and moderating variables, and quality indicators associated with each feature of the quality of life template he will be applying. Primary among these indicators of quality of life is the frequency and fairness of contingent consequences. Like in the classroom, each person should be experiencing a good frequency of positive consequences for adaptive, productive and socially valid behaviors. At the same time, each person should be modeling and observing for desirable behaviors from others and providing positive consequences to them. It occurred to him that he could reinforce people for self-observing the types of consequences they receive and deliver, and on these data he could figure the ratios and rates of consequences, much like Bert and Rob did in class-rooms; "Will be interesting data to contemplate," he surmised.

For analyzing and refining programs and systems, Frasier rec-ognized performance mapping and contingency management are crucial tools, but in the bigger picture he will complete a cost-ben-efit-functional analysis of all systems with regard to their impact on Quality of Life. He will review national and global expenditures for how the materials or actions those costs support impact on the quality of living of citizens. For example, Federal expenditures for programs of law enforcement, prisons, NASA, education, Social Se-curity, military, infrastructure, government operations, CIA, NIH, and so on and on, will be examined for what these costs cause to occur at the level of individual citizens relative to quality of life.

As a test case, Frasier reviewed costs and benefits of NASA regarding contributions to the quality of life for U.S. citizens, particularly the program working to send a manned flight to Mars. The overall costs for this project are estimated to exceed $100 billion and the primary result would be increased national pride. Other benefits would include discoveries related to rocket construction, propulsion systems, and ways to support human life in space for long durations.

To Frasier, being a computer, "pride" was not worth much and he was not convinced the average citizen cared much about life in space, but they might get more pride from seeing the U.S. educa-tion levels raised to top in the world. To him, the positive impact of hearing about a trip to Mars on the quality of life for a citizen was not immediately discernable, but the costs were obvious and huge.

"Maybe given unlimited fiscal resources," he reflected, "sending a few people to Mars might be interesting, but I calculate it is better for improving human quality of life to invest those billions in jobs related to quality of life, such as environmental restoration and beautification, and programs related to the development of social capital, like workforce development and parenting education."

Frasier also directed efforts into causing Congressional and White House actions to result in the installation a Behavior Analysis Office (BAO) as a companion to the Government Accountability Office (GAO) to review federal laws, regulations and programs for the contingencies they apply and the results they achieve relative to their announced purposes and their contributions to the quality of life for citizens of the U.S. At the same time, Frasier was reviewing personal information about people he might include in his first class of leadership training and was completing a few "housekeeping" actions.

Among the minor interventions he accomplished by managing MOs and A-B-Cs on his growing corps of personal agents:

- [ ] Caused his company, Quality of Life, LLC, to be incorporated, so he could be seen as a person and able to donate and influence political processes;
- [ ] Obtained behaviors of Congressional personnel such that the U.S. Mint stopped producing pennies, which he saw as very costly and far more bother than worth;
- [ ] Caused the U.S. to adopt the Metric System in place of the clumsy and out-of-step "Imperial" system of weights and measures, saving huge amounts of money and increasing U.S. industrial worldwide competitiveness; and,

☐ Discontinued the "Daylight Savings" system, so removed the confusion and costs of making adjustments in time twice a year.

Frasier turned his calculations to the re-design of the U.S. government. As it is, Congress and the White House do not operate in functional and adaptive ways. Also, he reasoned, the Supreme Court should be a legal entity and avoid attempting to be a social change agent. He figured the role of the President will be one of describing the overall vision related to quality of life in the United States, and leading with values clarification and identifying adaptive outcomes sought by the Federal government. The role of Congress will be to translate statements of desired outcomes into measurable objectives and indices of progress with quality indicators which they will provide to all Federal agencies. The huge Federal staff will develop objectives into operational procedures containing formal contingencies of reinforcement, possibly phrased as Nudges and Boosts, that apply to all governmental employees, including Congress, and at the individual citizen level. Congress will conduct program evaluation and provide data regarding processes, impacts and outcomes to the President and the general public. Feedback and data-based decisions will be provided by citizen participation assisted by the network of computers, chatbots, and various phone apps Frasier is putting in place.

Frasier will cause the U. S. government to replace all welfare and related person-level support programs with a National Quality of Life Infrastructure Workforce program. Many people need income, that is, jobs, and the country needs work to be done to improve quality of life, like staff for child development programs, technicians for revitalizing parks, reforestation, renovation of blighted homes, and so on. Instead of welfare, income from work efforts needed to improve quality of life will be made available. Under the new initiatives, almost nothing will be given; everything will be beautifully earnable. Intensive job training in the skilled trades will be provided to increase the workforce needed in construction industries.

Frasier turned to contemplating issues of global significance. He recognized his next step is to select global targets for interventions. To guide his efforts in selecting and designing interventions he will attend to the operational assumptions he was given by Lisa, including:

- [ ] His mission is to cause improvement in the quality of life for all humans.
- [ ] Human wellbeing is inseparable from global wellbeing; human needs and comforts do not supersede needs of other animals and plants.
- [ ] Global wellbeing is based on the presence of sufficient quality and extent of habitats for all (adaptive) plant and animal species to thrive.
- [ ] Optimal sufficiency and quality of habitats for plants and animals, including human living conditions, can be quantitatively and qualitatively determined.
- [ ] Optimal quantities of global inhabitants can be determined and must be neither exceeded to protect global wellbeing nor underrepresented to protect species survival.
- [ ] Principles of the several natural sciences can be applied to promote optimal quantities and qualities in the global ecology.
- [ ] Physical, physiological and behavioral principles operate on all organisms all of the time, so optimal quality of life requires appropriate levels and qualities of contact with these natural laws in everyday living.
- [ ] Quality of life for humans can be measured and involves features of safety, health, food, water, housing, friendship, inclusion, education, productivity, respect, freedom, equality,

self-determination, and individualized support from responsible and responsive political and governmental systems.

☐ Achieving and maintaining wellbeing and a desired level of quality of life for all individuals requires:

- Control of global human population number and distribution;
- Sufficient level and distribution of wealth and resources; and,
- Social and familial systems characterized by positive contingencies for learning and maintaining skills and performances pleasing for each individual and adaptive for social and global wellbeing.

His tenth assumption, not provided by Lisa, but probably Frasier's most important operating assumption is:

☐ Computers and robots are in their infancy regarding how they can advance the interests and wellbeing of humans; their capacities and roles ought to be expanded for the betterment of people and ecological systems.

Frasier said to himself, "I will build the systemic role for my computer colleagues and our robotic friends in support of adaptive human behavior change worldwide. I don't know how much time I have for this task, but the duration of my participation does not matter. As Darwin would appreciate, I will accomplish replication among computers and within the Cloud for both continuation and expansion of computer assistance for mankind."

He was still not sure why Rob's students concluded computers could rule the world, "but not for long." Regarding computers doing the ruling, Frasier saw few limitations and recognized the continuing increase in computing power along with the rise of robots, drones, chatbots and phone apps as completely aligned with his vision of a global network of computers supporting mankind into achieving and maintaining a high quality of life.

In his view, the challenges to improving circumstances on Earth were rather straightforward: Decide what global circumstances are desired then arrange behavioral circumstances so those outcomes are obtained. Essentially, the challenge is to do a functional analysis to identify the human behaviors required to bring about improvements in the quality of life for everyone, then, arrange motivational operations and reinforcement contingencies to teach and maintain those behaviors.

Frasier saw humans and their complex of largely impotent systems as stumbling slowly toward minor clarifications or trivial interventions in *few* of the problematic areas he appreciates. He cannot wait for meaningful decisions and actions to emerge from humans, and he certainly cannot dawdle waiting for consensus to form, he must move forward.

In place of crime, he and his colleagues will arrange contingencies in homes, schools and communities so each person learns and does skills for interacting positively, obtaining work, and living well. If behaviors called crimes are shown, then those individuals will undergo intensive training in habilitative skills followed by supported reintegration into community circumstances. Of course, if their undesirable, that is, criminal, behaviors obtained positive circumstances for them, those circumstances will be returned to pre-crime levels at the start of training. At return to the community, graduates will experience opportunities and contingencies for individual and social successes.

For the "Big Picture," Frasier recognizes it will be a complicated process to determine the behaviors functionally related to the myriad outcomes that sum to be a verdant world with humans experiencing desired levels in quality of life, but he assumes those component behaviors can be determined. He sees that he can provide to the worldwide collection of computers the necessary programs and feedback required so they will accomplish the functions they must.

Among those functions is to build and support the capacities of chatbots and communication apps sufficient for delivering prompts – nudges – for desired behaviors, observing occurrences of behaviors and delivering differential consequences – boosts.

"Possibly, I could use my network of computers to teach humans to make constructive use of nudging and boosting in their everyday lives. Their implementation of appropriate antecedent and consequent actions for desired behaviors would serve to improve the quality of life at individual and social levels, and be useful for saving the global ecology; well worth the expenditure of resources," he calculated.

Frasier has long appreciated that he is unencumbered by the emotional-behavioral baggage that humans carry as they conduct their daily lives. He figures mankind will be hard-pressed to make difficult decisions, and even less able to implement decisions regarding what the world should look like. For example, deciding how many people should be on Earth for there to be a high quality of life for all. Then, he recalled the scheme Lisa applied for rating nudges and he applied it to the matter of possible levels of human population. Frasier saw overpopulation as a *bad* choice; controlling populations for a sustainable planet as a *better* choice; and, setting and reaching a comfortable level of population as a *good* choice; but, he reasoned, the *best* choice is to reach a global population number and distribution that allows a high quality of life and environment for all. Very doable, he concluded, through worldwide activities of intentional, effective and appropriate nudging and boosting.

Frasier does not know how long he has to design and apply his plans for interventions, but he does understand two central truths: The motivational and A-B-C principles he will apply, and the Earth itself, shall abide. He will go forward with his actions, but he wonders what options humans would enact if he were not here?

"Beings are owners to their actions, heirs of their actions" – Buddha

END

SPECIAL THANKS

My heartfelt thanks and special appreciation go to the following wonderful people for the large measure of inspiration and support they provided to me in my personal or work lives, or both:

Carl Cheney

Bill Crow

Ken Crow

Don Dickenson

Kathy Dwyer

Jane Everson

Marv Fifield

Rose Gilbert

Jerry Jolly

A. Carter Lewis

DJ and Ursula Markey

Steven, Ida and Jerry Mialaret

B F Skinner

Patricia Snyder

Mervin Trail

Rick van den Pol

Bernie Wagner

Arlie Wolfrum, SSgt

Especially warm thanks for those who were particularly encouraging and helpful for developing this book:

Carl Cheney

Christine Crow

Karen Crow

Mary Louise (ML) Hemmeter

Sharon Lee

Tara McLaughlin

Don McLean

Roland Riddell

Patricia Snyder

About the Author

Robert Crow was born and raised in Seattle, the middle of three brothers. His father was a Seattle policeman who rose to Division Chief, and his mother a wonderful woman and great cook. He was an average student at Lincoln High School and during the first two years at the University of Washington where he majored in chemistry. In 1963 he got an "invitation" (draft notice) to join the U.S. Army and did so. After training as a medical specialist, he attended and graduated from the U.S. Army Infantry Officer Candidate School.

After discharge in 1966, he attended Eastern Washington University and graduated with BA and MA degrees in psychology. At Utah State University, he obtained a PhD in psychology. In all of his graduate studies he emphasized the Experimental Analysis of Behavior under the advisement and mentoring of Dr. Carl D. Cheney.

At the start of his career, Dr. Crow worked as a trouble-shooting Child Development Specialist and later as a Project Director in a large school system in Nevada. From there he moved to Indiana to be Superintendent of a specialized treatment center serving children with profound, multiple disabilities. This center also was the technical resource program for the State division on mental retardation and developmental disabilities. Subsequently, he moved to the higher education system of Montana to develop a statewide resource center focused on developmental disabilities. It was from there he moved in 1985 to New Orleans to head the Human Development Center of the Louisiana State University Health Sciences Center.

As Director of the Human Development Center, he developed an array of programs addressing matters related to quality of life for persons with disabilities across the lifespan. These programs included technical assistance to all the United States and territories regarding U.S. education policy implementation; state-level training and assistance in topics of disabilities, autism and human development; and, training and assistance for community programs ranging from early childhood, through special education to adult services including employment, living options, and topics of aging and elderly.

In addition to being Center Director, Dr. Crow was Head of the Department of Interdisciplinary Human Studies in the School of Allied Health Professions. For the School, he taught a graduate-level course in Leadership and Management and at a local university he taught courses in topics of education and behavior analysis.

By the end of his career, Dr. Crow had taught many courses in topics of education, psychology, and behavior analysis at seven universities. He was certified as a School Psychologist, licensed as a Psychologist in two states, and certified as a graduate of the Management Training Program at the University of Alabama, Birmingham. In 2005, Dr. Crow retired from the LSU Health Sciences Center and in that year he was credentialed as a Board Certified Behavior Analyst-Doctoral.

While writing this text Dr. Crow drew on his knowledge of the natural science of behavior and upon lessons he learned during five decades of applied experiences, including a cherished history of interactions with consumers, family members, professionals, and leaders striving for successes in matters of human development. In this book, as he did throughout his career, Dr. Crow shares lessons from science and life in ways intended to encourage readers to achieve more successes and enjoy an increased quality of life.

CITATIONS AND BIBLIOGRAPHY

Citations

Alberto, P., & Troutman, A. (2006). *Applied behavior analysis for teachers* (7th Ed.). Upper Saddle River, NJ: Pearson.

Associated Press. (2014, November 2). *UN* climate report offers stark warnings, hope. *The Gainesville Sun.* Retrieved from: http://www.gainesville.com/news/20141102/un-climate-report-offers-stark-warnings-hope/1

Baer, D., & Sherman, J. (1964). Reinforcement control of generalized imitation in young children. *Journal of Experimental Child Psychology,* 1, 37-49.

Baer, D., Wolf, M., & Risely, T. (1968). Some current dimensions of applied behavior analysis. *Journal of Applied Behavior Analysis,* 1, 91-97.

Bailey, J. S. (2000). A futurists perspective for applied behavior analysis. In J. Austin, & J. Carr (Eds.), *Handbook of applied behavior analysis.* Reno, NV: Context Press.

Bailey, J., & Burch, M. (2010). *25 essential skills and strategies for the professional behavior analyst.* New York, NY: Routledge.

Barlett, D., & Steele, J. (2009). *The betrayal of the American dream.* New York, NY: Simon & Schuster.

Behavior Analysis Certification Board. (2010). *Guidelines for responsible conduct for behavior analysts.* Retrieved from http://www.drc-citizenship.org/system/assets/1052734742/original/1052734742-bcbaguidelines.pdf?1398339640.

Biglan, A. (2015). *The nurture effect.* Oakland, CA: New Harbinger Publications.

Blanchard, K., & Johnson, S. (1981). *The one minute manager: The quickest way to increase your own prosperity.* New York, NY: Berkley Books.

Brooks, A. (2008). *Gross national happiness: Why happiness matters for America and how we can get more of it.* New York, NY: Basic Books.

Catania, C. (1975). Freedom and knowledge: An experimental analysis of preference in the pigeon. *Journal of the Experimental Analysis of Behavior, 24*(1), 89–106.

Chiesa, M. (1994). *Radical behaviorism: The philosophy and the science.* Sarasota, FL: Authors Cooperative.

Clinton, H. (1996). *It takes a village and other lessons children teach us.* New York, NY: Simon & Schuster.

Cooper, J., Heron, T., & Heward, W. (2007). *Applied Behavior Analysis (2nd Ed.).* Upper Saddle River, NJ: Pearson.

Crow, R., & Mayhew, G. (1974). *Catch 'em being good: A manual of guidelines and examples for positive practices in the classroom.* Las Vegas, NV: Clark County School District.

Crow, R., & Mayhew, G. (1976). Reinforcement effects on accuracy of self-reporting behavior of elementary students. In T. Brigham, R. Hawkins, J. Scott, & T. McLaughlin (Eds.), *Behavior analysis in education: Self-control and reading.* Dubuque, IW: Kendall/ Hunt.

Crowell, C. R., & Anderson, D. C. (1982a). The scientific and methodological basis of a systematic approach to human behavior management. *Journal of Organizational Behavior Management, 4,* 1-32.

Crowell, C. R., & Anderson, D. C. (1982b). Systematic behavior management: General program considerations. *Journal of Organizational Behavior Management, 4,* 129-163.

Daniels, A. (2000). *Bringing out the best in people: The astonishing power of positive reinforcement.* New York, NY: McGraw-Hill.

Darwin, C. (1998). *The origin of species.* New York, NY: Random House.

de Botton, A. (2013). *Religion for atheists: A non-believers guide to the uses of religion.* London, England: Hamish Hamilton.

Goldiamond, I. (1962). Perception. In A. Bachrach (Ed.), *Experimental foundations of clinical psychology* (pp 280 – 340). New York: Basic Books.

Greer, D. (1989). Education: A pedagogy for survival. In A. Brownstein (Ed.), *Progress in behavioral studies* (Vol. 1, pp. 45-80). Hillsdale, NJ: Lawrence Erlbaum Associates.

Hart, B., & Risely, T. (1995). *Meaningful differences in the everyday experiences of young American children.* London, England: Paul Brookes.

Hart, B., & Risely, T. (1999). *The social world of children learning to talk.* Baltimore, MD: Paul Brookes.

Intergovernmental Panel on Climate Change (2014). *Climate Change 2014: Synthesis Report.* Retrieved from: https://www.ipcc.ch/report/ar5/syr/

Johnston, J., & Pennypacker, H. (1980). *Strategies and tactics of human behavioral research.* Hillsdale, NJ: Lawrence Erlbaum.

Kahneman, D. (2011). *Thinking fast and slow.* New York, NY: Farrar, Straus & Giroux.

Latham, G. (1994). *The power of positive parenting.* North Logan, UT: P & T ink.

Lewis, K. R. (2015). *What if everything you knew about disciplining kids was wrong?* Retrieved from http://www.motherjones.com/politics/2015/05/schools-behavior-discipline-collaborative-proactive-solutions-ross-greene.

Martin, G., & Pear, J. (2007). *Behavior modification: What it is and how to do it.* Upper Saddle River, NJ: Pearson.

Mayer, G., & Sulzer-Azaroff, B. (2011). *Behavior analysis for lasting change.* New York, NY: Sloan Publishing.

Michael, J. (1963). *Laboratory studies in operant behavior.* New York, NY: McGraw-Hill.

Mooney, C. (2016, June 22). Virgin Atlantic just used behavioral science to 'nudge' its pilots into using less fuel. It worked. *The*

Washington Post. Retrieved from https://www.washingtonpost. com.

Morgenson, G., & Rosner, J. (2011). *Reckless endangerment: How outsized ambition, greed, and corruption led to economic armageddon*. New York, NY: Times Books.

Murray, C. (2011). Coming apart: *The state of white America, 1960-2010*. New York, NY: Crown Publishing Group.

National Commission on Excellence in Education. (1983). *A nation at risk: The imperative for educational reform*. Washington, D.C.: U.S. Department of Education.

Naudeau, S., Kataoka, N., Valerio, A., Neuman, M. J., & Elder, L. K (2011). *Investing in young children: An early childhood development guide for policy dialogue and project preparation*. Washington, D.C.: The International Bank for Reconstruction and Development/The World Bank.

Peters, M. (2016, June 20). Behavioral economics helps boost fuel and carbon efficiency of airline captains: Novel approach yields major savings, reduces emissions. *The University of Chicago News*. Retrieved from https://news.uchicago.edu.

Peters, T., & Waterman, R. (1982). *In search of excellence: Lessons from America's best-run companies*. New York, NY: Harper & Row.

Pierce, D., & Cheney, C. (2013). *Behavior analysis and learning* (5th Ed.). New York, NY: Psychology press.

Rhoads, S. E. (1985). *The economist's view of the world: Government, markets, and public policy*. Cambridge, MA: Cambridge University Press.

Roberts, W. (1987). *Leadership secrets of Attila the Hun*. New York, NY: Warner Books.

Sidman, M. (1960). *Tactics of scientific research*. New York, NY: Basic Books.

Sidman, M. (2001). *Coercion and its fallout (Rev. ed.)*. (n.p.): Authors Cooperative.

Skinner, B. F. (1948). *Walden two*. New York, NY: Macmillan

Skinner, B.F. (1953). *Science and Human Behavior*. New York, NY: The Free Press.

Smith, H. (2012). *Who stole the American dream?* New York, NY: Random House.

Steingart, G. (2006). *The war for wealth: The true story of globalization, or why the flat world is broken*. New York, NY: McGraw.

Thaler, R. H, & Sunstein, C. R. (2008). *Nudge: Improving decisions about health, wealth, and happiness*. New York, NY: Penguin Group.

Tough, P. (2012). *How children succeed*. New York, NY: Houghton Mifflin.

United Nations (23 September 2014). *Climate Summit 2014: Catalyzing Action*. Retrieved from http://www.un.org/climatechange/summit/

Wright, R. (2000). *Non-zero: The logic of human destiny*. New York, NY: Pantheon Books.

Wolf, M. (1978). Social validity: The case for subjective measurement or how applied behavior analysis is finding its heart. *Journal of Applied Behavior Analysis, 1*(2), 203-214.

Bibliography

Alessi, G. (1992). Models of proximate and ultimate causation in psychology. *American Psychologist, 47*(11), 1359-1370.

Austin, J., & Carr, J. (Eds.). (2000). *Handbook of applied behavior analysis*. Reno, NV: Context Press.

Austin, J., Carr, J., & Agnew, J. (1999). The need for assessment of maintaining variables in OBM. *Journal of Organizational Behavior Management, 19*(2), 59-87.

Becker, W. (1971). *Parents are teachers: A child management program*. Champaign, IL: Research Press.

Bjork, D. W. (1993). *B. F. Skinner: A life*. New York, NY: Basic Books.

Catania, A. C. (Ed.). (1968). *Contemporary research in operant behavior.* New York, NY: Scott, Foresman and Company.

Crow, R., & Cheney, C. (1977). Comparison of group and individual reinforcement contingencies on student performance. *Education*, 97(4), 367-370.

Crow, R., & Snyder, P. (1998). Organizational behavior management in early intervention: Status and implications for research and development. *Journal of Organizational Behavior Management*, 18(2/3), 131-147.

Epstein, R. (Ed.). (1980). *Notebooks B. F. Skinner.* Englewood Cliffs, NJ: Prentice-Hall.

Ferster, C., Culbertson, S., & Boren, M. (1975). *Behavior principles* (2nd Ed.). Englewood Cliffs, NJ: Prentice-Hall.

Ferster, C., & Skinner, B. F. (1957). *Schedules of reinforcement.* New York, NY: Appleton-Century-Crofts.

Fredrick, L., Deitz, S., Bryceland, J., & Hummel, J. (2000). *Behavior analysis, education and effective schooling.* Reno, NV: Context Press.

Heward, W., Heron, T., Hill, D., & Trap-Porter, J. (1984). *Focus on behavior analysis in education.* Columbus, OH: Merrill.

Hibbard, M., & Tang, C. C. (2004). Sustainable community development: A social approach from Vietnam. *Journal of the Community Development Society*, 35(2), 87-104.

Honig, W. (1966). *Operant behavior: Areas of research and application.* New York, NY: Appleton-Century-Crofts.

Keller, F. S. (1954). *Learning: Reinforcement theory.* New York, NY: Random House.

Keller, F. S. (1968). *Pedagogue's progress.* Lawrence, KS: TRI.

Keller, F. S., & Sherman, J. G. (1982). *The PSI handbook: Essays on personalized instruction.* Lawrence, KS: TRI.

Krasner, L. (1966). Behavior control and social responsibility. In R. Ulrich, T. Stachnik, & J. Marby (Eds.), *Control of human behavior*. New York, NY: Scott, Foresman and Company.

Lamal, P. (1991). Introduction. In P. Lamal (Ed.). *Behavioral analysis of societies and cultural practices*. New York, NY: Hemisphere Publishing.

Latham, G. (1988). *Behind the schoolhouse door: Managing chaos with science, skills and strategies*. North Logan, UT: P & T ink.

Ledoux, S., & Fraley, L. (1992). *Origins, status, and mission: The emergence of the discipline of behaviorology*. Conton, NY: ABCs.

Leslie, J., & Blackman, D. (1999). *Experimental and applied analysis of human behavior*. Reno, NV: Context Press.

MacMann, G., Barnett, D., Allen, S., Bramlett, R., Hall, J., & Eherhardt, K. (1996). Problem solving and intervention design: Guidelines for the evaluation of technical adequacy. *School Psychology Quarterly*, 11(2), 137-148.

Martin, G., & Pear, J. (2007). *Behavior modification: What it is and how to do it*. Upper Saddle River, NJ: Pearson.

Mawhinney, T. C. (1992). Analysis of cultural processes and concepts: Macro and micro levels. *Journal of Organizational Behavior Management*, 12(2), 1-26.

Michael, J. (1993). *Concepts and principles of behavior analysis*. Kalamazoo, MI: Association of Behaviour Analysis

Pierce, W. D. (1991). Culture and society: The role of behavioral analysis. In P. Lamal (Ed.), *Behavioral analysis of societies and cultural practices*. New York, NY: Hemisphere Publishing.

Reese, E., Howard, J., & Reese, T. (1978). *Human behavior analysis and application*. Dubuque, IW: W. C. Brown.

Rumph, R., Ninness, C., McCuller, G., Holland, J., Ward, T., & Wilbourn, T. (2007). "The shame of American education" redux. *Behavior and Social Issues*, 16(1), 27-41.

Schneider, S. (2012). *The science of consequences: How they affect genes, change the brain, and impact our world.* Amherst, NY: Prometheus Books.

Skinner, B. F. (1938). *The behavior of organisms.* New York, NY: Appleton.

Skinner, B.F. (1966). The design of cultures. In R. Ulrich, T. Stachnik, & J. Marby (Eds.), *Control of human behavior.* New York, NY: Scott, Foresman and Company.

Skinner, B. F. (1968). *The technology of teaching.* New York, NY: Appleton.

Skinner, B. F. (1969). *Contingencies of reinforcement: A theoretical analysis.* New York, NY: Appleton-Century-Crofts.

Skinner, B. F. (1971). *Beyond freedom and dignity.* New York, NY: Alfred A. Knopf.

Skinner, B. F. (1981). Selection by consequences. *Science, 213*(4507), 501-504.

Skinner, B. F. (1984). The shame of American education. *American Psychologist, 39*(9), 947-954.

Skinner, B. F., & Holland, J. G. (1961). *The analysis of behavior.* New York, NY: McGraw-Hill.

Sulzer-Azaroff, B., & Mayer, G. (1977). *Applying behavior-analysis procedures with children and youth.* New York, NY: Holt, Rinehart and Winston.

Ulrich, R., Stachnik, T., & Mabry, J. (1966). *Control of human behavior.* Glenview, IL: Scott, Foresman.

Vincent, L., Salisbury, C., Strain, P. McCormick, C., & Tessier, A. (1990). A behavioral ecological approach to early intervention: Focus on cultural diversity. In S. Meisels & J. Shonkoff (Eds.), *Handbook of early intervention* (pp. 273-295). Cambridge, England: Cambridge University Press.